Understanding Leadership Perspectives

Matthew R. Fairholm • Gilbert W. Fairholm

Understanding Leadership Perspectives

Theoretical and Practical Approaches

 Springer

Matthew R. Fairholm
University of South Dakota
Vermillion, South Dakota
USA

Gilbert W. Fairholm
Virginia Commonwealth University
Richmond, Virginia
USA

ISBN: 978-0-387-84901-0   e-ISBN: 978-0-387-84902-7
DOI: 10.1007/978-0-387-84902-7

Library of Congress Control Number: 2008940907

Building on a solid foundation is essential to success in any endeavor. My intellectual foundations have been formed more by my father than any other influence. I am grateful for his example and for our various conversations, many of which took place way before my interest in leadership studies formally emerged. More importantly, though, he and my mother have given me a broader, eternal foundation of faith and character and my sister and brothers have been constant examples of all that is best in people. As I, with my dear wife, Shannon, form a foundation for our family, I am grateful for her love, insight, patience, and example. I too am grateful for our sons Carl, Benjamin, Nathan, and William and for the light and wisdom I gain as I interact with them. I see in Shannon and our four sons the leadership I crave to understand. To them all I dedicate this effort and give my thanks and love.

Matt Fairholm, Vermillion, SD

Writing is essentially a solitary activity. While any author relies for both insight and context on a phalanx of extant research and researchers, the task of creating a unique perspective on any topic and logically fleshing it out is most often still done alone - except in this case. I am grateful that this time I could collaborate with an insightful and perceptive colleague, my son, Matthew. I am indebted to him both for his scholarship and his - and his sister and brothers' - example. They have always set the pattern of leadership for me.

Gil Fairholm, Richmond, VA

Contents

List of Figures

List of Tables

Introduction

It is a "fact" that people seem to know what leadership is and yet often disagree with each other when they talk about it. Most puzzling is that we all seem to think we are right. We all think we know what we are talking about, even when we disagree. And, collectively, we have disagreed on a definition of leadership for over the 100 years of its "modern" lifetime. There are about as many different understandings of what leadership is as there are writers on the topic.

Competing and Conflicting Values: The Cause of the Problem

We propose here that these multiple disagreements and misunderstandings sprout more from the individual's personal system of values and the perspective (or mind-set) that those values engender than they do from a lack of rational leadership sophistication. That is, our personal perspective about leadership influences how we view work and measure the success of our and others' leadership. The fact that, in our attempts to define more clearly that which we call leadership, such people as Genghis Khan and Gandhi, Hitler and Churchill, Caesar and Christ, Martin Luther King, Jr. and Pol Pot are mentioned side by side without embarrassment or concern is a testament to the progress still needing to be made in understanding, accepting, and implementing leadership.

Our understanding of this basic and widespread organizational relationship has been recast several times over the past 100 years. Analysis of this stream of ideas gives rise to several core concepts around which researchers have developed elaborate structures to define and describe leadership. The task we all face is to rethink our definition of leadership in ways most people will accept as intrinsically true in the face of the countless opinions and biases – mind-sets – we have created from our experience as and with our leaders. This is the challenge of this book: one we think is resolved within these pages.

Rethinking a leadership definition is, perhaps, the most difficult problem faced by practitioners and researchers alike. The problem is that each person has developed a mind-set that defines his or her perspective of leadership truth and, hence, any ideas about leadership that differ from this mental perspective are generally rejected out of

M.R. Fairholm and G.W. Fairholm, *Understanding Leadership Perspectives*,
DOI: 10.1007/978-0-387-84902-7_0, © Springer Science + Business Media, LLC 2009

hand. Indeed, we do not easily move out of one mind-set into another. What we believe to be true given our particular experience often seems to be the *only* truth. Often we need some outside force to trigger reevaluation and rethinking. That triggering force to intellectual growth may be a new idea, a new situation, a new value, a new boss, or some other significant emotional event – maybe, even, a new book.

The Research Foundation

This book is founded on two pillars: one, a model of five leadership mind-sets common in the last 100 years first presented in Gilbert W. Fairholm's (1998a, 1998b) book, *Perspectives on Leadership: From the Science of Management to its Spiritual Heart*; and two, Matthew R. Fairholm's (2002) dissertation, *Conceiving Leadership: Exploring Five Perspectives of Leadership by Investigating the Conceptions and Experiences of Selected Metropolitan Washington Area Municipal Managers*, which analyzed and validated the perspectives model (see the Appendix for more details). The data collected confirm there are five distinct perspectives of leadership evident in the 100-year history of leadership study and practice. The resulting model defines the five perspectives in terms of descriptions of leadership in action, leadership tools and behaviors, and the way leaders approach their relationship to followers. The five perspectives are related hierarchically so that they progressively encompass a unique perspective of the leadership phenomenon.

The Purposes of Leadership

The data also confirm the simple observation that leadership is not merely ensuring rules and procedures are efficiently carried out. Surely it includes productivity goals, but it is more than that. Fundamentally, it deals with people in relationships. This view opens tremendous possibilities for leaders and workers to experience personal growth and to be a positive influence in helping group members and those in the larger society live better lives, for the inescapable purpose of leadership is to change lives. By their actions, through the programs they manage, and in their personal behavior, leaders act to create a culture of individual trust, progress, and growth. Only in this activity is leadership enduring because it changes people at the level of self-definition, allows them to be different, better, more whole – complete – than they were before the leadership occurred. This is the essence, and the result, of leadership: helping others to develop and mature and, in the process, maturing ourselves.

The Leadership Perspectives Model

The 1998 Fairholm Perspectives model proposed an interrelated hierarchy of mind-sets about what leadership is; these mindsets have characterized the 100-plus year life span of modern leadership study. Since then literally hundreds of books, articles, and essays have been published that take a "perspectives" viewpoint describing various elements and aspects of leadership. Unlike *Perspectives on Leadership*, most contemporary studies mostly focused on only a few elements of the whole picture. The Leadership Perspectives Model (LPM) described herein emerged in part as a result of studying the attitudes and values of practicing organizational leaders, in part from analysis of available past and contemporary literature, in part from observation of leaders in action, and in part from the authors' personal experiences both as leaders and as followers of leaders – some good, some not.

The LPM defines a kind of leadership based in the values of the leader transposed to the group. Depending on the values-set of the individual leader, he or she may see leadership as (1) a synonym for management, (2) an element of excellence management, (3) a reflection of that leader's values-set, (4) an establishing of a values-laden culture he or she creates to facilitate group action, or (5) an outgrowth of the leader's core spiritual values. It is unclear which of these mind-sets is the correct one to delineate leadership. What is clear is that our core values define us, determine the goals we seek and the methods we will use to attain them, and dictate our measures of success.

Everybody has values and these values trigger our behavior. Necessarily, then, leadership takes place in a situation pregnant with values. The leader must act and influence at the level of values, because values are more powerful than plans, policy, procedure, or system. They define the person of the leader – and each follower – and constitute the measures of personal success and acceptability of others' actions. Absent shared values, the organization becomes just a crowd of people. The power of our values in shaping our individual and collective lives is obvious. Unfortunately, this truth did not find its way into past leadership models.

Given the importance of leadership in today's world, we cannot ignore this powerful way to think about and understand the leadership process. Rethinking leadership in values terms promises to help us appreciate more fully the leader–follower relationship and the values-laden culture in which it takes place. But, to make it work for us requires that we reconsider our present perspective about what leadership is and open our minds to new ways of thinking about, practicing, and measuring leadership action.

The Process of Leadership

The leader is a servant first and then a boss, if even a boss at all. Many of the problems we have as leaders result because we tend to reverse this phenomenon. That is, we concentrate overmuch on bossing our followers – making them do what *we* want – instead of serving them by helping them be the best they can be in their jobs and otherwise. True leadership and service cannot be separated (Greenleaf 1977). This is the message of leadership through the ages. The great leaders are and always have been of service to their followers first and then leaders into a new, better, more productive life. Unfortunately, past theory ignores this truth.

The LPM ultimately defines leadership as a task of service, of facilitating a values transfer – (1) through the leader's example, (2) through forming cultures within which followers can come to trust their leaders enough to follow them, and (3) by reflecting their authentic core self, their soul or spirit – in their relationships within the group and with all stakeholders. This task is not for the faint-hearted. It requires a bold meekness that all serious research ought to require, for through meekness comes a more sure understanding of what is being explored.

However, to present our research as nothing more than interesting information seems a disservice to our readers. Our intention is not disinterested intellectual curiosity, but rather it is to help our readers to rethink the comprehensiveness of the leadership mind-set they hold and to identify or create a map (or even the road itself) to the improvement of self, society, and our surroundings through a more thoughtful, enlightened, and practical understanding of leadership.

This book investigates how leaders conceive of and, importantly, apply leadership. It reassesses the kernels of truth gleaned from past study of leader action and proposes a more precise conception of leadership. The authors present a fully developed LPM which identifies unique leadership elements that concretely define and delimit the practice of the kind of leadership implied in each of the five individual perspectives. These elements flesh out an operational definition and define techniques of practice. They are categorized in terms of (1) Leadership in Action Descriptions, (2) Tools and Behavior, and (3) Approaches to Followers. These categories are applied to each of the five leadership perspectives to show how leadership changes with the mental perspective adopted by the individual. We conclude that the LPM incorporates operationally useful definitional elements that are valid in differentiating the five leadership perspectives, that the leadership perspectives are themselves valid and accurately reflect unique conceptions of leadership, and that the five leadership perspectives relate to each other in hierarchical ways.

Chapter 1
Intellectual Threads of Modern Leadership Studies

Defining leadership is a relatively recent academic activity, though the phenomenon of leadership has been ever present in human relations. Stogdill (1974) reviewed more than 3,000 studies directly related to leadership since this concept was introduced in the 1800s. Many propose definitions unique from any other writer's. Obviously, these studies have not closed the book on leadership research. In fact many analysts lament the lack of progress made in understanding and defining leadership. Bennis and Nanus (1985) conclude that so many have worked so hard to do so little. And Rost (1991) concludes that these attempts to define leadership have been anything but yielding of concrete answers. He uses words such as "confusing," "varied," "disorganized," "idiosyncratic," "muddled," and "unrewarding." Yet research continues, definitions proliferate, and leadership remains an enigma.

Rather than reflecting cynically on past efforts, Yukl (1988) says we need to draw new conceptualizations of leadership that give us a better, more thorough grasp of this elusive social phenomenon. Trying to integrate past leadership theories into an overarching supermodel of leadership, as Yukl tried, may prove impossible. Rather, we need to rethink the body of information amassed about leadership and try to find the substance of truth contained in some of this work and discard the myths and opinions making up the bulk of other studies. The task is not synthesis, but reduction of the data about leader action to its essential core – its values construct.

We Know It When We See It

As players in the interpersonal world of group activity, people have their own conceptions of leadership; that is, "we know it when we see it." While many researchers recognize this, few study leadership with that notion in mind. Past researchers have failed to account for this personal, even intimate, proclivity to define leadership. They ignore the personal values, individualized frames of reference, world views, and personal cultural constructs that ask each of us to answer for ourselves the question, "What is leadership?" We all need to rethink our own

M.R. Fairholm and G.W. Fairholm, *Understanding Leadership Perspectives*,
DOI: 10.1007/978-0-387-84902-7_1, © Springer Science + Business Media, LLC 2009

values mindset and begin work on understanding different leadership mindsets within which people operate and which they use to measure the success or failure of leadership.

Building on the growing body of research, the authors have reconceptualized past research findings to help the reader understand the threads of leadership theory. We have developed and present here the Leadership Perspective Model (LPM), which points to more comprehensive understanding of leadership in terms of ever-more encompassing and transcendent individual mental perceptions about leadership.

The Four Historical Threads of Leadership Thought

What makes a leader? What is leadership? What do leaders do? After more than a hundred years of modern study, these remain cogent questions. Many writers have offered either general or specific answers, but the discussion continues unabated. We need to understand past theory and rethink its application, if any exists, to present practice. Four threads of leadership thought help us understand the evolution of leadership's study: (1) TraitTheory (2) Behavior Theory, (3) Situational Theory, and (4) the newly conceptualized Values Theory.

Seen in terms of values, the first three threads lean toward a reductive methodology for understanding leadership by aggregating data about leaders, their behavior, and situations in which they find themselves. Sanchez (1988) suggests that examining leadership theory using these three threads provides a useful framework for analyzing the evolution of leadership thought. He cites Lewin's (1951) model of behavior as a reasonable foundation for examining these three elements of leadership (Colvin 1996). Lewin's model suggests that behavior depends upon the individuals involved and the circumstances of each individual's environment or situation, or $B = F(P, S)$: behavior is a function of person and situation. Colvin (1996) similarly describes the historical threads of leadership to include the leader as a person, the leader's behavior, and the leadership demands of the situation.

The first three approaches consider leadership in terms of what the leader is, what the leader does, and in which situation a leader is effective. Although all three of the historical threads mentioned above are still commonly used as a framework for understanding leadership, a new way of approaching leadership theory goes beyond these assumptions. In fact, many, if not all, of the leadership theories growing from the first three threads focus on skills, structure, and system concepts that are firmly within the realm of management, not leadership. At their worst, the past management-oriented frameworks divert our thinking from real leadership principles. At best they are only precursors and ingredients of values leadership – they contain parts of the guiding values and behaviors central to true leadership, but not its essential whole. Nevertheless, they are parts of our understanding and need to be considered in the development of a comprehensive theory of leadership such as the LPM.

Seen in terms of this emerging theoretical thread, the trait, behavior, and situational models constitute elements of a values-focus on leadership and not full-blown theories of leadership in their own right. The fourth thread, values leadership, moves us more in the proper direction, focusing on the distinctive nature of leadership. It moves the discussion toward a more holistic approach to interpret leadership. It changes the discussion from the leader to the phenomenon of leadership. This thread examines the relationships between leader and follower and the activity of sharing, or coming to share, common values, purposes, ideals, goals, and meaning in group and personal pursuits. This thread also points to the inevitable emergence of the perspectives approach upon which the LPM is based.

Trait Models: Who the Leader Is

The first modern theoretical thread examines the leader's traits of character. Trait theory deals with the capacities, talents, and person of the leader. An early iteration of trait theory focused on people who occupied significant positions and impacted societies in important ways – the great people of their time. The so-called Great Man (Person) model proposed that individuals become leaders because they are born with superior qualities that differentiate them from others. The contemporary version of this model argues that common character traits, if identifiable in recognized leaders, would help others develop their leadership capacities.

The search for the set of qualities that these superior individuals possessed began first by identifying generalities. For example, the idea that strength of personality equated to leadership was a consistent theme (Bingham 1927; Bogardus 1934; Bowden 1926; Kilbourne 1935). From these general discussions of the influence of personality, other studies tried to identify the set of qualities or traits that defined leadership across the board. Stogdill's (1974) review of leadership trait studies identified the following as important in successful leaders: chronological age, height, weight, physique, energy, health, appearance, fluency of speech, intelligence, scholarship, knowledge, judgment and decision, insight, originality, dominance, initiative, persistence, ambition, responsibility, integrity and conviction, self-confidence, mood control or mood optimism, emotional control, social and economic status, social activity and mobility, biosocial activity, social skills, popularity and prestige, cooperation, patterns of leadership traits that differ with situation, and the potential for transferability and persistence of leadership. Other studies focused on physical characteristics, social background, intelligence and ability, personality, task-related characteristics, and social characteristics (Stogdill 1974). The focus on the last two categories presages the beginnings of behavioral theory. Interestingly, Schein's (1989) study of women and leadership concluded that the traits of leadership are virtually identical between men and women, though some scholars disagree (Rosener 1990).

Broadening the Great Person theory, Scott (1973) discusses a theory of significant people. Significant people are the administrative elite who control the mind and techniques of others because they do significant jobs and are superior to everyone else. Their justification is not to control, but rather to improve efficiency. Since people will benefit from the techniques, which are not based on notions of control, Scott considers them to be morally correct. The result of improved efficiency will enable the elite to handle crisis situations better than before. An equation representing this concept is as follows: $AE + MT = SP$ (administrative elite + mind techniques = significant people). Leaders, presumably, have more developed mind techniques.

Charismatic leadership also is rooted in trait theory, though it is a topic of considerable debate. Conger and Kanungo (1988) call charisma the elusive factor in organizational effectiveness. Nadler and Tushman (1990) say that charismatic leadership, which involves enabling, energizing, and envisioning, is critical during times of strategic organizational change. Valle (1999) suggests charisma, in conjunction with crisis and culture, helps define successful leadership in contemporary organizations. Sashkin (1982), however, views charisma as a replacement for leadership, not a trait that leaders necessarily possess. Rutan and Rice (1981) question even whether charismatic leadership is an asset or a liability to organizations. The potential for good and evil is too significant to ignore because charismatic leaders influence others by appearing more than human.

Although the traits of leaders appear to be implicit in most discussion of leaders and leadership, this leadership model needs to be rethought. Traits alone cannot define the leadership construct. They need to be linked with other leadership requirements such as behavior and situation and more importantly with values, passion, spirit, and meaning-making. For example, Bennis (1982) used trait theory in his study of how organizations translate intention into reality in a cohort of 90 CEOs of reputable companies to identify specific qualities of leadership. Sashkin (1989) concluded that to understand leadership, one must consider personal characteristics as well as behaviors and situations.

More recent research has refocused interest in a purer form of trait studies. Jaques and Clement's (1991) work suggests that certain people are innately better suited to leadership roles (reminiscent of older foci on the debates about significant people and great men). A more direct reexamination of trait theory and leadership comes from Kirkpatrick and Locke (1991), who argue that though leadership study has moved beyond traits to behaviors and situational approaches, a shift back to a modified trait theory involving the personal qualities of leaders is occurring. They identified six traits leaders possess as distinct from nonleaders, but they argue that these traits are simply necessary, not sufficient, for success. Possessing these qualities gives individuals an advantage over others in the quest to be leaders; it does not predestine them to leadership. And, more recently, the work by Goleman (1995) on emotional intelligence harkens back to the trait theorists.

Trait theory is a constant in leadership studies. It is seemingly the most obvious avenue for researchers to embark upon, assuming, as it does, that leadership is simply an aggregation of the qualities of good leaders. While trait theory has its uses, the quest for a single list of universal qualities still eludes researchers. Theories of who the leader is help us understand one important aspect of leadership– the character of the individual leader. They do not do much to predict future leaders or anticipate leader behavior. They are of even less help in leadership development training. New, more operationally specific theories were needed and theorists turned their attention to another thread, this one focusing on the leader's behavior.

Behavior Theory: What the Leader Does

The second thread in the fabric of leadership is behavioral in nature. Behavior theory has attracted attention since the mid-twentieth century. The rationale is that concentrating on studying observable behavior may be more operationally useful than looking at traits. Most behavioralists focused on the top of the organizational hierarchy to understand management-cum-leadership practice (Argyris 1957; Barnard 1938a, b; Follett 1926, 1998; Gouldner 1954; Gulick 1937; Homans 1950; Maslow 1943; Taylor 1915; Whyte 1956). The assumption was that those at the top were more often than not called leaders. Therefore, what they did in their headship roles, the logic went, was leadership. The roots of the confusion that persists to this day between what is leadership and what is management are easy to see in the behavioral mindset.

The classic Ohio State and University of Michigan studies on leadership were the prime examples of and the watershed events for the development of behavior theory in leadership research. Hemphill (1950) and others discerned from factor analysis research two main elements of leadership behavior: consideration and initiation of structure. The contemporaneous Michigan studies verified these findings in describing relationship building and task-focused leadership orientations. Although the research questions and conclusions of each study were slightly different, the similarities are significant.

Coming out of these beginnings, Stogdill and Coons (1957) edited a series of research efforts describing and measuring leadership behavior. Jay (1968) popularized managerial tactics by using the advice and wisdom of Niccolo Machiavelli. Blake and Mouton (1964) developed a behaviorally based grid describing leadership behavior and positing an ideal leader type based on the two factors of the Ohio State studies. Gardner's (1987) review of the tasks of leadership moved the discussion from management to leadership, but retained the focus on leader behavior. And, in many ways, writers on total quality management (Deming 1986; Juran 1989) add the behavior approach to good managerial leadership.

Gardner's (1990) argument that most leadership behaviors are learned opened the door for many to write about organizational learning and leadership (Kouzes and Posner 1990; Senge 1990; Heifetz 1994; Hughes et al. 1993; Howard 2002). Much of what could be learned centered on the power relationships that are inevitable in the leadership dynamic, even though that dynamic was not yet clearly defined (Fairholm 1993). Much of the contemporary practices of leadership, and especially leadership development training, emerged based on modern illustrations of behavior theory (Drucker 1990; Kotter 1996; Vaill 1996; Collins and Porras 1997).

Tannenbaum and Schmidt (1973) saw leader behavior as a continuum ranging from manager-centered to subordinate-centered behavior. Davis and Luthans (1984) concluded that behavior represented environmental cues, discriminative stimuli, and results of behaviors that form a behavioral contingency for action. Leaders lead as they determine the occasion or provide needed stimulus for the evocation of follower behavior. Likert (1961) defined four basic leader behavior patterns – from highly job-centered to highly people-centered – elaborating McGregor's (1960) Theory X and Theory Y assumptions.

Interaction-expectancy theories emphasize the expectancy factor in the leader–follower relationship (Homens 1956). Leaders, Homens says, act to initiate structure-facilitating interaction, and leadership is the act of initiating structure. Stogdill and Coons (1957) develop an expectancy-reinforcement theory that defines the leader's role as setting mutually confirmed expectations about follower performances and the interactions followers can provide to the group. Evans (1970) and others suggest that leaders could determine the follower's perception of the rewards available to them, and hence, the leadership task is to determine the follower's perception of the behaviors required to get needed rewards. And Yukl (1988) postulates that leaders are to train, increasing follower task skills. A leader's consideration of others and a decentralized decision-making process, he argues, increase subordinate motivation, and, in turn, follower skill enhancement and motivation increase overall effectiveness.

Perceptual and cognitive theories focus on analysis and rational-deductive approaches to leadership. In attribution theory, leadership activity is dependent on what we think leaders should be and do. We see leader behavior and infer causes of these behaviors to be various personal traits or external constraints. We assume that the causes are a function of an experience-based rational process internalized by the leader. Classical behavior research is a more scientific approach to leadership study because behaviors can be seen, observed, measured, and potentially mimicked much more easily than traits, especially if traits were found to be innate to the person (Stogdill and Coons 1957).

Behavior theories provide a way for people to copy what other leaders have done, but the behaviors, in the end, do not prove to be generalizable. Importantly, they began the intellectual exercise to view leadership as something apart from the leader: a set of actions, attitudes, and values that involve the individual leader in intimate, personal ways. Behavior theory is where much of the confusion between leadership and management theory originated. The rise of this research focus coincided with the efforts to understand the rigors of management and executive authority in the industrial age. As a result, most past leadership theories in this vein were, in reality, management theories. Behavior theory, like trait theory, is a useful thread in weaving the full fabric of leadership, but neither theory is enough – singly or collectively. Consequently, the next intellectual thread added the dimension of situation – where leadership happens.

Situational Theory: Where Leadership Takes Place

Situational theory flows from the idea that behavior theory is not adequate for the complicated world of work and society because specific behaviors are most useful only in specific kinds of situations. Although there is a specific theory of leadership labeled "contingency theory" (Fiedler 1967), in the broadest sense this theory, also known as situational leadership theory, tries to define leadership through what leaders can do in specific situations that differ because of internal and external forces. In this sense, leadership is not definable without considering the specific situational context.

Situational theory argues that situations determine what leaders do and that behaviors must be linked to – be congruent with – the specific environment at hand. Situational theory, contingency theory, and the humanistic models of leadership followed. Researchers looked both at a wide range of variables that could influence leadership style and at different situations that would call for various leadership behaviors or call forth those individuals who have leadership traits. Situation theorists prioritize critical factors in the environmental situation, which impacts leader behavior, in which individual leaders operate. Thus, organization size, worker maturity, task complexity, or a variety of other so-called critical contingencies conditions leadership. According to this theory, situational factors are finite and vary according to several contingencies. A given leader behavior can be effective in only certain kinds of situations and not in others.

Contingency theorists posit the criticality of discrete factors in the situation in which individual leaders operate. These factors influence leader behavior and need to be part of a theory of leadership. That is, leadership must change with the situation or the situation must change to the kind of leadership exercised. Two versions of this theory are popular. The first, path-goal theory, involves a concentration on follower reactions to leader behavior. The second, contingency theory, concerns itself with the cluster of complex forces at work in the corporation that affect leader activity. Organization size, worker maturity, task complexity, or other so-called critical contingencies affect leadership action.

Homans (1950) develops a theory of leadership using three basic variables: action, interaction, and sentiments. Hemphill (1954) studied leadership in terms of the situations in which group roles and tasks are dependent upon the varying interactions between structure and the office of the positional authority. Evans (1970) suggests that the consideration or relationship aspects of leadership depend upon the availability of rewards and the paths through which those rewards are obtained. Fiedler's (1967) classic contingency theory model suggests that leadership effectiveness depends upon demands imposed by the situation in that task-oriented leaders are more effective in very easy and very difficult situations, and relationship-focused leaders do better in situations that impose moderate demands on the leader. Many researchers have used Fiedler's approach and his Least Preferred Coworkers (LPC) methodology to verify his hypotheses (Cheng 1982; Offermann 1984; Rice and Kastenbaum 1983; Shouksmith 1983).

Hollander (1978) suggests practical guidelines for leadership interactions in different group circumstances. Hersey and Blanchard (1979) built upon the behavioral work of Blake and Mouton (1964) and suggest that the best leadership style depends upon the situation and the development of the leader and the follower, concluding that empirical studies find that there is no normatively "best" style of leadership and that effectiveness depends upon the leader, the follower, and situational elements. However, Nicholls (1985) argued that the Hersey and Blanchard model violates three logical principles: consistency, continuity, and conformity. Nicholls' model posits a smooth progression of the leader from leader as parent to the leader as developer, and balances the task and relationship orientations in the leader's style. His model performs all the functions of the Hersey and Blanchard model in relating leadership style to the situation, while avoiding the problems inherent in the original's fundamental flaws.

Hunt, et al. (1981) describe the testing of a model of leadership effectiveness that centers on nine macrovariables and the idea of leadership discretion. Their macrovariables were represented by the complexity of the environment, context, and structure of a unit. Vecchio and Gobdel (1984) studied the vertical dyad linkage model of leadership, suggesting that the type and distribution of leader and follower interaction determine leader effectiveness. They determined that in-group status was associated with higher performance ratings and greater satisfaction with supervision, and reduced the propensity to quit. Objective measures of actual job performance yielded results that were congruent with the prediction of a positive correlation with subordinate in-group status. Triandis (1993) contributed to this line of thought by studying leadership in terms of triads.

Stimpson and Reuel (1984) studied the variable of gender in determining the kind of styles managers adopt. Results showed that managers tended to model the style of their boss and that females evidenced this tendency to a greater degree than males. Furthermore, when the boss was female, male subordinate managers became somewhat more participative than the boss, while female subordinate managers became more authoritarian. Vroom and Yetton (1973) developed a contingency model of decision-making to determine effective leadership behaviors in different situations. Heilman et al. (1984) were some of the many researchers who examined the validity of Vroom and Yetton's contingency model. They determined that the perspective of the individual viewing a leader influences the way in which he or she evaluates that leader's task effectiveness. Data from this study indicate a consistently more favorable affective response to the participative than to the autocratic leader, regardless of the subject's perspective or the circumstances.

Vroom and Yetton (1973) joined some accepted facts about leadership behavior to a rational structure and determined that some factors are most likely to result in leader success. For example, leaders ought to be directive when they are confident that they know what to do and when followers do not know. Exchange theory compares leader–follower relationships to economic transactions. Group members contribute at a cost to them and receive returns at a cost to group members. Interaction continues because members find the social exchange mutually rewarding. Effective leadership implies a fair exchange between leader and follower, when each party can satisfy the expectations of the other on a fair basis.

Versions of situational theory, called humanistic models of leadership, focus on the development of effective and cohesive organizations. They see a basic tension between the individual-in-the-group and the group. Their theories consider the so-called human factors in proposing models that accommodate both forces in the relationship. Humanistic theorists combine both behavior and situational elements to define an organizational surround that counters some factors that otherwise would be considered essentially antagonistic to human desires. The central theoretical problem is to devise a theory of leadership that allows for needed control without thwarting the individual's motives. The aim of leadership for the humanists is to change the corporation to provide freedom for individuals to realize their own potential for fulfillment and at the same time contribute to the firm's goals.

Contingency theory, especially in combination with trait and behavior theory, offered useful avenues of research into what makes leaders effective. Nevertheless, neither trait, nor behavior, nor contingency theory recognized the emotive and inspirational attachment that leaders tend to evoke in followers no matter what the situation. Contingency theory disappointed some thinkers because it reduced leadership to "it all depends."

To answer this lack of certainty about what makes an effective leader, some researchers began to rethink leadership as separate and distinct from leaders and conceive of it as a theory of social interaction or an organizational philosophy. In recent years it has been difficult to separate these new theoretical threads from each other as they morph from one concept to another. These new avenues of research included follower dynamics, relationships, intrinsic and extrinsic motivation, organizational culture, organizational change, and power in an effort to understand what variables influenced the effectiveness of leaders. Until now, they all have ignored values as the trigger of human action and the centerpiece of leadership, an omission this book resolves.

Values-Oriented Theory: The Fourth Theoretical Thread

Called "Values Leadership," a new and growing body of research focuses on the values of both leader and led that serve as the *raison d'être* for individual and group actions. Thus, a values leader fosters an environment where people have freedom of thought, are comfortable talking about their different values and aspirations, and can take action to realize their values-laden vision with no fear of persecution or retribution. The leader's authenticity is key as leaders try to impact organizational dynamics such as creativity, relationships, and innovation and attempt to create trusting work environments. Inspired leaders give voice to followers, serve them, listen to them, and positively impact their lives. Research generated in the last decade of the twentieth century begins to deal with these factors of the leader–follower relationship that previous models ignored. What is needed is a new thread, one that focuses fully on leadership as a discrete technology with separate systems of behaviors, techniques, and methods. Such a theory is found in the new theory of values-oriented leadership.

Shortcomings of Leadership Threads: Confusing Leadership and Management

The problem with past theories is that they fail to distinguish unique leadership tasks, skills, behaviors, or thought processes from those of management. Although situation and behavior theories form the nexus of current leadership studies, both are still rather focused on close control of workers and the situation. The job is to make every person, system, activity, program, and policy countable, measurable, predictable, and therefore controllable. These emphases may be important in managing things, but many object to them as the basis for leading people. Past so-called leadership theories stress this kind of control and are really nothing more than theories of management. Some, actually many, even use the two words inter-changeably, thereby confusing the issue and making contemporary leadership notions irrelevant to reality. But leadership is not management. Something else is needed; some new thinking is called for.

Leadership subscribes to a different reality than management. Leaders think differently, value things differently, and relate to others differently. Selznick(1957) argues that they infuse the group with values. Leaders have their own unique expectations for followers and seek different results from individuals and from the group than do managers. They impact stakeholder groups in volitional ways, not through formal authority mechanisms. Leadership and management use separate technologies, with different agendas, motivations, personal histories, and thought processes. Given these essential differences between leadership and management, any theory that combines the two systems of behavior and ideology must necessarily be faulty because it would ignore essential features of each or else over-emphasize features of one to the detriment of the other. This argument is made more obvious as we study the different leadership perspectives outlined in this book.

However, here we must make a clear distinction. Just as management and leadership are terms to be distinguished, the terms "leader" and "leadership" are also not synonymous, nor are they interchangeable. The confusion and imprecise use of each term in describing certain phenomena may be at the core of the confusion (and dissension) among those who study the topic. The confusion often stems from the methods used to study leadership. Some researchers view leadership study from a reductionist perspective – they aggregate lessons learned from case studies of leaders to deduce the "essence" of leadership.

Their view is that leaders define leadership. Another approach to leadership research, however, views leadership as something beyond the sum of individual leader styles, behaviors, and qualities. In this approach, *leadership* encompasses a unique conception of individual interaction. That is, leaders do not define leadership; rather, leadership defines what a leader is, what a leader does, and who may be labeled a leader. One perspective is very much an aggregation or mechanistic system. The other is much more a philosophy.

The philosophical approach frees us of the notions that leadership is positional, hierarchical, or managerial and allows for leadership to be more pervasive in organizations and life because leadership is not tied to structure, special qualities, or birth. It moves us from mundane, cookie-cutter approaches to power relationships and allows us to accept creativity, flexibility, and inherent, emerging order. The approach is inspirational rather than merely motivational. The quest for this more holistic approach is to study what leadership actually is. The attempt, it is assumed, will yield different and more precise definitions of leadership than we have had in the past and will, as a consequence, change our definitions of leader based on the elements of these more precise definitions.

Values Leadership: Beyond Reductionism

When researchers focus on a broader, more philosophical values conception of leadership, the emphasis is not on studying specific leaders in specific situations, doing specific things. Rather, the focus is on the common relationship elements exhibited over time which characterize this thing called "leadership" – the less definable aspects of relationship between people. The elements of this relationship deal more with values, morals, culture, inspiration, motivation, needs, wants, aspirations, hopes, desires, influence, power, and the like. Such values-based theories are an early (late 1980s and early 1990) example of a shift in methodologies. This shift began to distinguish leadership and management and change our focus from the leader to the phenomenon of leadership. Burns attempted this in his 1978 book, but only recently a fully holistic view of leadership has emerged.

Basically, values leadership theorists believed that there was something unique about leadership that transcended the situation and remained constant despite the contingencies. Values-based transformational theory defines this something as the leader tapping into long-held beliefs and personal or organizational values that inspire others to move in certain directions and develop in certain ways (Bass and Avolio 1994; Bennis and Nanus 1985; Burns 1978; Covey 1992; Cuoto 1993; DePree 1989; Fairholm 1991; Greenleaf 1977; Manz and Sims 1989; O'Toole 1996; Quinn and McGrath 1985; Rost 1991). The primary leadership role is recognizing the need to integrate the values of all followers into programs and actions that facilitate development of both leader and led. Leaders evidence their personal values as they create a culture that fosters stakeholder expression in the workplace and nurtures the whole person at work (Krishnakumar and Neck 2002). Leaders who do this enhance organizational performance and long-term success (Herman and Gioia 1998; Neal et al. 1999). They facilitate creativity (Freshman 1999), honesty and trust (Wagner-Marsh and Conley 1999), personal fulfillment (Burack 1999), and commitment to goals (Delbecq 1999). The leadership task is to align with human nature and to change the culture from a task focus to one that attends to the needs of followers' values and expectations (Fairholm and Fairholm 2000). Such leadership fosters values that help people become their best selves through creating, living within, and encouraging shared culture based on such values (Schein 1992). This values leadership philosophy allows a leader to overcome the pathologies of today's organizations and societies because it recognizes the need to develop the individual, letting him or her express values and flourish independently, while maintaining a functioning organization that fulfills its goals in an excellent manner.

In a more practical sense, values leadership encompasses the actions of leaders who internalize and legitimize group values and teach these values to followers who internalize and express them in their individual behaviors. In this sense, leaders are teachers with a unique capacity to understand the values that enervate a group and individuals and to communicate them effectively (Tichy 1997). Upon these principles also rests the communitarian notion of the good society, one that trusts its members to behave in a way that reflects their values because they are core beliefs, not because they fear public officials or are motivated by economic gains (Etzioni 1996). In this way, leaders create a culture of trust that allows individuals to act in ways supportive of the group values and goals while enhancing their autonomy because of self-led activity (Fairholm and Fairholm 2000; Fairholm 1994; Kouzes and Posner 1993; Mitchell 1993).

Values leadership, then, is the philosophy that seeks to meld individual actions into a unified system focused on group desired outcomes and is only possible if a few criteria are met. First, the members of the organization must share common values. Second, leadership has to be thought of as the purview of all members of the group and not just the heads. Third, the focus of leadership must be individual development and the fulfillment of group goals. And fourth, shared, intrinsic values must be the basis for all leader action. Values become the bridge that links the individual or groups of individuals with the tasks that are required or expected of the group. Instead of studying the leader, values leadership theory engages the entire process of leadership, taking into account such attributes as traits, behavior, and situations, but not being dependent on or limited by them. It is a transcendent point of view that intends a holistic understanding of leadership. To understand better that holistic view, we have to understand the relational aspects, the transforming effects, and the moral philosophy of leadership.

Leadership Happens in Relationships

Leadership is relational. It is an interpersonal connection between the leader and the constituents based on mutual needs and interests. Kouzes and Posner (1993) argue that leadership is a reciprocal relationship between those who choose to lead and those who choose to follow. Unless we have a relationship, there is no venue within which to practice leadership. It is something we experience in an interaction with another human being. Leadership is a form of consciousness in which people are aware that they exist in a state of interconnectedness with all life and seek to live in a manner that nourishes and honors that relationship at all levels of activity. Jacobsen (1994) indicates that there is a powerful inference that the leader's values and leadership itself are related. Values theory is not related to any one style or model of leadership but can be viewed across all types of leadership equally (Zwart 2000). Leaders view the realms of personal and group values and the secular world as inherent in each other – that is, all leadership is values-laden and relationship-based.

Leadership Is Transforming of the Individual

Burns (1978) identified two types of leadership: transactional and transforming. The relationship between most managers and followers is transactional. On the other hand, values leadership describes a situation in which the leader chooses a vision grounded in his or her values and recognizes followers' strengths and interests. The result of this leadership is mutual stimulation and elevation that convert – change – followers into leaders and may convert leaders into moral agents. Transforming leadership implies changing the individual as well as the group to enable leaders and followers to reach higher levels of accomplishment and self-motivation. It releases human potential for the collective pursuit of common goals (Fairholm 1994). Leaders set peoples' spirits free and enable them to become more than they might have thought possible. Values leadership focuses first on improving the leader's own sense of self, his or her spirituality as a precursor to elevating the human spirit of others. This leadership has a transforming effect on both leader and led, raising the level of human conduct and ethical aspiration of both.

The Moral Philosophy of Leadership: What Greenleaf and Burns Began

Much of values-based transformational theory owes its beginnings to the work of Robert Greenleaf and James MacGregor Burns in the late 1970s. Greenleaf (1977) proposed a thesis he himself labeled unpopular: that servants emerge as leaders and that we should follow only servant-leaders. Greenleaf describes how service, first and foremost, qualifies one for leadership and that service is the distinctive nature of true leaders. In *Servant Leadership*, Greenleaf traces this idea from conception to potential application, but he peppers the discussion with a serious focus on the need for and the ways to serve. He moves the discussion of leadership toward an explicitly moral dimension and an overarching social relationship phenomenon.

Greenleaf defines servant leadership as the natural feeling that one first wants to serve. This conscious choice brings one to aspire to lead. The difference manifests itself in the care taken by the servant to make sure that other people's highest priority needs are being met. A characteristic of servant leadership is to serve the real needs of people, needs that can only be discovered by listening. Greenleaf asserts that leadership is about choosing to serve others and making available resources that serve a higher purpose, and in turn, give meaning to work.

He suggests that there is a moral principle emerging that guides leadership, and perhaps always has: the only authority deserving one's allegiance is that which is freely and knowingly granted by the led to the leader in response to, and in proportion to, the clearly evident servant nature of the leader. Adherents to this will not casually accept authority of existing institutions. Rather, they will freely respond only to individuals who are recognized as leaders because they are proven and trusted as servants. Servant leaders constantly ask four major questions: (1) Are other people's highest priority needs being served? (2) Do those served grow as persons? (3) Do they, while being served, become healthier, wiser, freer, more autonomous, and more likely themselves to become servants? (4) Is there a positive effect on the less privileged in society? Or will they at least not be further deprived? Ultimately, Greenleaf's servant leadership model assumes that the only way to change a society (or just keep it going) is to produce enough people who simply want to serve.

In *Leadership* (1978), Burns adds to this philosophical orientation. He is not trying to develop a list of qualities or even techniques that "leaders" in the past have developed or used. Rather, he delves into the true nature of leadership – not what it looks like, but what it conceptually is and hence also points toward a general theory of moral leadership. Burns explicitly states that there should be a "school of leadership," that leadership is a legitimate field of study. This field should, he argues, marry the heretofore elitist literature on leadership and the populistic literature on followership.

Burns begins this marriage by differentiating between transactional and transforming leadership, helping us to initiate a recognition of the difference between management and leadership. Transforming leadership is a personal attribute of leaders, not just a formal aspect of organizational structure or design. These leaders, therefore, become models for others to follow. Transforming leaders inspire, change, and energize their followers to become their best selves. His greatest, self-stated concern, however, is with the idea of moral leadership and its power, influence, and capacity to change and inspire people.

For transforming leadership to be authentic, it must incorporate a central core of moral values. The leader taps into and shapes the common values, goals, needs, and wants to develop and elevate others in accordance to the mutually agreed upon values and then fosters appropriate changes. Leaders address the needs, wants, and values of their followers (and their own) and, therefore, serve as an independent force in changing the makeup of the followers' values set through gratifying motives. Authentic transforming leaders are engaged in the moral uplift of their followers; they share mutually rewarding visions of success and empower them to transform those visions into realities. They know themselves, their strengths and weaknesses, and how to fully exploit their strengths and compensate for their weaknesses. Transforming leaders are not the mirror image of the transactional leader. Rather, they are an enriched transactional leader (Bass and Avolio 1994) – a transactional leader who is also charismatic in such a way that pushes collaborators to go further than what is formally demanded of them.

Transactional leadership (Burns 1978) is in play when someone takes the lead in working with others with the objective of exchanging things of value. A purchase of something for consideration is an example of an exchange, as is trading goods for other goods, or providing psychic rewards for desired action. A transaction is a bargain in which involved parties recognize that their purposes are related insofar as the present transaction will advance their purposes. But, the relationship is temporary and bargainers have no enduring links holding them together. Leadership in this context is episodic: nothing binds leader and follower together in a mutual and continuing pursuit of a higher purpose beyond the actual transaction. Transactional leadership is therefore defined as an economic exchange relationship. The transactional leader is exclusively concerned with the results of the relationship and focuses his or her work on negotiating extrinsic exchanges and on controlling the actions of his or her collaborators so that they follow the leader's will. Transactional leadership depends on contingent reinforcement (Bass and Avolio 1994), and, therefore, good transactional leaders use skills of negotiation, are authoritarian, even aggressive, and seek maximum benefit from the economic relationship that they have created. However, the benefits from transactions remain tangible and extrinsic. There is no consideration of other higher level value-added partnerships.

However, Burns goes beyond transactional and transforming leadership definitions toward an implementation of a general theory of moral leadership, developed in part by understanding the transforming and transactional distinction but not by the institutionalization of this distinction in management texts and consulting practices. For the cursory reader, his observations of these two "leaderships" become the point, instead of serving to elucidate the more general point of leadership that he was trying to develop.

Burns creates a theoretical leadership model that contains definitions and perspectives so that the study of leadership practice will be both more focused and more accurate. Much of his definitional work revolves around the concepts of power, motives, and values. Power and the power-wielder need little comment here; motives and values deserve more attention. From his conceptual work on values and motives, and drawing upon the themes outlined earlier, Burns develops a general theory of leadership. His theory is not limited to the governmental or corporate world, but applies also to the social world, the family, the volunteer group, and the work unit. His conception of leadership goes beyond political theory and historical biographies that he uses to develop his themes. He argues that leadership is, at heart, philosophical: it involves a relationship of engagement between the leader and follower based on common purpose and collective needs. The key to leadership is the discerning of key values and motives of both the leader and follower and, in accordance with them, elevating others to a higher sense of performance, fulfillment, autonomy, and purpose.

The development of this general theoretical framework of leadership has dramatically altered the study and application of leadership principles. Burns' work is an essential part of any study into the true nature, purpose, and applicability of leadership in today's organizations. Not everyone accepts this approach. Perhaps this explains why some of the recent literature on leadership misses the point about understanding leadership holistically, focusing instead on the checklists and measurements of "effective leadership" and often confusing true leadership with management functions. Burns' great service to the study of leadership may lie less in the popular distinction between transactional and transforming leadership (though this ushers in the contemporary distinctions between the technologies of leadership and those of management) and more in the elevation of leadership as a philosophical and developmental relationship between people who share common purpose, motivations, and values.

Both Greenleaf and Burns deserve recognition for their part in enhancing the study and practice of leadership by transcending the traditional focus on the leader and focusing on the more pervasive, holistic philosophy of leadership. Such a holistic approach informs values-based theories of leadership and, in fact, forms the foundation of the LPM. It attempts to define leadership by its implementation, its tools and behaviors, and its approaches to followers and, through that understanding of leadership, see whether someone may or may not be called a leader.

The Leadership Mindset: Alternative Ways to Think About Leadership

Central to this book is the idea that the title of "leader" does not necessarily denote true leadership, nor does the absence of the title signify the absence of leadership. Understanding the role and function of leadership is the single most important intellectual task of this generation, and leadership is the most needed skill. The reason is simple: leaders play a major role in helping us shape our lives. Leaders define business and its practice. They determine the character of society. They define our teams, groups, and communities. They set and administer government policy. In all walks of life, leaders' behaviors set the course others follow and determine the measures used to account for group actions taken. Success in the new millennium, as in the past one, will depend on how well leaders understand their roles, the leadership process, and their own as well as their groups' values and vision. Their behaviors set the course others follow and determine the values and other measures used to account for group actions.

However, people have alternative value-orientations, different ways of viewing the world. These values not only shape how they internalize observation and externalize belief sets, they also determine how they measure success. Thus, defining leadership is an intensely personal activity limited by our individual values or our mental state of being, that is, the unique set of our mind at any given point in time. Our leadership perspective defines what we mean when we say "leadership" and shapes how we view successful leadership in ourselves or in others; it is the criteria we use to determine who is and who is not our personal leader.

The stumbling block to understanding the true nature of leadership is due, in part, to the way we structure ideas and thinking. Defining leadership is limited only by our unique world views and personal values paradigms. Leaders must be capable of leading and managing teams, employees, and other leaders with identities and belief systems different from their own (Howard 2002). Recent research adds several models useful to leadership theory-building. For example, Gibbons (1999) analyzes gaps in existing theory-building efforts in contemporary leadership literature and clarifies measurement and definitional issues and assesses the assumptions and claims of spirit at work in validity terms. Korac-Kakabadse et al. (2002) describe the characteristics of values leadership as those interested in moral, social, and political reforms. And, Fry (2003) describes a causal theory of leadership using an intrinsic model that incorporates vision, hope (faith), and altruistic love. This emerging research prefigures a basis of personal perspective upon which a full-blown model can be fleshed out.

The idea that leadership is in the mind of the individual and that his or her leadership perspective is true for them regardless of the objective reality is new in leadership studies, but it is not new in other fields. The idea of alternative mental perspectives is supported by both the social sciences and psychology. Several contemporary models serve to illustrate the intellectual support for this view. Drath and Palus (1994) take a constructivist approach to describe leadership as meaning creation. Bolman and Deal (1984, 1997) think that leader–follower relationships or frames are metaphors that dramatically influence a leader's organizational stance and the group activities that take place. Thus, leadership is contingent on the metaphor the organization has chosen to use to describe the condition or nature of the organization. Several writers describe organizational culture in similar ways, ascribing to a given culture the power to shape members' thoughts, actions, and behaviors (Herzberg 1984; Hofstede 1993; Quinn and McGrath 1985; Schein 1992). Certainly cultural differences in member behavior are obvious to even the casual observer. People of different national, ethnic, religious, corporate, or other origins behave differently, measure success differently, and value material and intellectual things differently. Barker (1992) popularized the word "paradigm" to describe a pattern of integrating thoughts, actions, and practices people and groups adopt to define their personal world. Graves (1970) talks of "states of being," or levels of personal existence that determine our actions, affect our relationships, and measure our success.

Cultural Filters

Each of us filters our perceptions, our values, and our experience though our unique culture (Herzberg 1984; Hofstede 1993; Quinn and McGrath 1985; Schein 1992). Part of the confusion and imprecision we see in the literature has to do with this personal cultural life filter through which we view leadership. As we move through life, we change those around us and are changed by them. Our cultural biases are very often more important than objective reality. Our individual perception of what leaders do takes on meaning in the context of our cultural experiences as both leader and follower of another's leadership. Accepting as valid any other understanding of leadership than our personal one is, obviously, beyond our own experience and impossible.

Paradigms

A paradigm is a set of rules groups adopt, often implicitly, that define the boundaries of the acceptable. It tells us how to behave in order to be successful. Our paradigm provides a model for how problems are solved, people are to be treated, and individual and group actions interpreted. Barker (1992) defines a paradigm as a set of organizational realities, such as values, beliefs, traditional practices, methods, tools, attitudes, and behaviors. Social group members construct paradigms to integrate their thoughts, actions, and practices. A leadership paradigm consists of the rules and standards as well as accepted examples of leadership practice, laws, theories, applications, and work relationships in a corporation or team.

The power of paradigms is that they affect our ability to see the world. Quite literally, what is obvious to one person may be totally invisible to another. Thus, those people who see leadership as position-based cannot accept the idea that leaders can occupy positions in the middle or lower reaches of the organization as rational. Similarly, people who see leadership as management cannot accept as plausible any notion that leaders ought to deal with a follower's spiritual side as well as his or her skills.

States of Being

An interesting way to think about leadership relationships within the group and the world is in terms of "states of being," or "levels of existence" (Graves 1970). Graves builds an interpersonal relationships model that emphasizes the power of individual values and personal perception, or point of view, in shaping our thoughts and actions. Graves' work confirms the perspectival approach in concluding that whatever level of existence we are in determines our values and therefore our actions, our relationships, and our measures of success for self and for others. A person in a given level uses the mindset of that level to solve problems and choose his or her course of action in relationships with others. Our preferences about leadership are appropriate to that reality. If we were in another state, we would act differently, using alternative values and ethics to judge the appropriateness of our behavior and our cohorts'. Growth is marked by progressive subordination of older, lower-order behavioral systems to newer higher-level behavioral systems. However, some people arrive in one state and cannot move to another. Others stay in one level for a time and regress to a lower order. Regardless of the level, when we are in a given level we have only the degree of freedom to think about an issue granted by that level.

Each of these researchers describes a mindset or point of view, a personal perspective, that may or may not reflect reality, but which individuals adopt based on their set of values as a way to make sense of the dynamic interactive process called leadership. Regardless of the focus, the mindset we adopt orders our thinking and makes understanding easier. While in a specific mindset, whether we see it as management, values setting, trust building, or spiritually focused, we can understand leadership only in terms of our unique set of values that form the parameters of our point of view. Unless something extraordinary happens, we cannot accept other points of view as credible. Practically speaking, each one of us is locked into our current mental biases about leadership, or any other seminal idea, and need heroic measures to move out of it.

Thus, defining leadership is an intensely personal activity limited by our distinctive paradigms or our mental state of being, our unique "mental world" defined by our ideas and experience. Our cumulative experience creates a mindset that lets us see our world more globally than our local experience. But, at the same time, it creates a kind of prison that constrains our freedom of action. The mental perspective we construct both frees us to function within its parameters and limits our ability to think beyond its borders. Over time, this individualized mental perspective will change as our experiences change. But, while we are in a given "fabricated" frame of reference we may not be able to even accept the idea that other perspectives exist or that they may be more useful to us than our currently held perspective.

We can conceive of our leadership mindset in terms of increasingly complex levels of mental and emotional awareness. While we are in one reality we may understand less complex realities but not fully comprehend those more complex ones. We may even think that another level of understanding is not even credible. Leadership, therefore, is a phenomenon best described as an holarchical system (Koestler 1970) of ever more encompassing and transcendent perspectives of social interaction based on such personal elements as values, vision, direction of action, and free choice.

While leadership may indeed encompass certain discrete elements, the individual's ability to understand or apply those elements may be limited by the mental perspectives they (and, perhaps, their followers) bring to organizational and social life. It is in this direction that research may be fruitfully focused to determine leadership concepts that would inform both the theory and practice of leadership. Rethinking leadership research to focus on a perspective approach will let practitioner and analyst alike understand the leadership phenomenon holistically. The next likely step in leadership thought is to look at leadership in broader, more philosophical, more holistic terms, recognizing that individual perspectives are brought to bear on understanding leadership. Discovering what those perspectives are is the purpose of this book.

Levels of Leadership

In sum, different people can view a given example of leadership differently. That is, leadership may be the same – practiced in the same way for the same results, using the same technologies – but depending on how we look at it, we see it in vastly different light. How we see it depends on what mindset we occupy. Using a personal example for illustrative purposes, the authors can say that they have observed and experienced at least five levels of understanding about what leaders do and the leadership process. Initially our view of leadership was technical, scientific, procedural, and managerial. Later, we saw leadership as a function of only excellent managerial performance. Still later, as we observed leaders getting others to do what they (the leader) wanted done, without exercising control, our focus turned to the idea that leadership was a process of getting followers to share the leader's vision and values.

Later still, we expanded that idea to include the perception of leadership as a culture-creation task; these created cultures, however, must support high levels of interactive mutual trust. Neither shared values nor trust cultures seem to explain leader success. It is clear now that leadership is the job of transforming the core nature or character of the leader, of the corporation, and of people themselves. In this perspective, we can accept the kernel of truth in each of the other states of being. They all have value. Each contributes to and supports the progressively higher levels. All point to leadership as a function of spirit.

Which of these states of being you, the reader, bring to leadership will depend on your past experiences and cumulative wisdom. Only time will tell which is the real, authentic, objective truth. However, each mindset adds incrementally to our collective insight about the leadership task. In the meantime, rethinking our perception of what leadership is, while seemingly extreme, or even, ridiculous, may be interesting and educational. It may even be an event sufficient to move you to another state, another perspective about what leadership truly is.

These five mental models mark the 100-year-plus history of intellectual thought to full understanding of leadership. Each has had its period of prominence in the past. Each is true in that it helps describe some part(s) of the leadership task. They each lay out a logical, rational – although incomplete – pattern of leader action. It is only together that they define the full picture. Below are brief descriptions of the different levels of leadership that form the basis for this book.

- Leadership as (Scientific) Management – Leadership equals management in that it focuses on getting others to do work the leader wants done, essentially separating the planning (management) from the doing (labor).

- Leadership as Excellence Management – Leadership emphasizes quality and productivity process improvement rather than just product and people over either product or process, and requires the management of values, attitudes and organizational aims within a framework of quality improvement.

- Values Leadership – Leadership is the integration of group behavior and shared values through setting values and teaching them to followers through an articulated vision that leads to excellent products and service, mutual growth, and enhanced self-determination.

- Trust Culture Leadership – Leadership is a process of building cultures within which leader and follower (in an essentially voluntary relationship, perhaps from a variety of individual cultural contexts) trust each other to accomplish mutually valued goals using agreed-upon processes.

- Spiritual (Whole-Soul) Leadership – Leadership is the integration of the components of work and self – of the leader and each follower – into a comprehensive system that fosters continuous growth, improvement, self-awareness, and self-leadership so that leaders see each worker as a whole person with a variety of skills, knowledge, and abilities that invariably go beyond the narrow confines of job needs.

Perhaps each of us has to move through each leadership mindset, accepting one before we are ready to experience the next. This book is intended to help the traveler see the landmarks guiding this movement. It is also intended to raise the possibility that the path you are on now is not the only one, and may not be the best to meet your leadership needs in the twenty-first century.

Summary and Conclusions

In very general terms, these five perspectives are an elaboration of one general theme: values are central to the leadership phenomenon. The notion that values play a key role in leadership provides a way to frame the variety of individual perspectives about values, organizations, and leadership. The first two perspectives focus on values that relate to organizational hierarchy and authority. The last three take into account a more personal approach to values. Values leadership makes the case for values displacement as the task of leadership. The next perspective goes further to generalize shared values in a culture characterized by mutual, interactive trust. The final perspective makes the case that when engaging in leadership not all the values the leader holds are important, but only the core, soul values, the ones we just will not compromise, define the true essence of leadership just as they define the leader as a person.

This model suggests that while there is a kind of evolutionary order to our understanding, each leadership mindset has adherents today. They can be ranked hierarchically, or more precisely holarchically, along a continuum from managerial control to spiritual holism. These leadership perspectives might best be illustrated as relating to each other in terms of concentric circles where each circle is of itself a complete picture of leadership for some. For others, however, there exist perspectives that encompass and transcend previous perspectives (see Fig. 1).

As mentioned earlier, researchers attempt repeatedly to answer the question "What does it really mean to be a leader?" But the focus of many, if not most, is on the leader, as if to say leadership can only be understood by studying specific individuals in specific situations. There are some, though, who go beyond the mere study of leaders. Recognizing that studying individual leaders may not facilitate a better understanding of leadership, these researchers reject, implicitly or explicitly, the idea that leadership per se is a summation of the qualities, behaviors, or situational responses of individuals in a position of prominence. To study leaders is not, in this sense, to study leadership.

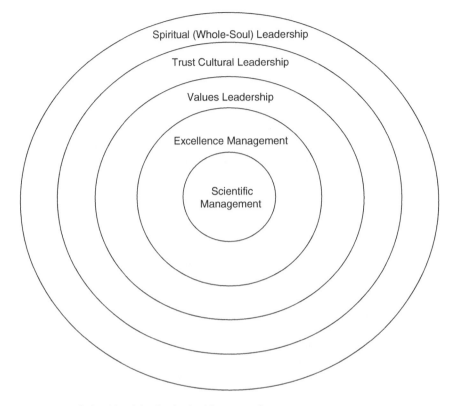

Fig. 1 Interrelationship of the five leadership perspectives

The development of leaders is a significant individual and public goal. It is, however, dependent upon the conception of leadership. There is an implicit acceptance that leadership is something more expansive than the title "leader" and that an integrated understanding of leadership requires a broader, more holistic approach. That is, one must try to understand the essential nature of leadership.

Chapter 2
The Leadership Perspectives Model

Leadership is a reality that people accept, and even long for, but rarely understand enough to describe accurately. To understand the true significance of leadership, the analyst must explicitly determine the difference between management and leadership. In the past, the idea of leadership has suffered as it has been defined at best as being synonymous with good management and at worst as just another skill that makes up the competent manager.

One useful difference between management and leadership that others sometimes make implicitly is the idea that headship – the person filling the top box in the organizational chart – is not always leadership, even though much of the literature assumes it is. Differentiating between the structure of headship and the philosophy of leadership allows the concept of leadership to be spread throughout the organization, allowing any worker to develop into a leader in his or her own right.

Leadership is the art of influencing people to accomplish organizational goals, while management is the science of specifying and implementing means needed to accomplish these ends. In a sense, the pure leader is a philosopher and the pure manager is a technologist. As a person moves up the organizational ladder to higher and higher levels of responsibility, a point is reached, presumably, where the nature and scope of required competencies change. The incumbent no longer practices management skills but moves (or should move) on to something else – to leadership focused on values, change in the character of the institution, and issues of long-term survival. What was learned on the way up has little value once one reaches the top of the hierarchy, because what one does there is (or should be) so different. We can also observe that the kind of true leadership emerging from hierarchical development is not dependent on an organizational hierarchy at all, but can be manifest in any social, collective activity.

This insight about leadership begins to clarify some of the confusion that all too often characterizes modern leadership thought. Accepting this organizational reality, researchers are beginning to record the presence of divergent views of leadership in the literature and in observed practice. Frameworks to understand these differing views are just now emerging. This book outlines one such framework: The Leadership Perspectives Model (LPM).

M.R. Fairholm and G.W. Fairholm, *Understanding Leadership Perspectives*,
DOI: 10.1007/978-0-387-84902-7_2, © Springer Science+Business Media, LLC 2009

Leadership Perspectives: The Fifth Thread
of Leadership Research

While the practice of leadership is easily recognized in social and organizational life, the theory of leadership continues to be refined. From trait to behavior to contingency theory, from values-based theory to a distinction between leadership and management, researchers are attempting to better understand leadership. Although leadership studies may isolate some specific definitional elements, these elements may not be understood fully nor put into practice at all except through the individual's conception of what leadership is. Discovering those perspectives builds upon the four research threads discussed in Chapter 1 and constitutes a fifth thread of leadership research. This fifth thread is the perspectives approach to leadership theory and practice.

The theoretical model introduced in Chapter 1 posits five leadership perspectives arranged in a hierarchical pattern with the higher encompassing the lower levels. Graphically, this model can be depicted as five concentric circles, each building upon the lower-order perspectives (see Fig. 1). Identifying these perspectives rests on observation of leaders in action and on analysis of available literature. Much of that research has been anecdotal in character. Experience, reason, and anecdote have always had their place in leadership studies. But new research using content analysis techniques, coupled with interviews of randomly selected midlevel executives, provides specific validation of both the five perspectives and their hierarchical nature.

The LPM includes more comprehensive and operationally verifiable activities and approaches to leading others than do many other leadership theories, historical or contemporary. This model precisely identifies unique elements of each perspective and uses this new insight to validate both the descriptive and prescriptive potential of the LPM approach. That is, the LPM represents a theory in the traditions of the social sciences.

The LPM perspectives approach demonstrates that individuals hold alternative conceptions of what leadership actually is and use their conception to measure their leadership activities and that of others. Each of us draws upon our own mental conception to judge whether or not others are exercising leadership. Frustration and confusion surrounding the definitions of leadership and the lack of agreement on what leadership is can be explained by understanding that each individual has a unique concept of the phenomenon. Judging which of the conceptions is right or not is a significant question, but the intent in this chapter is simply to offer an intellectual foundation for the LPM itself.

Research Validation of the Five Leadership Perspectives

The Leadership Perspectives Model (LPM) is soundly based on both research and practice and is useful, as theory should be, for both descriptive and prescriptive purposes. It is descriptive in the sense of exploring how one may perceive leadership and positioning that perspective into an overarching leadership model. The LPM explains the activities, tools, approaches, and techniques required to be effective or successful within each of the five perspectives. The five perspectives, themselves, are legitimate constructs that aid understanding about how individuals may view leadership and together outline a comprehensive leadership model.

Data suggest that leadership is more than the simple aggregation of those perspectives. These data illustrate that successive perspectives encompass and transcend previous perspectives. Furthermore, the tools and behaviors of a "lower-order" perspective may be the building blocks for the tools and behaviors of succeeding perspectives. Importantly, as one moves up the hierarchy of leadership perspectives, the tools, behaviors, and approaches one uses are themselves encompassed and transcended so as to be obsolete or even antithetical to the activities of a higher-order perspective. Illustrative of this point is one executive interviewed who suggested that the things she did and believed as a first-line manager were totally different than the things she does and believes now as a senior executive. The skills and perspectives she used in getting to her position were no longer effective in that position. As she progressed through different perspectives of what leadership meant to her, she also progressed through different tools and behaviors needed to practice it.

The leadership construct outlined in Chapter 1 is based on the following assumptions that were validated in the research. The first is that the five leadership perspectives can be delimited by specific operational categories and elements, and the second is that each is distinguishable in the workplace. These first two assumptions of the LPM exploit the notion that individuals conceive of leadership in distinct and discernable ways. The third assumption explores whether and how these perspectives relate to each other in a way that helps clarify the leadership phenomenon. The third assumption is that the perspectives are related to each other in a hierarchy (or more precisely a holarchy) in that each perspective encompasses and transcends the previous, making what might be viewed as a hierarchy of leadership conceptions. Koestler (1970) defines a holon as any stable portion of a social hierarchy that displays rule-governed behavior and/or structural constancy. Each holon can stand on its own, without reference to the other subunits. In essence, each leadership perspective in the LPM is a holon. Looking downward, each subunit serves as an encompassing whole. In this sense, looking down the hierarchy, each perspective looks like a complete view of leadership. Looking upward, each unit serves to point toward larger, more encompassing ways of engaging or understanding the whole notion. In this sense, each perspective points to and grounds a broader, more holistic view of leadership. Hence, the LPM explains not only five distinct leadership perspectives, but also how each perspective builds toward a higher, more encompassing and transcendent view of leadership. The end result is a more comprehensive and holistic understanding of the leadership phenomenon.

Identifying Operational Categories and Leadership Elements

The basic constructs or perspectives of the LPM include the following notions of leadership, which will be more fully explained in the subsequent pages: Leadership as (Scientific) Management, Leadership as Excellence Management, Values Leadership, Trust Culture Leadership, and Spiritual (Whole-Soul) Leadership. Identifying each perspective as unique requires us to present distinct activities or behaviors or philosophies peculiar to each. The research and theory development identifies three operational task categories that are useful in fleshing out the LPM. These operational categories are further divided into 40 specific leadership elements. These categories and elements constitute the skeleton of the Leadership Perspective Model and serve as the basis for analysis of each perspective.

To make the five perspectives useful in everyday work, leaders must know three concepts. These three notions form the basis of the operational categories in the model: (1) the criteria for differentiating what each perspective really means in action, (2) what specific sets of behaviors or techniques make that perspective apparent in social interaction, and (3) how each perspective sees the leader–follower relationship in interaction. These three operational categories of analysis help us see each leadership perspective in practice. They are generic enough to be useful across the perspectives but offer a chance to define unique criteria or leadership elements that are specific to each. The three operational categories are defined in the following way:

> *Leadership in Action Description* – This category of leadership elements describes what a perspective looks like when implemented. It explains the goals of each perspective and gives a specific logical and practical meaning to each perspective. It is the verbal expression of the leadership philosophy inherent in the perspective.

> *Tools and Behaviors* – Elements in this category specify the behaviors needed and/or the tools of engagement for each leadership perspective. They point to the individual's capacity to "do leadership" in terms of a perspective's essential characteristics. Although relatively few in number, they pinpoint key ideas that distinguish each perspective and have proven to be useful in doing so.

> *Approach to Followers* – This category highlights the basic position in which a leader places himself or herself in relation to follower(s) in a given perspective. This category proves to be a powerful distinguisher of perspectives.

While the operational categories developed to analyze each perspective seem almost common-sensical, the specific variables within each category may not be so readily evident. Table 1 notes several authors who illustrate each perspective. Indeed, there is a vast literature backing up, explaining, and supporting various assumptions and activities within each perspective. The key is to identify specific leadership elements unique to each perspective. Rather than strain the patience of readers with a long elaboration of the research supporting these five leadership perspectives, the table shows how the variables help define the leadership perspectives. The elements specified for each leadership perspective are supported by the literature and are more fully developed in succeeding chapters. The operational categories show how the different Leadership in Action Descriptions, Tools and Behaviors, and the leader's personal Approaches to Followers may influence the identification and differentiation of the perspectives in the LPM. Working in concert, the perspectives, the operational categories, and the leadership elements complete the LPM (see Fig. 2).

Table 1 Intellectual foundation of the Leadership Perspectives Model: leadership elements and leadership literature

Leadership perspective	Leadership elements	Illustrative citations
Scientific management	Ensure efficient use of resources to ensure group activity is controlled and predictable	Gilbreth 1912; Gulick and Urwick 1937; Seckler-Hudson 1955; Taylor 1915
	Ensure verifiably optimal productivity and resource allocation	Drucker 1954; Gilbreth 1912; Gulick and Urwick 1937; Selznick 1957; Taylor 1915
	Measuring/appraising/rewarding individual performance	Box 1999; Bozeman 1993; Drucker 1954; Gilbreth 1912; Millett 1954; Newcomer 1997
	Organizing (to include such things as budgeting, staffing)	Drucker 1954, 1966; Gulick 1937; Seckler-Hudson 1951
	Planning (to include such things as coordination and reporting)	Drucker 1966; Malmberg 1999; Mintzberg 1975; Price 1965
	Incentivization	House 1996; Kohn 1993; Drucker 1954
	Control	Dowd 1936; Drucker 1954; Gouldner 1954; Jay 1968; Taylor 1915
	Direction	Drucker 1966; Mintzberg 1975; Price 1965
Excellence management	Foster continuous process improvement environment for increased service and productivity levels	Deming 1986; Juran 1989; Ross 1993
	Transform the environment and perceptions of followers to encourage innovation, high-quality products, and excellent services	Deming 1986; Juran 1989; Peters and Waterman 1982; Rago 1996
	Focusing on process improvement	Davis and Luthans 1984; Deming 1986; Ross 1993
	Listening actively	Fairholm 1991; Hefitz and Laurie 1998
	Being accessible (to include such things as managing by walking around, open-door policies)	Deming 1986; Hefitz and Laurie 1998
	Motivation	Deming 1986; Herzberg 1987; Herzberg et al. 1959; Hughes et al. 1993; Juran 1989; McGregor et al. 1966; Roethlisberger 1956
	Engaging people in problem definition and solution	Deming 1986; Rago 1996; Vroom and Jago 1988
	Expressing common courtesy/respect	Deming 1986; Fairholm 1998a

(continued)

Table 1 (continued)

Leadership perspective	Leadership elements	Illustrative citations
Values leadership	Help individual become proactive contributors to group action based on shared values and agreed upon goals	Barnard 1938a; Fairholm 1991; Kouzes and Posner 1990; Sullivan and Harper 1996
	Encourage high organizational performance and self-led followers	Bennis and Nanus 1985; Fairholm 1991; Kotter 1996; Manz and Sims 1989; Rosenbach and Taylor 1989; Rost 1991
	Setting and enforcing values	Conger 1991; Covey 1992; Fairholm 1991; Frost and Egri 1990; Nirenberg 1998; O'Toole 1996
	Visioning	Barker 1992; Collins and Porras 1997; Kouzes and Posner 1990; Nanus 1992; Sashkin 1989; Thornberry 1997; Cleveland 1972
	Focusing communication around the vision	Felton 1995; Kouzes and Posner 1990; Sashkin 1989; Sashkin and Rosenbach 1998
	Values prioritization	Bennis 1982; Burns 1978; Covey 1992; Fairholm 1998b; Kidder 1995
	Teaching/coaching	Fairholm 1991; Rost 1991; Tichy 1997
	Empowering (fostering ownership)	McFarland et al. 1993; O'Toole 1996; Rost 1991; Sullivan and Harper 1996
Trust culture leadership	Ensure cultures conducive to mutual trust and unified collective action	Dreilinger 1998; Fairholm 1998b; Kouzes and Posner 1993; Schein 1992; Malmberg 1999; Mitchell 1993
	Prioritization of mutual cultural values and organizational conduct in terms of those values	Hofstede 1993; Hollander 1997; Schein 1992; Selznick 1957
	Creating and maintaining culture through visioning	Collins and Porras 1997; Schein 1992
	Sharing governance	Fairholm 1994; Gardner 1990; Kaufman 1969; Rosenbach and Taylor 1989; Rost 1991
	Measuring/appraising/rewarding group performance	Fairholm 1994; Fraser 1978; Gardner 1990; Luke 1998
	Trust	Fairholm 1994; Kouzes and Posner 1993; Fairholm 1998a; Fairholm and Fairholm 2000
	Team building	Luke 1998; Sashkin and Sashkin 1994; Tuckman 1965; Fairholm 1998a; Nolan and Harty 1984
	Fostering a shared culture	Conger 1991; Quinn and McGrath 1985; Schein 1992; Wildavsky 1984; Nolan and Harty 1984

Spiritual (whole-soul) leadership	Relate to individuals such that concern for the whole person is paramount in raising each other to higher levels of awareness and action	Argyris 1957; Burns 1978; Cound 1987; DePree 1989; Herzberg 1984; Levit 1992; Fairholm 1998a
	Best in people is liberated in a context of continuous improvement of self, culture, and service delivery	Autry 1992; Jacobsen 1994; Manz and Sims 1989; Nelson 1997; Senge 1998
	Developing and enabling individual wholeness in a community (team) context	Barnard 1938b; Cound 1987; Drath and Palus 1994; Herzberg 1984; Vaill 1989; Greenleaf 1977
	Fostering an intelligent organization	Senge 1990, 1998; Vaill 1996
	Setting moral standards	Barnard 1938b; Burns 1978; Covey 1992; Gini 1997; Prince 1995
	Inspiration	Berry 1997; Burns 1978; Fairholm 1997; Greenleaf 1977; Wheatley 1999
	Liberating followers to build community and promote stewardship	Block 1993; DePree 1992; Fairholm 1997; Vaill 1989; Wheatley and Kellner-Rogers 1998
	Modeling a service orientation	Greenleaf 1977, 1998

Some general leadership concepts, also found in the literature, such as "taking risks" or "being bold" emerge from the research data along with the elements described above. Such concepts are not included in the LPM model as distinctive elements because they do not clearly differentiate among the leadership perspectives. Rather, they reflect a notion of how a leader may respond to or react to different situations and can apply to each of the five perspectives, as well as to how other organizational actors – e.g., managers, technicians, specialists – may behave. They are not distinct enough to identify a particular perspective. More specifically in relation to the LPM, whether one is being bold or taking risks may be dependent upon how one views the leadership phenomenon itself. Taking risks in the

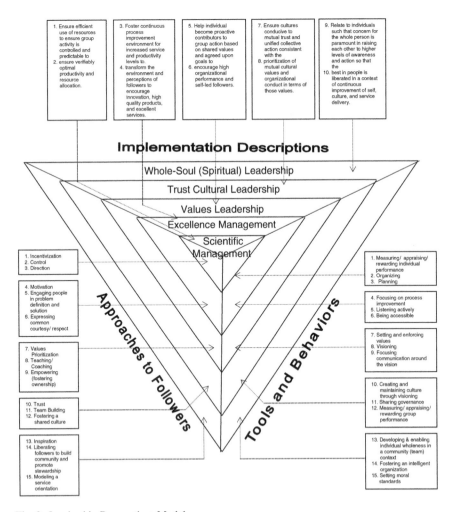

Fig. 2 Leadership Perspectives Model

Excellence Management Perspective may not reflect the same notion as that of someone who is taking risks within the Trust Culture Leadership perspective or any of the other perspectives. The leadership elements identified and described in this research serve to distinguish unique leadership perspectives so that, for instance, when assumptions of leader success are made, one is able to analyze their efficacy.

It should be noted that cultural impediments to clear thinking about leadership may make it difficult for people to describe or practice leadership. In essence, because of cultural constraints people may lack the leadership vocabulary to describe what leaders really do because they have been trained to think and write about organizational life in the managerial terms generated in the industrial revolution. Hence, a leadership element such as "Values Prioritization" may receive relatively little comment by study respondents within a perspective because people may lack an appropriate descriptive vocabulary because of their managerial conditioning. However, actual practice of leadership is not hindered by the respondent's constrained vocabulary. That is why such concepts of Incentivization and Values Prioritization are included in the data, although those terms were not generally explicitly stated.

Understanding these categories lets us begin to refine and flesh out the original model outlined in Chapter 1. Each leadership perspective may be better shown in relationship to one another as concentric triangles, each side identified as one of the operational categories defined and described above with the corresponding leadership elements. Figure 2 depicts the basic structure of the LPM in two dimensions.

Leadership as (Scientific) Management

People who accept this leadership perspective emphasize the leader's management role and highlight ideas such as controlling interpersonal relations, making decisions, aligning individual member actions and perceptions with corporate goals, planning, budgeting, and directing the effort of the several followers engaged in the work. This role involves leaders in ensuring that group activity is timed, controlled, and predictable. Chronologically, Leadership as (Scientific) Management is the first modern leadership perspective. Summarizing this perspective based on the research supporting the LPM, we can define this perspective as follows:

Leaders in Action Description: Leaders in this perspective ensure efficient use of resources to ensure group activity is controlled and predictable to assure verifiably optimal productivity and resource allocation.

Tools and Behavior: These leaders Direct others and Measure, Appraise, and Reward Individual Performance. They organize (which includes budgeting and staffing) and plan (including coordination and reporting). This is the most significant operational category in defining this perspective. Highly significant leadership elements are direction and planning.

Approach to Followers: Their interaction with followers involves incentivization, control, and direction.

Leadership as Excellence Management

This second perspective emphasizes high-quality, excellence management as the real function of leadership. The idea is that the excellent leader performs the duties of a manager, but with a quality focus that gives confidence to the rest of the organization. They are catalysts, bringing out the best in workers, fostering worker innovation, and igniting creativity. While still managerial in nature, this perspective introduces the careful reader to some of the core values that have guided leaders throughout time such as quality, concern for excellence, stakeholder development, and values of integrity, caring, creativity, and service. The descriptors for this perspective include the following:

Leaders in Action Description: Fostering a Continuous Process Improvement Environment for Increased Service and Productivity Levels and Transforming the Environment and Perceptions of Followers to Encourage Innovation, High-Quality Products, and Excellent Services. Transforming the Environment is the second most helpful leadership element identified by study respondents.

Tools and Behavior: Focusing on process improvement, Listening actively, Being accessible (including managing by walking around, open-door policies, etc.).

Approach to Followers: Motivation is the most useful leadership element to define this perspective. Others include Engaging People in Problem Definition and Solutions, Expressing Common Courtesy and Respect. This operational category most significantly characterizes this perspective.

Values Leadership

The key idea in this perspective is simple: everybody has values and these values trigger their behavior. If the leader wants to lead others, he or she must ensure first that the group shares common values and that these values provide both the goals (the group vision) and the measures of group and individual success. This conception of leadership proposes a kind of leadership rooted in the reality of human nature and conduct. It accepts the idea that individual and group action is values-driven. Its purposes place individual change and development equal to group productivity. It can be characterized as follows:

Leaders in Action Description: Help individuals become proactive contributors to group action based on shared values and agreed upon goals to encourage high organizational performance and self-led followers.

Tools and Behavior: This category best identifies this perspective. Visioning is the most descriptive of its action element, along with Setting and Enforcing Values and Focusing Communication around the Vision.

Approach to Followers: Values Prioritization, Teaching/Coaching – recognized as a key leadership element by many respondents – Empowering (i.e. fostering ownership).

Trust Culture Leadership

A logical extension of the Values Leadership Perspective is the idea that the leader's task is to build a culture of shared values where people can come to trust each other enough to work together. Trust is central to leadership in organizations because followers are people who choose to follow leaders. It is the glue holding the organization and its programs and people together. Leaders with this perspective see the leader's role as not so much a characteristic of the individual leader as it is a condition of the culture he or she creates. Although leadership may be spontaneous at times, most often it is a result of specific, planned actions to create an environment conducive to internal harmony around values and ideals the leader and follower share or come to share. The key value to share and promote is trust. This perspective is characterized by the following:

> *Leadership in Action Description:* The key elements here are Ensuring That Cultures Created Are Conducive to Mutual Trust, Fostering Unified Collective Action Consistent with the Prioritization of Mutual Cultural Values, and Ensuring that Organizational Conduct is consistent with the terms of those values.
>
> *Tools and Behavior:* Measuring, Appraising, and Rewarding Group Performance is the most descriptive leadership element for this perspective. Others include Creating and Maintaining Culture through Visioning and leader action to share Governance among coworkers.
>
> *Approach to Followers:* This perspective is best characterized in its approach to followers especially the elements of Team Building. Trust and Fostering a Shared Culture are also useful descriptors.

Spiritual Leadership

There is growing research support for the idea that leadership comes out of the leader's inner core spirit. We have long known of the powerful, if implicit, impact of the spirit on decisions affecting our work. Part of the most recent pressures toward reinvention of the organization is to invent corporate structures that recognize and respond to human needs for self-expression. The reasons are obvious: a leader or group member with a clear sense of their own spirit foundation and that of their coworkers can have greater transforming effect on the organization, its forms, structures, and processes than some formal reorganization plan. Leaders need people who are able to flourish in an environment of interactive trust, shared vision, and common values. A leader who is comfortable with himself or herself is happy and strong and can convey these qualities to others. They can, in this way, be a part of another's spirituality and increase effectiveness as a result. Descriptors of this perspective include the following:

Leaders in Action Description: Relate to individuals such that concern for the whole person is paramount in raising each other to higher levels of awareness and action so that the best in people is liberated in a context of continuous improvement of self, culture, and service delivery.

Tools and Behavior: Developing and Enabling Individual Wholeness in a Community (Team) Context, Fostering an Intelligent Organization, and Setting Moral Standards are the leadership elements most descriptive of this perspective, especially Setting Moral Standards.

Approach to Followers: Inspiration and Liberating followers to build community and promote stewardship. Modeling a service orientation.

Overview of the Five Perspectives

Research resulting in the development of the operational categories and leadership elements summarized above confirms that they are useful in describing and differentiating unique leadership perspectives. Together they help to distinguish the leadership perspectives since surveyed executives noted all of these elements in their responses. The Approaches to Followers Category of elements most distinctly distinguish three of the leadership perspectives. The Values Leadership and Spiritual (Whole-Soul) Leadership perspectives, however, were better defined by the elements of the Tools and Behavior category. Overall, however, the specific tools and behaviors that leaders use or describe in "doing leadership" are more helpful in differentiating leadership perspectives than leadership elements in the other two operational categories.

Interestingly, the most popular leadership element for each perspective is found within its most distinctive operational category. In essence, this means that what a leader is most likely to do in a particular perspective is encompassed within its most distinctive operational category. This finding highlights the fact that a perspective can be distinguished by identifying its elements and categories. An exception is found with the Scientific Management Perspective. Here, the top operational category is Tools and Behaviors and the top element is found in the category Approaches to Followers. The cause for this may be, though, that the element "direction," which incorporates the idea of decision-making, is seen by some as a behavior tool, not as a way of relating to others.

In sum:

For Scientific Management, the elements of Direction (including decision-making) and Planning are most useful in describing this perspective. The tools and behaviors indicative of this perspective generally distinguish it from other perspectives.

For Excellence Management, the data confirmed that Motivation, Transforming the Environment, Perceptions of Followers to Encourage Innovation, High-Quality Products, and Excellent Services are most useful, with the general set of Approaches to Followers being most distinctive.

For the Values Leadership Perspective, the Tools and Behaviors category elements are most distinctive, with Visioning and Teaching/Coaching as the most useful elements to describe this perspective.

Trust Culture Leadership depends most on Approaches to Followers to distinguish itself from other perspectives, with Team-building and the idea of Measuring and Rewarding Group Performance as requisite elements.

Spiritual Leadership is most distinctively defined in the Tools and Behaviors operational category, with the elements of Setting Moral Standards and Inspiration as identifying elements.

Each of the five perspectives defines and describes a unique set of leader actions and behaviors and a leadership mindset that differs substantively from the others. Expertly understanding the categories of Leadership in Action, Tools and Behaviors, and Approaches to Followers in one perspective is insufficient to describe leadership in another. Individual leaders who are effective in one perspective will not find that they can accept another perspective without altering their leadership behavior and exercising different operational tools and orientations. Further detail about each perspective helps us see how each element within the categories illustrates the unique nature of each perspective.

Another useful aspect of this research is that the leadership elements produced are confirmed by anecdotal data extracted from respondent essays and interviews. These data verify that the different categories and elements of the LPM are reflected in the way people talk and write about leadership. They also bring us to the conclusion that the modeled perspectives are apparent in the everyday actions of people involved in collegial life. In other words, there are people in the world who define leadership in terms of each separate perspective; there are people who occupy each perspective. Surveyed respondents included at least one, though often multiple, mention of leadership elements descriptive of a given perspective. The Scientific Management Perspective was the most commonly described perspective, receiving 24% of the total identified elements. The Excellence Management Perspective received the least of the total descriptions at 15%. Significantly, each of the leadership elements is illustrated and reinforced in the essays. The five modeled perspectives appear from these data to be legitimate and reflective of the real world.

The data also show that individual respondents are not always exclusive in the leadership perspective they defined, mixing and matching elements from different perspectives. This suggests that individuals may conceive of leadership in complex ways or that they are in the process of developing or changing their conceptions by adding elements of some perspectives to previous ideas. Skeptics may be tempted to conclude that "pure forms" of the leadership perspectives do not exist, that the five perspectives are not distinct, and that the LPM does not describe reality, but rather is merely an ideal leadership taxonomy. This conclusion is strongly refuted by the data. Pure forms of four of the leadership perspectives are discussed by several respondents. Furthermore, other essays reflect a clear majority of leadership elements found in a single perspective. Indeed 15% of the study respondents reflect a single leadership perspective.

The exception is the Excellence Management Perspective. No pure form of this perspective is described in the essays. This may be the result of the perspective's positioning between a perspective that focuses on more traditional management foundations and the others that deal with the relatively new, even revolutionary, idea of values leadership. In essence, the Excellence Management Perspective forms a bridge between control technologies and values-based relationships or culture creation technologies. As a bridge, it necessarily will reflect a mixture of the two.

Each of these five perspectives has its particular adherents and illustrates that leadership is best understood in terms of ever more encompassing and transcendent perspectives, as the LPM theory suggests. The data offer meaningful support of the core proposition that suggests, for example, that persons who hold to the Scientific Management Perspective see no difference between management and leadership as they have been identified in past leadership literature. Speaking of this dichotomy, one interview respondent said, "The current fad says management is less than leadership. I don't see the dichotomy and we are downplaying management. It is hard to distinguish the two, if at all." Another study subject, in responding to what an "ideal boss" would think leadership is, stated that "there is no hard line to see between leadership and management. Getting things done is what both are all about. My boss would see leadership as essential but not exclusive component of the job… management is necessary. Leadership and management are less distinguishable than people are trying to do. Leadership and management are the same in essence." Still another interview response summed it up by saying the following: "A manager or leader? No real difference in definition." These interview responses are strong indicators that the theoretical definitions of Scientific Management are valid.

Comments from other subjects confirm, however, the theoretical distinctions between leadership and management that undergird the Values Leadership Perspective and the other two perspectives that encompass it. One interviewee, reflecting the Values Leadership Perspective, opened by saying, "I struggle with answering this. I call myself a leader and am trying to think it through. Leadership is different from managing people." The respondent then revealed that "in this current job, I jumped right into management (there was a lot wrong in that area) and I was frustrated that I hadn't taken the time to do the leadership. Now I am starting from scratch all over focusing on the 'leadership piece' because the office still did not function well." Another example from an interview validating the difference between leadership and management suggests "leadership… is not management. Management is keeping things working, in control, where they are. Leadership is striving to take people and the organization somewhere." This comment is illustrative of much of the organizational change and values leadership literature (Kotter 1990; Fairholm 1991).

The Hierarchical (Holarchical) Pattern of Perspectives of Leadership

The LPM asserts that succeeding perspectives encompass and transcend previous perspectives and are organized into a hierarchy with individual leaders moving from lower- to higher-order perspectives as their personal or group situation changes. In this sense, the data also confirm that fewer individuals are able to describe higher-order leadership perspectives in clear ways, because they do not believe in them or because they have not been exposed to them or, perhaps, because those perspectives lack the support of historical theory. This may also suggest that fewer people have internalized the principles of trust, cultural, or whole-soul leadership perspectives, because they have not yet "progressed" to these more encompassing and transcendent perspectives (Miller and Cook-Greuter 1999).

Knowing that individuals view leadership from multiple perspectives suggests that they are undergoing transitions from one perspective to another and that they retain the vocabulary and principles of the previous perspective as they also try to internalize and express the vocabulary and principles of the perspective they are beginning to adopt. This supports the observed tendency for individual leaders to move from one perspective to another and lends evidence that succeeding perspectives encompass and transcend previous perspectives in some hierarchical relationship.

The relationship between the primary and secondary perspectives emphasized in each essay is progressive in nature. This relationship illustrates a general evolutionary trend from lower-order to higher perspectives. Research establishes that leaders adhering to Leadership as Scientific Management Perspective showed that attachment but generally did not reflect a secondary perspective. This is natural, given that people in this mindset cannot easily conceive of other points of view about what leadership is. Values-Leadership-oriented executives typically showed Scientific Management as their secondary perspective. Persons with Trust Leadership as their primary perspective displayed either or both Values Leadership or Scientific Management as their secondary perspectives. And those with a Whole-Soul Leadership perspective selected either or both values leadership or Trust Leadership Perspectives as their fall-back perspective. And, given the character of the Excellence Management Perspective, adherents to this mindset showed secondary perspectives of Scientific Management and/or Values Leadership, illustrative of its bridging role.

Moving from One Perspective to Another

As individuals mature in organizational life and assume greater positional authority and responsibility, it is reasonable to think that their perspective of leadership may progress as well. The findings summarizing the management-oriented leadership perspectives suggest that at lower levels, many managers do not distinguish leadership from management and focus more on task, direction, efficiency, and effectiveness, as discussed in the analysis of the Operational Categories for each perspective. Managers in the middle levels of organizational structure begin to differentiate leadership and management as they relate to others in engaging, respectful, and accessible ways. One interview respondent in the Excellence Management Perspective said, "Leadership is about making decisions on policies that helps you get the job done. But I think there is a difference between leadership and management." This reveals a change, or progression, in this person's thinking about leadership and points to further refinement of his or her own perspective.

Interview subjects also believe that individuals progress from one perspective to another. One mid-level manager within the Spiritual (Whole-Soul) Leadership perspective stated bluntly that "my views have changed over a number of years." Another response from a senior executive within the Trust Culture Leadership indicates this change: "If you were to ask me five years ago I would have a different answer, I'd have different thoughts." These statements lend evidence to support the idea that people can and do move from one perspective to another and that the movement is toward higher-order perspectives – perspectives that are more encompassing and that transcend previous conceptions.

The way this progression occurs may be found in the following statement from a senior executive holding the Values Leadership Perspective. This individual suggests that movement occurs through trying out new things and seeing what works: "Leadership has a personal component to it. I don't treat everybody the same. I treat them the way they want to be treated. I give them what they want. I really did this once and it worked in the unit, but it is hard to do. Early in this job, I didn't do that and I found myself in a rough place. Understanding values and skills sets – that is the beginning of the relationship." As this individual understands different aspects of the job, especially aspects dealing with values and relationships, new ideas and technologies began to emerge and be viewed as successful.

This progression may, in fact, create the situation where previous technologies, ideas, and activities that made an individual successful in one perspective are no longer useful or successful in higher-order perspectives. A senior executive within the Whole-Soul perspective sums this up by observing, "The skills and activities that got you to this point, you now need to abandon to be successful where you are now (higher up in organization). At a certain point the skills, tools, and techniques are not enough. What you need is to comfort, assist and be concerned about others and love them." Such comments reinforce the idea of development beyond previous practices.

Both interview and essay data verify that the five perspectives relate in a hierarchical manner and that individuals may, through trial and error, increasing awareness, and/or increasing levels of responsibility in the organization, progress from one perspective to another – from lower-order to higher-order perspectives. Importantly, the data corroborate an important element of the foundational theory of the LPM: the philosophy, tools, behavior, and follower relationships deemed useful in lower-order perspective must be adapted or replaced if one is to be successful in higher perspectives. The LPM encompasses the idea that it is possible to expand one's understanding of leadership by emphasizing certain ways of describing leadership in action, certain tools and behaviors, and certain approaches to followers. It does not assume, however, that one must necessarily move from one perspective to another, but it does suggest that that movement can and often does occur.

Leadership Perspectives Are Not Styles

When talking about leadership, respondents recognized the need for flexibility as they relate to their stakeholders. They were also consistent in the way they described leadership. In other words, respondents reflected a sincere and intellectually appealing approach to leadership that they felt comfortably fit their views on how they interact with other people and how other people interact with them. These are not expressions of calculated activities to achieve some specific goal or achieve a particular agenda. Rather, respondents' comments underscore a comprehensive feeling, an individual paradigm, or a mindset that defines generic leadership despite the vagaries of organizational life, task needs, or interpersonal relationship differences.

Past leadership theorists admit that leaders can alter their style to match the specifics of people, situation, or task (Hersey and Blanchard 1979; Nicholls 1985; Triandis 1993). These theorists grant that individuals may have a predominant style to which they usually default. They also suggest that the styles are easily adaptable by individuals so that they can deal effectively with any situation that may arise. In this sense, past leadership theory, like the perspectives approach described here, is both descriptive, outlining the basic leadership styles, and prescriptive, describing the style that is most effective in certain situations. However, unlike situational leadership theory, the perspectives approach rejects the idea that an individual can or should be comfortable switching perspectives according to some analysis of the organization or followership. The perspective a person holds defines (1) the truth to them about leadership, (2) the leader's job, (3) how one analyzes the organization, (4) how one measures success in the leadership activity, and (5) how they view followership. Switching leadership perspectives to accommodate some temporary context, then, is problematic at best and impossible at the extreme.

The perspective one holds acts as a measuring rod, a yardstick, and the perceived truth about leadership that defines how one views success in the leadership of others and their own leadership. It also defines how the individual may view the purposes or structure of organizational life in general and interpersonal relationships; it is a kind of philosophy of leadership. In that sense, morphing from one perspective to another and back again to accommodate multiple situations, as is suggested by theories linked to leadership styles, is not a possibility. An individual may progress toward a different, more encompassing perspective, but once achieved, that perspective defines one's activities and becomes the default paradigm for leader action and analysis. The perspectives are not leadership styles to be changed on a whim. Rather, leadership perspectives are paradigms or world views (leadership philosophies) that need not necessarily change over a lifetime but may be fostered through concerted training efforts and the integration of profound professional and continual living experiences.

This conclusion could have a significant impact on the way one chooses to train leaders. Instead of concentrating training efforts on how to handle observable situations most effectively, leadership training may need to concentrate on exposing participants to different views – different perspectives – of leadership. As trainers define characteristics or principles of the several leadership perspectives, they can then train participants to have the ability to recognize where they are on the hierarchy of leadership perspectives and the opportunity to adopt more encompassing points of view. The LPM also provides an implicit outline of specific training modules (the Operational Categories and Leadership Elements) to help trainees develop their capacity to function successfully in a given perspective.

Bridging the Leadership–Management Divide

In light of the above, the debate about whether or not leadership is a part of management becomes crucial. Because individuals are influenced so greatly by their perspective, it is difficult to see how one might be able to frame a discussion of leadership that might convince someone holding a lower-order perspective of leadership that there is value in moving toward a higher-order perspective. Perhaps, this is where the efforts to differentiate management from leadership are most useful, not only in studying leadership, but also in training others on the subject. Leadership and management have been defined as different concepts with different technologies (Baruch 1998; Kotter 1990; Nirenberg 1998; Zaleznik 1977). Available literature also suggests that other theorists disagree that the two are the same or that one is a subset of the other (Drucker 1954; Whetton and Cameron 1998). The LPM approach to understanding leadership offers a way to validate the observations of both camps while also distinguishing more fully the two concepts of leadership and management.

Burns (1978) offers a dichotomy of interpersonal relationships within work life, as well as in all other aspects of society. Interestingly, even while Burns distinguishes transactional approaches from transforming approaches, he suggests that both approaches are leadership. He stops short of suggesting that transactional leadership is management and transforming leadership is leadership. Others that followed him, however, do make that distinction. To Burns, both approaches are leadership, yet each hold distinct conceptions of the purposes, values, and motivations of the relationships being forged. Indeed, Burns does not necessarily distinguish management from leadership, but he suggests that there are two perspectives of leadership that rely on a relationship focus and a values connotation. However, the nature of the relationships and the values inherent in them differ substantively and substantially.

From Burns' work, others began the effort to clarify the work of management and the work of leadership. This current debate captures the attention of many leadership trainers, organizational consultants, practitioners, and academics. The either/or nature of the debate flies in the face of Burns' original theory from which the current debate emanated. However, the debate has served to further define and refine the complex sets of activities that occur in organizational and societal settings. Similar to Burns' original reluctance to drop the term "leadership" from the distinction between transactional and transforming relationships, the perspectives approach also suggests that what are currently known as management activities may still be viewed as leadership by some. Additionally, like the current debate to distinguish management from leadership, the LPM suggests that, at a certain point, what is perceived as leadership at the higher levels of the perspectives hierarchy differs so dramatically from what is perceived as leadership in the lower order of the hierarchy that a differentiation is useful and inevitable.

The research findings regarding the Excellence Management Perspective may be useful in bridging the past and present theories and point out how future discussion may unfold. As discussed earlier, the Excellence Management Perspective was not as distinct as the other four perspectives, even though specific leadership elements defining that perspective were evident in the data. The data suggest that the Excellence Management Perspective serves as a transition between what is found in the Scientific Management Perspective and the Values Leadership Perspective. Interview data reflecting Excellence Management were filled with key components of Scientific Management, such as control, decision-making, order, and management vs. labor, and key elements of the Values Leadership Perspective such as vision, values prioritization, and teaching/coaching. The Excellence Management Perspective reflects a transition from what Burns would call transactional and transforming leadership to what current leadership theorists would debate are management and leadership technologies. This bridge perspective may allow for some individuals to see the potential for perspectival growth. Of course, people who hold to the Excellence Management conception need not necessarily move to higher-order perspectives, but these individuals may tend to be ambivalent about the discussion of management vs. leadership, since they clearly are comfortable operating in a mindset that combines key elements of both.

Table 2 summarizes how this research may offer a unifying foundation for much of the leadership literature of the past, present, and future. Understanding how the five perspectives relate to past and present research helps both to clarify the perspectives themselves and to create avenues of future research. As the findings of this research indicate, the LPM accurately reflects valid conceptions of leadership. Understanding further the nature of the hierarchical relationship found in the data, the organizational and individual emphases of the perspectives approach and the role of values in each of the five perspectives is essential and is explored in succeeding chapters.

Table 2 Links between leadership research past, present, and future

Burns's dichotomy (the past)	Current literature distinction (the present)	Leadership perspectives (the future)
Transactional leadership	Management technology	Scientific management
Bridge – elements of transactional and transforming leadership (or management and leadership)		Excellence management
Transforming leadership	Leadership technology	
		Values leadership
		Trust culture leadership
		Whole-soul leadership

Summary and Conclusions

While the practice of leadership is something people recognize in social and organizational life, the theory of leadership is continuing to be refined. From trait to behavior to contingency theory, from values-based-transformation theory to a distinction between leadership and management, researchers and theorists are attempting to understand leadership better with a clear knowledge that we are not yet there. Perhaps the next step in leadership thought is to look at leadership in broader, more philosophical and more holistic terms, recognizing that individual perspectives are brought to bear on understanding leadership. Although leadership may contain certain elements, these elements may not be understood fully nor put into practice at all, except through individual conceptions of what leadership is. Discovering what those perspectives are builds upon the four previous research threads discussed in Chapters 1 and 2 and constitutes a fifth thread of leadership research.

Chapter 3
Leadership as Management

The Western myth of managerial man is one of the dominant myths of our age, the central feature of which is the idea of managerial control over others' acts and behaviors. For most people, leadership, or a position of leadership, equals a management role with its accompanying tasks and techniques – its technology of control, making decisions, aligning and setting corporate goals, planning, budgeting and directing the effort of the several followers engaged in work. The manager role entails insuring that group activity is timed, programmed, controlled, and predictable. Acceptance of management in business, government, and all other social groups is pervasive and powerful in society. It defines those human attributes thought appropriate to success in the formal corporation, such as competition, ambition, and financial astuteness. In the early days of this century, and even today, management was given prominence over other, some arguably more important, human activities related to emotional needs, wider family relationships, and social or intellectual aspirations. For many, management has become the metaphor of the twentieth century, encompassing work, workers, and work cultures.

There is overwhelming evidence that management is a powerful and needed force in group action. The evidence that this is also a necessary element in leadership is less well documented. Indeed, we need to rethink our perhaps faulty assumptions that leadership is nothing more than what managers do.

Evolution of the Manager as Leader

Modern professional management came of age in the last decade of the nineteenth and the first of the twentieth century, the heyday of Scientific Management. Early in the development of Scientific Management, Taylor (1915) and others advocated increased human freedom in the workplace. They saw the head of any social group as someone who was equally concerned with the work and the workers, someone whom we would today call a leader. As social groups became larger and more complex, these head people began to move away from this personal kind of leadership to impersonal, objective management of the group's growingly complex resources.

M.R. Fairholm and G.W. Fairholm, *Understanding Leadership Perspectives*,
DOI: 10.1007/978-0-387-84902-7_3, © Springer Science + Business Media, LLC 2009

The personal, human focus was quickly discarded in the enthusiasm for efficiency and top-down control, which held promise of easily coping with the expanding social, governmental, and business climate. This top-down management model quickly became the sign of American management as a whole and the basis of Scientific Management theory, despite the fact that it is antithetical to both the psychological and the spiritual makeup of human beings and is not validated by a complementary model in other areas of society (Wilsey 1995). Nevertheless, management by measuring and controlling people and product became the hallmark of American management practice.

Therefore, to understand leadership and the nature of its development, we must first understand its management roots. Management is the science or art of achieving goals through people. Whatever the title given, be it middle manager, boss, foreman/woman, director, owner, team or project leader, or department head, the task remains constant: to get the job done and keep the people motivated while operating within numerous restrictions such as time, limited resources, rules, and tradition.

To properly consider managerial work, it is necessary to put management in the context of the organization. In the early twentieth century, the sociologist Weber (1921) offered the bureaucratic model as the best system of management of the rapidly expanding German economy. At the turn of the twentieth century, Henri Fayol reduced the work of managers to a series of universal laws abstracted from a study of the best organizations. In the 1930s, Gulick (1937) summarized the work of the manager into seven universal functions such as planning, budgeting, staffing, and decision-making. Since then, the theory has been elaborated multiple times over.

Modern Management Theories

The modern manager was created out of the ferment of the Industrial Revolution and the genius of a few pioneer observers of and thinkers about the workplace, its operations, and its control. Their work has produced the professional managers who now occupy decision-making positions in virtually every social institution in the industrialized world. Proper understanding of this phenomenon asks the reader to put the work of managers – management – in context of its history. Unlike the evolution of leadership over the ages, modern management theory has a short history. Its beginnings date only to the period around the turn of the nineteenth to the twentieth centuries. We also date our understanding of the leadership-as-management perspective from this period. This early management model emerged as a set of principles and practices that were predictive of success in getting other people to do the organization's work. The brief review of the evolution of this perspective outlined below follows the chronology of traditional research and highlights some of the leadership elements noted later.

Scientific Management

Taylor (1915) is generally acknowledged to be the father of the Scientific Management movement. His central focus is on productivity improvement and efficiency. Scientific Management is unique not so much in its central purposes, but in the technologies by which it attempts to achieve efficiencies. The techniques in Scientific Management reflect Taylor's belief that the planning of tasks must be separated from the doing. Taylor applied hard science methods to the problems of attaining management efficiencies. He relied on observation, measurement, and experimentation to help solve production and control problems. He depended heavily on incentives to attract and keep workers producing at high levels of effort. Scientific study of production processes and the payment of high wages, he said, could best solve industrial efficiency issues. That is, the most efficient work will be done as managers design work methods based on scientific research and pay workers high wages to ensure that workers use scientifically developed work methods.

Regulating work through carefully designed standard operating procedures ensured that both levels of production and quality were maintained. Managers had the responsibility to develop these standard practices. They were also charged with recruiting, training, and then supervising work using elaborate incentive systems to induce workers to perform within the confines of these scientific techniques.

Other researchers contributed to and made fashionable various versions of Scientific Management. In the early decades of this century, one of the most popular was a model of the manager's job that divided the tasks of management into seven distinct functions. Credited to Luther Gulick and a number of British researchers (Gulick and Urwick 1937), Organization and Methods (or simply OM) centered on seven tasks managers perform summarized under the mnemonic POSDCORB (Planning, Organizing, Staffing, Direction, Coordination, Reporting, Budgeting). The skills defined by POSDCORB are technical. Managers became known by their specialty. Thus, we see managers as budgeters, personnelists, supervisors, etc. The virtue of this model is in its clarity and simplicity. The manager's job can be conveniently divided up into actions to further one or more of these functions. According to the theory, that is what managers do.

Supplementing Taylor's focus on task and technique, Fayol (1916), a French scientific manager, concentrated on the generic functions of management. He summarized managerial work into six organizational activities or functions: technical, commercial, financial, security, accounting, and managerial functions. He also identified a number of principles of management, including the following:

- Division of Work (specialization of labor)
- Authority and Responsibility
- Unity of Command (workers report to one boss)
- Unity of Direction
- Subordination of individual to the general interest
- Remuneration of Personnel
- Equity

- Scalar (hierarchical) chain
- Order (everything in its proper place)
- Esprit de corps
- Stability of staff tenure
- Initiative (thinking and then executing a plan)

Fayol touted these principles of management as universal: effective in any organization in any field. Building on Fayol's principles of organization, managerial activities or functions focused on universal principles. The major managerial functions adduced from this research include planning, organizing, directing, controlling, and deciding. Of course, other functions are also identified in this body of research, but these five seem to be the most universally mentioned.

Managerial functions should not be confused with organizational functions such as finance, production, engineering, sales, and marketing. Organizational functions deal with structural processes whereas the managerial functions relate more directly to individual manager action. These functions can and are performed by managers assigned in each structural unit. Thus, there is planning, organizing, direction, controlling, and decisions made in production, engineering, finance, sales, and marketing units. Managerial functions are also distinct from a variety of on-going technical functions in any organization. These nonmanagerial tasks are critical to success and are most often delegated to subordinates. They include tasks such as scheduling, auditing, reporting, measuring, filing, etc. Of course, a manager may perform these tasks himself or herself, but when doing so he or she is not involved in management.

Position or title is not as important in identifying managerial work as is the nature of the work actually done by the incumbent. Thus, a nonmanager may perform managerial tasks such as planning. When doing that work, the employee is performing a managerial function. Similarly, a manager may undertake to schedule workers and work and thus be engaged in the technical function of scheduling. In either case, the work done, not the title held, determines whether the person is functioning as a manager or a technician.

Scientific Management remains an important influence on modern management thinking and practice (Stoney 2001). The value of a well-considered and well-defined procedure, process, and system for the organization is uniformly advocated by respected analysts to ensure superior performance and drive the ways in which mangers devise, control, and communicate strategy (Beaver 2002). Grounded in system dynamics (Georgantzas and Ritchie-Dunham 2003), the insights provided by science and the scientific method let modern managers also focus their attention on the combined effects of direct, human dynamics and structural effectiveness.

Behavioral Science Approaches

Early work in the Leadership-as-management perspective also included consideration of a behavioral approach. This approach applies the methods and findings of the sciences of psychology, social psychology, sociology, and anthropology to help understand organizational behavior. The most famous and significant behavioral science application occurred in the series of experiments at the Hawthorne, Illinois Plant of Western Electric Company, during the late 1920s and early 1930s. The Hawthorne studies initially sought to further test Scientific Management ideas. They began by investigating the relationship between physical conditions of the workplace and employee productivity. They soon found that the social variables between researchers and the worker subjects were more important than the physical variables within which they worked as factors affecting productivity.

This unexpected outcome began widespread study of human behavior in the workplace. Elton Mayo, a principal consultant in the Hawthorne studies, is generally considered the founder of the field of industrial and human relations. For Mayo (1945), rather than being a hindrance in productivity, human relations became a broad new field of study capable of improving both morale and productivity. The manager-as-leader now needed to be expert in another new technology: the science of human relations.

These studies in part expanded traditional Scientific Management and in part conflicted with some defined principles. The studies also added new factors to the mix of issues facing the leader-manager. For example, piecework systems in use often led to conflicts between workers and time-and-motion study experts. They also found that in addition to being a formal arrangement of functions, the firm is a complex social system whose success depends on the appropriate application of behavioral science principles

Leaders imbued with the leadership-as-management philosophy seek employee satisfaction and morale as prime goals, because their underlying assumption is that high morale leads to high productivity. Recent research indicates that this assumption is oversimplified. Behavioral science approaches also include studies of motivation, the study of organization as a social system, the assessment of the impact of informal as well as formal corporation structure, and identify "leadership's" relationship to corporate success.

With the addition of leadership studies to the behavioral science approach to management, researchers entered a new dimension. They began the formal process of studying the organization as a complex of employee motivation. They began to view the corporation as both a social and a technical system and to study the process of interpersonal communications and employee development. Mintzberg (1975) challenged the Scientific-Management-based model as the way to define management. In his experience, managers did not do POSDCORB functions. They did something else as they accomplished planning, organizing, etc. Mintzberg gave us two sets of ideas to use in thinking about, describing, and training for management. The first is a set of characteristics of managerial work that operate independently of process or function and the second is a listing of descriptive tasks all managers perform for their organizations. The job characteristics include the following:

1. Managers produce a great quantity of work at an unrelenting pace.
2. They favor variety, fragmentation, and brevity.

3. They prefer explicit issues that are on the current agenda, not long-term seminal issues.
4. Managers are at the center of a communication network of contacts.
5. They prefer verbal media in communicating.
6. They seek to be in control of their own affairs.

And the ten managerial tasks divided into three functional areas include the following:

Interpersonal roles	1. Figurehead
	2. Leader
	3. Liaison
Informational roles	4. Nerve center (focal point for the communication network)
	5. Disseminator
	6. Spokesman
Decisional roles	7. Entrepreneur
	8. Disturbance handler
	9. Negotiator
	10. Resource allocator

Mintzberg defined skills that managers need which are more complex than POSDCORB tasks. They are political skills requiring negotiation and compromise, technical skills of communicating accurately, behavioral skills of coordination, conflict resolution, and innovation and creative skills. Mintzberg's model is clearly behavioral. But, intellectually and operationally, it is still fully in the orbit of Scientific Management and sees the leader in terms of managerial control. Also, Mintzberg (1975) added to our understanding of this perspective of leadership by suggesting a set of managerial characteristics and by outlining various roles that managers (read, also, leaders) play in organizations.

Behavioralism is currently being superseded by newer leadership paradigms, among them spiritual leadership. Spiritual leadership is partially supported by behavioral theory as it emphasizes organizational learning (Bierly et al. 2000) and unifying and building viable work and social communities (Cavanaugh et al. 2001). Behavioral ideas are also implicit in elements of spiritual leadership that connect coworkers to each other, as well as to the work itself. Furthermore, Cacioppe (2000) argues that these leaders have a key function in the evolution of groups by helping link all organizational levels: individual, team, and corporate.

These additions to the mix challenge traditional management theory and ask us all to rethink our present points of view about leadership. Yet, conventional thinking about the manager as the leader is still common in society.

Emerging Functions/Issues of Management

Management practice has for a 100 years been things – not people – oriented. Although effective in meeting production-of-things tasks, the organizations in which we work today do not engage so much in the production of tangible objects. Much of today's work is to produce information, facts, and ideas. And the knowledge-workers creating and using these facts want involvement; they want to manage their own work lives and contribute to their level of competence, whether in a leadership position or not. Obviously, the traditional corporation does not lend itself to broadly distributed manipulation of ideas or broad involvement in planning and decision-making. Manipulation of knowledge requires flexibility, adaptability, and sometimes even waste. On the other hand, management fights waste by sponsoring programs of efficiency and tight supervisory control.

Plainly, work is changing (Pinchot and Pinchot 1994). We no longer need machine-like bureaucratic procedures. Rather, the movement is from unskilled work to knowledge work and from individual work to teamwork. We now ask our workers, and they are asking their leaders, to move from a system that once required single-skilled expertise to one requiring multiple skills. We are replacing coordination from above with cooperation among peers. The present circumstance has produced a situation where workers often do not need supervisors at all. The constant tension resulting from this condition of accelerating change places impossible pressures on traditional structures, on the people doing the work, and on their leaders.

The following more contemporary functions seem to more accurately describe management today. They find their roots in early Scientific Management or human relations models revived by recent research. They offer insight into the human nature of both manager and subordinate and represent a melding of these two pioneering theories.

Systems Management and Quantitative Management

Following on the initial study of management as a control mechanism, the systems approach is a modern contributor to management theory and technology. The historical event that triggered this approach to management was the development during World War II of Operations Research by the British military services. Operations Research's most enduring contribution was its legitimating of systems theory. The system approach lets researchers focus on studying whole situations and relationships rather than organizational subunits or other small segments. Systems theorists study the organization as a whole, not just a series of functions such as production, sales, engineering, or accounting. For them, productivity improvement is a function of the interaction of all components, not incremental improvement of individual units.

It is important to note that for this body of research, a system could mean a social system and have a behavioral orientation or it could mean the technical system and have a Scientific Management focus. Operations Research also introduced statistical quality control and other quantitative management methods into the discussion of management. The focus here is not so much on employee motivation, conflict resolution, or communications as it is on decision-making in these areas. This discipline has resulted in viewing the corporation as an interrelated decision-making system connected by communications channels, which direct information to decision points within the organization. The systems approach tends to view the corporation in information flow terms and the leader in technical, procedural terms.

Coming out of this branch of early management theory and practice are several techniques and tools still used and still descriptive of this approach to management. Program Evaluation and Review Technique (PERT) is one such tool. PERT is a planning and control method fully within the systems approach and used to control complex production systems. This approach cuts across functional department to provide leaders with detailed information about project status during all phases of design, production, and distribution. Critical Path Method is a similar tool, familiar to many scientific managers in late twentieth century America and the industrialized world as is Management by Objectives.

Organizational Structure and Management

The environment within which most people work is the corporation and its work teams. Today, we are moving beyond bureaucracy to reconstruct the patterns of our formal relationships to expand worker discretion (Pinchot and Pinchot 1994). We model the modern large- and smaller-scaled organizations after the classical bureaucracy: highly structured and geared to the production of tangible objects, where few leaders do little more than coordinate efforts in their small sphere, with no one caring about what anyone else is doing (Adair 1986). In many respects, life in large-scale organizations sometimes resembles life in a totalitarian state: workers are "labor bond-servants" of the manager who controls their life in detailed fashion. However, in business organizations as in governments, totalitarianism is incompatible with high performance. Indeed, the corporation and other large employers may be among the last bastions of a stifling bureaucratic dictatorship defined by chains of dominance and submission.

Today, though, our measurement systems are keyed to a money standard, and organizational structures mirror this. Accounting, auditing, control, and success itself are defined, measured, and compared in terms of the standard unit of money. We define any other values as ephemeral and irrelevant. Control over money makes managers successful. By converting all activity to numerical representations of money (and hence into numbers), we can compare, control, and prescribe everything which, then, can be processed, computerized, handled – in short, managed. The cynic would say that the manager knows the price of everything but the value of nothing. The leader, by contrast, focuses on the noncountable features of the corporation.

Organizational Coordination

A primary task of managerial leaders is to allocate available resources so that a balance is achieved among the competing interests of the several groups of stakeholders represented. Meeting the objectives of some stakeholders and not others would reduce effectiveness or even cause dissolution of the organization itself. People affiliate with any organization in order to satisfy their own objectives. Unless the corporation in doing its work also provides opportunity for stakeholders to satisfy their individual objectives, it will not be able to fully satisfy its own. The prime task of management planning is to coordinate these interests and set objectives that will help the organization survive, prosper, and meet the needs of all stakeholders.

Fundamentally, coordination is a by-product of hierarchy: thus, there can be no coordination without subordination. Successful coordinating activities follow from effectively carrying out the functions of planning, organizing, directing, deciding, and controlling. Lack of coordination between corporate units may also result from incompatible policies and procedures. Failure to define authority relationships clearly may also result in lack of coordination of efforts. Similarly, when managers fail to decide, control their resources effectively, or provide direction, it is impossible to predict the effectiveness of that corporate unit.

The Leadership Vs. Management Challenge

As noted earlier, leadership and management are congruent in neither concept nor practice. However, the debate surrounding this assumption continues today. The basic questions, historically and contemporarily, are whether or not what has formerly been identified as management is indeed the same thing as leadership, whether or not they are two subsets of each other, or whether or not they are two distinct concepts.

Since Taylor's (1915) Scientific Management approach to organizational efficiency, management has been central in the academic and practitioner's study and structuring of organizations. Taylor's work begins to illustrate the good and the bad of management (Weisbord 1987). Over time, the distinctions of good and bad have become deeper and more socially profound. The labor movement grew in opposition to the positional, hierarchical figure of management. The sterile approach of many managers became stereotypical of what was bad about organizational life. On the other hand, the industrial model, with its emphasis on management, is often given credit for much of the success of modern industrial America.

Yet, amid this study and practice of management, the meanings of words such as "management," "manager," "leader," and "leadership" were defined in various ways, often blurring and confusing the concepts. Efforts to study these concepts and to develop a vocabulary of leadership muddied the definitions and differences, if indeed differences existed at all. Some of the confusion may have been caused by the fact that more sophisticated management tools were developed alongside the notion that leadership was situational. Thus, the practices of a leader looked very much like good management practices.

Eventually, there arose recognition that management and leadership, although both important, may not be the same phenomenon. This is not to say that managers and leaders need be different individuals, though they may be, nor that there are normative judgments about the value of each. Simply, "doing leadership" and "doing management" are two different tasks. In *Leaders*, Bennis and Nanus (1985) make clear that managers focus on routine, they accomplish, and they are efficient. Conversely, leaders are masters of change, and they influence: they are effective. Mcfarland et al. (1993) also pointedly distinguish between the two, saying that in the past the distinctions between leadership and management were blurred, and they were often used interchangeably. Not so today.

Zaleznik (1977) suggests that organizations depend upon people who keep the processes moving along, ensure productivity, and control and schedule the use of appropriate resources, but organizations also need people who can infuse the organization with purpose and values, help determine the character of the organization, and ensure its long-term survival. The skills and competencies required to do the first critical activity are substantially different than those needed to do the second. The first is the domain of the manager; the second is the domain of the leader (Fairholm 1991). Although some authors and practitioners continue to confuse the two concepts or make no distinction (Drucker 1954; Whetton and Cameron 1998), increasingly, the literature is asserting that management is not leadership and leadership is not management.

Management is the act of controlling, counting, and supervising other people so that they perform in specific ways to increase the overall productivity of the system or operation (see Taylor 1915; see also Selznick 1957; Stodgill 1974). Nelson (1997) challenges whether that conception of management is sufficient in today's organizations. In his review of motivation in today's work environment, he explains that managers have fewer tools to influence employee behavior because coercion is no longer an option. Today's effective managers must create positive work environments that can influence, but not order, desired behavioral outcomes. In saying this, Nelson counsels that we need to change our understanding of how individuals relate to each other at work. Wheatley (1997) suggests that traditional management activities are used to change organizations by "tinkering with incentives" and reshuffling organizational pieces and parts. Furthermore, she says that thinking of management as engineering people or directing people into "perfect" workers is doomed unless the field rethinks its theory and develops a new model of headship.

But confusion persists about what, besides management, is necessary. Much of this confusion is due to a lack of precise definition. Nirenberg's 1998 study of organizational behavior textbooks reveals much about how leadership is presented in the literature and taught in schools. He concludes that textbook definitions of leadership are a collection of control theories that ignore essential aspects of leadership. These texts imply that leadership is achieved by promotion from worker roles. Given this situation, the term "manager" could easily replace "leader" in our definition without losing any meaning.

Further refining what leadership may be, some have explicitly differentiated headship and leadership, where headship refers to hierarchal position held. Differentiating between the structure of headship and the philosophy of leadership allows leadership to be distilled throughout the organization, thus encouraging the development of individuals at multiple levels into leaders in their own right. Baruch (1998) clarifies the distinction further in a study that explores how far leadership research has focused on the phenomenon of leadership by examining actual leadership cases or something he calls "appointmentship." For Baruch there is a real distinction: appointmentship is power and responsibilities over other people, granted through an external authority. Leadership comes to the individual as people recognize and are ready and willing to be influenced by that person. Ignoring the difference and referring to one phenomenon as if it were actually the other results in faulty group action and failed theory.

Kotter (1990) also differentiates between leadership and management, suggesting that management is about coping with complexity and leadership is about coping with change. These two activities demand different sets of skills and different organizational perspectives that substantially distinguish between the two activities. In a similar vein, Ackerman (1985) argues that leadership is followership based on personal attraction while management is followership based on acceptance or organizational position.

Any description of leadership, then, should distinguish it from management. This does not mean that one person cannot be both a leader and a manager. Just as quantum physics teaches us that light is both a particle and a wave but never simultaneously both, one individual may perform both management and leadership tasks at different times, but *not* at the same time (Wolf 1989). As the characteristics of particle light are distinct from the nature of wave light, so are the characteristics, perspectives, and values of management distinct from those of leadership. The two are complementary, but not synonymous. Leadership encompasses technologies and mindsets that are different, but not necessarily better, than management.

The problem with these and many other attempts to define the function of leadership in terms of the manager's work is that they emphasize one aspect of the overall task to the exclusion of the complete picture (Mintzberg 1975). Using only management theory gives an inaccurate description of the actual work of leaders. Simple observation supports a contention that leaders do not merely plan, direct, budget, etc. In studies of general managers conducted by Kotter (1990), he found that they spend much of their time interacting orally with workers. The manager's activities were often unplanned and the result of diversions such as unscheduled meetings and telephone calls. These conversations tended to be short, disjointed, and touch on a number of issues. These observational data support the idea that acting in their role places managers in positions to influence the actions of others in more than just functional, systemic, or procedural ways.

National and even global concerns affecting our society help shape the current pursuit of better, more directed leadership. Changes in population, culture, economy, and other demographic factors are global. These pressures supersede discrete institutional boundaries and override the parochial parameters of past theory and/or contemporary practice. Past theories of leadership based on management theory cannot sustain this assault. Still, the leadership-as-management perspective remained the foundation for much of the theory-building about leadership until as late as the last two decades.

Analysis of the Leadership as (Scientific) Management Perspective

Essentially, the leadership-as-management perspective assumes that leadership equals management in that it focuses on getting others to do work the leader wants done. Key fundamentals of this perspective include (1) efficient use of resources, (2) optimal productivity and resource allocation, (3) measuring, appraising, and rewarding individual performance, (4) organizing, (5) planning, (6) incentivization, (7) control, and (8) direction. These tasks are reflected in the research. Table 3 helps to summarize the intellectual contributions to these leadership-as-management model elements of a wide range of scholars writing in the past 100 years.

Table 3 Summary of scientific management theory research

Leadership perspective	Leadership elements	Illustrative citations
Scientific Management	Ensure efficient use of resources to ensure group activity is controlled and predictable	Gilbreth 1912; Gulick and Urwick 1937; Seckler-Hudson 1955; Taylor 1915
	Ensure verifiably optimal productivity and resource allocation	Drucker 1954; Gilbreth 1912; Gulick and Urwick 1937; Selznick 1957; Taylor 1915
	Measuring/appraising/rewarding individual performance	Box 1999; Bozeman 1993; Drucker 1954; Gilbreth 1912; Millett 1954; Newcomer 1997
	Organizing (to include such things as budgeting, staffing)	Drucker 1954, 1966; Gulick 1937; Seckler-Hudson 1951
	Planning (to include such things as coordination and reporting)	Drucker 1966; Malmberg 1999; Mintzberg 1975; Price 1965
	Incentivization	House 1996; Kohn 1993; Drucker 1954, Taylor 1915
	Control	Dowd 1936; Drucker 1954; Gouldner 1954; Jay 1968; Taylor 1915
	Direction	Drucker 1966; Mintzberg 1975; Price 1965

The leadership-as-management perspective is logical. It is clear, specific, and subject to control and verification. In essence, it equates leadership and management. Given the economy of nature (and dictionaries), we cannot stretch two meanings from one idea.

This first perspective in the LPM equates leadership with the type of management developed from the scientific management movement of the first years of the twentieth century (Fig. 3). At that time, considerable emphasis was placed on ensuring that managers understood the "best" ways to promote and maintain productivity among their employees. This body of thought legitimized and routinized the administration of almost all social organizations. The executive functions reviewed above operationalize this role. Essentially, this perspec-

Fig. 3 Leadership Perspectives Model – leadership as scientific management

tive assumes that leadership equals management in that it focuses on getting others to do work the leader wants done, essentially separating the planning (management) from the doing (labor).

Key elements of this perspective include control, prediction, verification, headship, and science-based measurement. The leadership elements that form and inform Leadership as (Scientific) Management for many people are powerful descriptors of what leadership really is. Analysis of study respondent comments confirms that both the Leadership in Action Descriptions, the Tools and Behaviors, and the Approach to Followers elements reflect traditional descriptions of management. In the following sections, current and past research are melded to provide the reader with a capsule description of this leadership perspective.

The following examples suggest that those who see themselves as leaders or managers function in ways directly reminiscent of traditional Scientific Management.

They describe leadership as ensuring efficient use of resources to guarantee that group activity is controlled and predictable and to ensure verifiably optimal productivity and resource allocation. They use measurement and appraisal as the basis of rewarding individual performance. They focus on the tools of organizing, budgeting, staffing, and planning as well as such techniques as coordination and reporting. They use financial, social, and professional incentives to control and direct followers. Control and organizational predictability is the hallmark of this perspective. Indeed, leaders harboring this perspective share descriptive characteristics with the traditional literature on management action.

The Scientific Management Perspective is most clearly identified in terms of the Leadership Element Direction within the category of Approach to Followers. Twenty-two percent of the content analysis data in this perspective are found to illustrate that element. One manager validated this element in the essays: "The final aspect of leadership is direction. Direction is one of the most important facets of leadership. Without direction your employees, projects, programs, and organization's mission, may come to a standstill."

Overall, 51% of the respondent comments describe the different Tools and Behaviors identified with this perspective. Among the five perspectives, this percentage is the highest, suggesting that the Scientific Management Perspective is most heavily focused on implementing certain skills and techniques rather than on emphasizing particular approaches to followers. The main leadership elements within each operational category identified are Direction, Planning, and Efficiency. Likewise, respondents describe Scientific Management as directive in nature, involving planning and meeting objectives, focusing on efficiency and effectiveness, and characterizing incumbents by the distance between leader and subordinate. The following is a sample of survey respondents' comments about what leadership is in general:

> Leadership is how you are able to get an individual or group to attain goals that you set forth. The goals are determined depending upon who is in charge of the organization, operation, or project.
>
> Leadership is a take charge person [sic] who first defines the mission and goals of an agency or program. You need to demonstrate an ability to take charge and bring the right people together... It is about directing, encouraging, and coaching.
>
> Subordinates follow the leader. Subordinates give you what you give them. Therefore, leaders need to model behavior so that the subordinates can aspire to something higher than where they are now.

Furthermore, interview subjects describe the tools and behaviors indicative of this leadership perspective. An unedited sample of the responses follows: "Good leaders must be a good manager"; "Decisiveness...can't be wishy-washy"; "Knowledge of subject, flexible, ability to synthesize different obstacles, ability to read body language and style of work or management"; "Taking charge"; "Credibility, consistency, predictability, decisiveness"; "Effective, talented, gets the job done, committed." These comments suggest that traditional competencies of management are important to leadership.

The following additional comments reflect how leaders in this perspective relate to followers. One subject said, "Leaders do and should distance themselves from those they lead – be more formal, don't socialize with them, hold your tongue. You act differently with coworkers once you are the leader." Another said, "A leader has to establish himself as a person who assumes the bulk of the responsibility. You need to develop lines of communication so that followers know their roles and assignments and so that they can give honest feedback to overcome leader isolation that often occurs. Leaders need to plan, find resources, and give staff the chance to grow. Leaders need to have the followers' best interests in mind, but it is not a democracy. Someone has to decide, and the subordinates need to bring to the leader the information or tools that he would need to get the job done. The leader than makes sure the subordinate can do it by having the right resources, training, education, cross-training, needs assessment, etc. A better product emerges as you cooperate like this." The general message here is one of exclusivity within a hierarchy, deference to authority, and unilateral decision-making.

These anecdotes reinforce that the following leadership elements are indicative of this managerial viewpoint about leadership and always have been. A more directed discussion of each of the leadership elements of the Leadership as (Scientific) Management perspective follows.

Efficient and Optimal Use of Resources

Scientific Management leaders describe leadership as ensuring effective use of resources to ensure group activity is controlled and predictable and to ensure verifiably optimal productivity and resource allocation. Managers allocate resources to all units in a planned and coherent way and with an expectation of success. Often this is done in terms of preset objectives that focus on the economic contribution of each work unit. Together they define the group's work effort and the proportion of total resources allocated to attain desired results.

Performance Measurement

Taylor and the early scientific managers developed much of the quality control and general management technologies used by today's managers. Scientific managers developed time study, motion study, and work measurement. The range of management decision systems introduced since Taylor's time that focuses on issues of measurement, including operations research, management science, and statistical quality control, all trace their origins to the Scientific Management movement. About this perspective, the subjects noted, "Leadership is, and can encompass rewarding efforts from those who have put in extra time on special projects, and extra time used to succeed with positive results for both personal and organizational needs." Another subject affirmed, "A leader must never show favoritism or be biased when counseling and disciplining. They must be able to show each individual what they did wrong, explain why it was wrong and then administer positive rein-forcement when the situation dictates. Their actions must be quick." And finally, "All staff or group members are individuals. They should be treated as such without playing favorites."

Employee appraisal is intended to measure how well the individual employees function within the organization. Performance measurement is usually based on personal traits or behavior. However, Deming (1986) denounced appraisal sys-tems as devastating: they nourish short-term performance, annihilate long-term planning, build fear, demolish teamwork, and encourage rivalry and politics. Appraisals produce negative consequences, such as high costs, deteriorating rela-tionships, decreased motivation, potential litigation, poor or false data, loss of self-esteem, and high turnover (Mohrman et al. 1989). The real solutions to organizational improvement are likely to involve corporate culture, commitment, and accountability.

Organization

Organizing deals with the formal relationships present in the organization and forming the organization itself. It is often pictured graphically as a diagram that groups activities and connects them via authority relationships and sometimes cer-tain communications channels. Classic Scientific Management and the behavioral approaches related to it form the foundation of the idea that leadership is simply management, or a subset of it. This kind of thinking guided the industrial revolu-tion, encouraged a management–labor bifurcation, and gave us the general vocabu-lary of traditional organizational theory. This vocabulary has hampered discussion of other leadership perspectives. The notions of management and organizational success inherent in this perspective have given rise to a number of significant organizational models and approaches. Review of these models brings the leader-ship-as-management perspective to focus.

Planning and Coordination

Planning includes developing strategic objectives, collecting past, present, and future data about the group's effort, markets, and clientele groups, and creating necessary policies and procedures to turn plans into reality. For the leadership element Planning study respondents reported that "the superiors gave out the orders and basically planned out the work strategy and the subordinates followed" and that "staff should have a clear idea about time limits and the completion of projects. Clear goals help employees to avoid wasting energy, and it avoids confusion. The department manager should establish goals for the staff." Leaders, respondents said, "construct a plan of action for achieving the desired results, considering the resources required and available. The plan should include benchmarks, milestones and factors for measuring the success of the plan."

The leader's perspective defines the rules of the games he or she plays. It establishes and defines the boundaries of action and tells us how to successfully behave inside those boundaries (Barker 1992). Fry (2003) contends that leaders are necessary for altering organizational design.

Incentivization

Taylor's (1915) work highlights incentives as a significant mode of getting workers to perform work in the "one best way." Using scientific methods, he relied on observation, measurement, and experimentation to help solve production and control problems. He then introduced incentives to attract and keep workers working at high levels of effort. Incentivization via payment of high wages, he says, could best solve industrial productivity and efficiency issues. That is, the most efficient work will be done as managers design work methods based on scientific research and pay workers high wages to ensure that workers use scientifically developed work methods. It is not encouraging enthusiasm or a simple formula to make people more responsible, or a bribery system. Rather, incentivization is providing a spark to motivate, stimulate, move, arouse, and encourage workers to strive for a personal best, while doing group work.

Control

The control process includes steps such as establishing standards, comparing actual performance with these standards, and taking corrective actions. Standards set include those of quality, quantity, cost, and time and material use. Control over work and workers are prime outcomes of the formal structure. It involves rules, procedures, and sanctions, and it is an interpersonal process. It involves worker's needs and desires to exert influence or power over others as well as feelings about others' control over us. A relatively well-understood idea, the element "Control" received only 4% of mentions by respondents favoring the Scientific Management Perspective. This result may be a reflection of people's uneasiness in confessing to outright control tactics, or it may be that for many people control is subsumed in the ideas found in the other leadership elements, such as Planning, Organizing, and Direction.

Generally, elements in the Approaches to Followers categories are most distinctive here. However, the analyst must look at an entire category rather than a single element. In this sense, then, the set of Tools and Behaviors that individuals use or describe in "doing leadership" is more helpful than the other operational categories in differentiating leadership perspectives.

Direction

Direction involves the manager in supervising subordinates toward the realization of the group's goals. Increasingly, this function is seen in motivational terms, using both physical and psychological rewards to ensure desired worker performance. Typically, however, Direction has a coercive undertone. In discussing the Leadership Element Direction, one respondent said, "The final aspect of leadership is direction. Direction is one of the most important facets of leadership. Without direction your employees, projects, programs, and [the] organization's mission, may come to a standstill." Another reported that "being able to direct employees brings ...confidence to make decisions." Still another said, "Leadership through instruction is when a leader can give clear defined instructions to those employees under his command. A leader must be able to define what is necessary to those employees so the project can be completed on time and within budget."

Summary and Conclusions

Since Taylor described *Scientific Management*, we have imposed a hard science behavioral focus on most human activities, including management activities. The effort has been to make management a science: measurable, precise, and repeatable. Leadership, too, has fallen victim to the pull of the scientific method since some see leadership as just another tool or skill of management. Even those who see it as a separate function have used hard-science techniques to build their theories. They have assumed hard-science goals of precision and predictability as the desired outcome measures. Such early definitions of leadership mirrored those of management in theory, process, techniques, and goals.

Historically, what has taken place in the modern corporation over the past century is a shift from leadership to management. This is the same shift that we have seen in the decline and fall of the ancient church, the Roman Imperial Army, and most other older social institutions. Where the ancient leader once held symbols of power, managers now hold them. Today's managers have adopted the ceremonial robes and perquisites formerly taken by tribal chiefs, priests, and generals. These almost sacred leadership symbols are only changed to conform to the needs of the modern managers and contemporary civilization. Instead of fancy robes, head dresses, and mystic ceremonies, we see them in today's academic gowns, corner offices, $2,000.00 business suits, and the fostered illusion that the manager has "the word" and is the center piece in the communication network.

The obvious intent is the same in both systems: to produce respect and obedience in subordinates. These perquisites of managerial power inspire a decent awe for the professional manager (or teacher, or lawyer, or doctor, etc.). They add a patina of pseudosacred solemnity and mystery to replace our innate needs for inspiration. For most of this century, headship was seen as much more a matter of ceremony than of personality and vision. The logistics expert has supplanted the charismatic hero in the military. In government, the shift has been from the appointed, hereditary, or revolutionary leaders to the calculating, power-preserving, authoritarian master-bureaucratic managers of today. The prophet of religion has been replaced by the managerial bishop of today. We have come to distrust charismatic powers in every aspect of society and have replaced them with pseudoceremonies that can be timed, organized, and controlled.

The fall of leadership and the rise of modern management have brought mixed results. It has allowed us to attain remarkable material progress. Surely modern management has produced fantastically complex organizations able to cope with the pluralistic needs and desires of a growing and demanding population. But the costs are also significant. Without the interpersonal bonding true leadership produces, we have created a working population characterized by alienation, anomie, and despair. Our measures of productivity in our organizations and as a society are down, morale is low, and creativity is falling (Freshman 1999).

Management is adept at producing tangible products. It is less proficient in producing motivated, inspired people. Managers are not trained to inspire, nor are their systems and theory geared to encouraging, independent follower action. Rather, managers are successful if they can direct desired behavior, control deviation, and punish recalcitrance. This propensity for control through uniformity is seen in our organizational structures, operating systems, reports, and management approaches. But as the authority of management spreads over the organization, quality deteriorates. Management shuns excellence. It thrives on repeatable performance geared to the lowest skilled employee. It feeds on controlled and controllable mediocrity.

But this is a persistent perspective, despite some of its critiques. One respondent aptly summed up the description of Leadership as Scientific Management: "Leadership is about one who could lead the resources that are available to achieve an end result. It is about identifying outcomes, pointing out where the ship needs to go and expressing the method and commitment to get there. It is about making the best decisions." Another respondent said that leadership is all about "[d]ecisiveness…be[ing] able to make decisions! Examples of good leaders are those who could fairly quickly make decisions. Too many waffle and can't make up their minds. Good or bad…make a decision. That is what leadership is all about…[a leader is] a person with the ability to quickly see the true goals, perceive the necessary resources, get those resources, and persuade others to follow decisions." Another suggests, "You need to get them there in the most efficient and effective manner. Leadership is so many things… I think it is what I said before, the ability or capacity to marshal a group of people to get them to follow your objectives and to design strategies and methods to reach the goal." Better summaries are hard to find. The comments highlight the idea of getting other people to do what the "leader" wants done in predictable, unilaterally decisive, and controlled ways. These kinds of quotations reflect the mindset, the perspective, of people who believe leadership is really about management and they reinforce the observation of many who hold this view.

Chapter 4
Leadership as Excellence Management

The idea that leadership characterizes only the excellent managers evolved from the leadership as scientific management perspective. It is essentially a transitional perspective rather than an operational one. Popular in the 1970s and 1980s, it focuses on performance excellence in managerial tasks. It centers on the leader's need to be sensitive to the workers' human relations needs along with the demands of productivity. Excellence-focused leaders are mature, horizon thinkers with a penchant for high-quality performance. They define their mission in terms of high quality and see leadership as broadly dispersed throughout the organization. They encourage creative use of systems and resources in responding to the pressures of the environment and the desired potential of the future. This accent on excellence encompasses the leader's ideas about self, followers, and their common corporate culture.

Historically second, this leadership perspective reformulates what has been called the excellence movement introduced by Peters and Waterman (1982). The excellence movement highlights systematic quality improvementswith an emphasis on the people involved in the processes, the processes themselves, and the quality of products produced. The work of leadership is to foster innovation in an environment of honest concern for all stakeholders. The Total Quality Movement(TQM) of the 1980s is closely linked to this accent on excellence.

The skills highlighted in the quality excellence movement link directly to the definitions of leadership found in this perspective. The general framework of Leadership as Excellence Management relies on acceptance of the value of quality as a guiding dictum. It involves organizational cultural change toward a service philosophy centered on meeting customer requirements through continuous process improvement, encouraging innovation, ensuring high quality, providing service, listening actively, being accessible, motivating, engaging people, and showing common courtesy. The mechanisms to achieve success include training, role modeling, sponsoring feedback and communication, recognizing good work, teambuilding, and satisfying customer demands. Thought of as a bridge perspective linking management to values leadership, Leadership as Excellence Management deserves attention as a bridge to values leadership.

M.R. Fairholm and G.W. Fairholm, *Understanding Leadership Perspectives*,
DOI: 10.1007/978-0-387-84902-7_4, © Springer Science + Business Media, LLC 2009

The Excellence Management Perspective

Unlike Leadership as Scientific Management, this perspective does not focus solely on direction or control, operational style, or productivity. Rather, Leadership as Excellence Management involves prioritizing ideas such as innovation, concern for customers, quality, and simple structures (Samuelson 1984). Drawing on the Japanese model, which used Deming's comprehensive quality approach, Gitlow and Gitlow (1987) predict a rise in quality for American organizations. They, and others like them, offer plans to raise American management and leadership to its former greatness, using the various systems of quality improvement.

Leadership excellence has emerged as both a technology and a value system. It is a mindset orientated toward the leader's role and defines it in service-to-others terms. Brassier (1985) defines it in strategic terms. She describes leaders as those who take confidence in a commitment to the development of the capacities of people. Leadership excellence requires no gimmicks, no complicated theory or philosophy, no new funding, and no great charisma (Calano and Salzman 1988). Evidence suggests that there are pockets of excellence in most organizations. They can be present in the most traditional productivity-oriented groups or in badly run organizations.

Historical Roots and the Modern Quest for Quality

The present day interest in leadership as a function of good management can trace its roots to the turn of the century interest in scientific management. Interest in good (e.g. high quality) management is, of course, not new. A focus on high-quality performance has always been a part of management and leadership. Lammermeyer's (1990) research shows that quality has been a factor since the earliest management systems. The actual beginnings of the excellence movement can be traced to the ancient past. Ancient civilizations valued high quality in individual and group performance (George 1968). The Phoenicians used a very effective corrective action program to maintain quality: they cut off the hand of the person responsible for unsatisfactory quality. According to Lammermeyer (1990), part of the ancient Phoenician housing construction standards stated that if a builder does not build a strong house, and it falls and kills the owner, the builder will be executed. Even our most fanatical advocates of high quality have not yet reached this level of urgency.

The early impetus of the scientific management movement was on quality, but this value quickly gave way to quantity in the drive for productivity improvement. The industrial revolution reconstituted the way work was done in much of the Western world, including America, by emphasizing the benefits of increased quantity to manufacturing and processing tasks. Quantity factors soon predominated and reduced the focus on individual and unit quality. Nevertheless, early scientific managers introduced us to technologies such as time-and-motion study, statistical quality control, use of standardized jigs and patterns, and similar techniques to focus worker and managers alike on repeatable quality performance. Thus, the American work force has been committed, motivated, and prepared educationally and psychologically to produce "things" at high levels.

The pressure is still intense to provide more and more things to a growing and demanding population. This pressure to produce has minimized the independent craftsman's role. As a result, much of the responsibility to secure high quality is built into corporate structures and systems, not in the attitudes and values of the organization's people. We even delegate the problem of increasing quality to third parties who examine worker product after-the-fact. Now inspectors, behavior modification experts who use psychology to induce – often via implied threats and/or bribes – workers to produce at predetermined levels, and quality control units have responsibility for quality. The results have been to continue to increase quantity at the expense of quality.

The 1970s and 1980s especially brought a renewed interest in making quality a value in contemporary American business and government cultures. Spurred by the successes of post World War II Japan in applying quality control techniques coupled with participative structures, some American organizations moved toward this technology. Current systems typically focus on a commitment to organization-wide quality, a customer service orientation, and measurement of performance effort. The quality movement also impacted leadership theory. It gave rise to the excellence movement most prevalent in the 1980s but still a minor thread in leadership theory. The origins of the most recent ideas about leadership as a focus on excellence stem from the work of Peters and Waterman (1982). Their book, *In Search of Excellence*, relates excellence to caring for others, innovation, and high-quality service, with innovation being the key factor. However, this innovation occurs within an environment of honest concern for all stakeholders.

For Peters and Austin (1985) leadership connotes the task of unleashing follower energy, building, freeing, and allowing for their growth. This definition recasts the dedicated, analytical manager as an enthusiastic coach-leader. These leaders strengthen followers and recognize in tangible ways their creative contributions. This recognition allows followers to grow and the corporation to prosper. To foster excellence in followers, leaders also need to allow them some control in their work and to let them know what the whole organization is all about. Excellent leaders create a culture that fosters excellence and develop cultures that incorporate the leader's values and practices. Excellent leaders instill a sense of vision of the potential of the individual and in the corporation as an institution.

Defining Quality Operationally

Dictionary definitions of quality include ideas of excellence. Some define quality as existing when successive articles of commerce have their characteristics more nearly like its fellows and more nearly approximating the designer's intent

(Lammermeyer 1990). Crosby (1984) defines quality as conforming to requirements. He says that we attain quality best by having everyone do it right the first time. And, Juran (1989) defines quality as freedom from waste, trouble, and failure. Others suggest that quality is meeting and exceeding informed customer needs. Still others define quality in global terms, suggesting that it is a composite of the organizational components such as the design, engineering, manufacturing, marketing, and maintenance a given product or service receives.

Defined this way, quality is a function of any work process, including customer satisfaction. Today, many place a strong emphasis on customer satisfaction, not engineering, in defining quality. They see quality as a way of managing, not a task of management. In this connection, too, the Leadership as Excellence Management Perspective is a bridging idea from sterile management to leadership using shared human values. Deming (1986), a founder of the so-called Third Wave of the industrial revolution, defines quality as the result of forecasting customer needs translated into product characteristics to create useful and dependable products. Quality is, in effect, creating a system that can deliver the product at the lowest possible price, consistent with both the customer's and producer's needs.

Accordingly, a key to excellence leadership is to surround the leader with excellent people. To do this, leaders need to understand their followers' capacities and their corporation's particular niche in society. Leaders must also be willing to innovate solutions in sometimes critical situations (Flom 1987). In this leadership perspective, there is an emphasis on values of high-quality service, innovation, and concern for stakeholders. Excellence leaders devolve responsibility on the work force. They use techniques such as quality circles (QCs) or workers councils that recognize, use, and honor the work force.

Excellence leaders create an organizational surround fostering these kinds of people values. Such a culture encourages and rewards effective leadership throughout the organization. It fosters program or task champions and features close interaction between leaders, workers, and customers at all levels. Corporate systems and values emphasize concern with process rather than just product and with people over either product or process (Porter et al. 1987).

The Quality Movement in America

Once quality was only one element among many in corporate management. In the Leadership as Excellence Management Perspective, it is the key element. In this mindset, quality is more a function of the attitudes and style of the leader and the culture he or she creates than it is a function of a specific managerial control system employed. Quality becomes a part of the values, purposes, and goals of both leaders and their followers. It is a part of the value system of corporate leaders and all stakeholders, not a separate add-on system. The focus is on "total quality."

Deming (1986) is credited with introducing this new "philosophy" of management when outlining his TQM ideas. In TQM, a leader is successful as he or she

(1) defines mission, (2) identifies system output, (3) identifies customers, (4) negotiates customers' requirement, (5) develops a "supplier specification" that details customer requirement and expectation, and (6) determines the necessary activities required to fulfill those requirements (Ross 1993). The key ideas in Deming's philosophy are subsumed in his 14 points or philosophical principles.

According to Deming, the leader's job is to transform the system from its current *modus operandi* to one consistent with the 14 principles he enunciates: (1) create consistency of purpose with a plan, (2) adopt the new philosophy of quality, (3) cease dependence on mass inspection, (4) end the practice of choosing suppliers based on price, (5) find problems and work continuously on the system, (6) use modern methods of training, (7) change from production numbers to quality, (8) drive out fear, (9) break down barriers between departments, (10) stop asking for productivity improvement without providing methods, (11) eliminate work standards that prescribe numerical quotas, (12) remove barriers to pride of workmanship, (13) institute vigorous education and retraining, and (14) create a structure in top management that will push these 13 points everyday.

Each of these principles helps define the process of qualitycreation. His principles speak to the need of creating constancy of purpose toward improvement of products and services. They guide leaders toward adopting a philosophy of quality and rejecting the idea that the work group can accept delays, mistakes, defective materials, or faulty workmanship. Deming's philosophy creates a new paradigm of leadership. It involves the use of prediction techniques and scientific methods, but it adds the essential element of building relationships, encouraging communication, and inculcating pride in and rewarding quality work to the work of management.

Deming assigns managers the tasks of working continually to improve the system, instituting modern methods of training, and introducing different methods of supervision of workers. He says that the responsibility of the foreman must change from counting units produced to assessing quality. Deming also advocates the elimination of fear, ensuring everyone's effective work for the company. Leaders, he says, break down the barriers between departments. They abolish numerical goals and slogans for the workers, asking instead for new levels of productivity without providing detailed methods that employees themselves can better supply. The intent of the Deming philosophy is to remove barriers that stand between workers and their right to pride of workmanship.

Deming advises leaders that excellence cannot come as we continue to set specific numerical goals. Abolishing numerical goals lets us focus, rather, on improving the process of work, not just its results. The leader's job is to work continually on improving the system. It is to create a management structure that will strive for high quality every day. Deming says that the responsibility of leader – from foreman to top management – must change from numbers to quality. One way to accomplish this is to drive out fear from the workplace. Leaders should not let bad news intimidate workers so that they can use the information to improve the processes and strive for lowest product price. In every essential respect, Deming's philosophy is a prescription for corporate change favoring a work environment emphasizing excellence. He asks leaders to begin to require constancy of purpose, including developing and promoting a long-term, corporate commitment to the aim/vision of improving the workplace.

Juran (1989) teaches a ten-step method for implementing quality similar to Deming's 14 principles. Juran's philosophy, however, centers on building awareness of the need and opportunity for improvement. He suggests that leaders set goals for improvement and organize to reach these goals. He supports establishment of quality councils to identify problems, select projects, appoint teams, and choose facilitators. His worker quality councils represent a new form of corporate governance based on values of quality, sharing, and participation. They provide training in quality techniques to workers, who then carry out projects to solve problems. Other elements of his philosophy involve giving recognition for quality performance, communicating quality enhancement skills developed by one council, and keeping score – that is, recording progress routinely to ensure all workers know and understand the organization's priority on quality performance. The bottom line of the Juran philosophy is making improvement part of the regular values, work systems, and processes of the company.

Crosby's (1984) view of quality and Lammermeyer's (1990) excellence focus both have a more managerial feel. Crosby proposes the following absolutes of quality management: quality is defined as conformance to requirements, not "goodness"; the formula for delivering quality is the prevention of poor quality through process control, not appraisal or correction; the performance standard is zero defects, not "good enough"; and rather than measure quality through indices, the measurement of quality is based on the price of nonconformance to the quality process.

Rago (1996) presents an example of excellence leadership in his case study of a planned TQM-type organizational transformation in a Texas State public agency. Although there were many successes over the course of events, they were marked by a series of struggles that had roots in a mixture of uncertainty regarding the next steps to take and in the need for the agency's senior managers to personally transform the way they go about their work. The struggle for managers to make this personal transformation is an important aspect of the study, and it is indicative of deeper leadership issues. Kee and Black (1985) also discuss overarching leadership concerns about bringing this perspective to the group's work. They suggest that implementing quality improvement ideas may face some distinct challenges to success, such as identifying the real customer(s), determining core values, and promoting risk-taking.

All together, the roles and functions of leadership in this perspective stress quality and productivity process improvement rather than just product and people over either product or process, and they require consideration of values, attitudes, and organizational aims within a quality framework. Some of the key elements of this perspective include being sensitive to the human relations needs of workers along with the productivity demands on them, improving the process, having a concern for performance excellence/quality, and focusing on stakeholder development and interaction.

In the excellence leadership model, the leader's job is to teach workers, customers, and indeed all stakeholders, what they need in the way of quality products and to value high-quality products or services. Most quality control experts see work process as the amalgam of workers, material, equipment, customers, suppliers, and all other stakeholders as well as the larger community within which the firm is housed. These leaders consciously engage in activities to ensure that all coworkers uniformly accept and value corporate goals and methods that revolve around high performance. They do this by manipulating scarce resources, recognizing outstanding performance, setting organizational values, and otherwise establishing expectations of excellence.

Methods to Improve Quality Performance

Leadership as Excellence Management incorporates quality improvement systems that cause stakeholders to accept the values underlying quality enhancement, not just as discrete tools or systems to control worker performance. In this sense, quality is the factor in managing the organizational culture, not task control or supervision. Leadership excellence focuses everyone's attention and energy on high-quality service. The leader's intent is to change coworkers so they internalize the quality valuein performing their work.

Attaining quality performance requires the concerted effort of all levels in the organization (Wharff 2004). The first step is to recognize that a quality improvement process can be beneficial to both the corporation and its individual members. Other steps involve specific training in improved techniques and institution of measurement systems to evaluate progress. Leaders are involved in creating and maintaining work systems that emphasize results, measurement of quality, and implementation performance (Danforth 1987). The search for quality extends to hiring, training, placement, and inspiration of coworkers. The quest for quality asks corporation members to accept the quality value and act in accordance with this mental standard. They do this via a variety of techniques seen every day in organizations worldwide and confirmed by study findings examined below.

The Leadership as Excellence Management Perspective appears to be an applied capacity. It is action-oriented, and often, it cannot be learned in classrooms. Of course, some leadership skills are acquired in the normal way through reading, studying, and analyzing theoretical propositions and principles. But leadership excellence is learned most fully as the leader models desired action. It is a dynamic process. Fairholm (1991) identified eight skills that seem to define the technology of excellence. They are as follows:

- The ability to assess the situation
- Sensitivity to evolving trends
- Political astuteness
- A refined sense of timing
- The capacity to build on employee strengths
- The capacity to be inspirational
- The ability to focus on a few key things
- Technical (job) competence

The factors that promote excellence in organizations include clarity of mission, clarity of vision, and effective leadership at the top. Excellence leaders select and support service champions or in-house entrepreneurs. They interact closely with both employees and customers. They understand cultures and work-community structure, emphasize process over product, and focus on human factors to get a high-quality product. These skill areas differ from much of the content of professional business school curricula. These schools teach quantitative analysis and rational decision-making as primary technologies. Unlike management, though, excellence management is more a political process of defining the situation, assessing the strengths of actors, sensing nuances in relationships, and acting to focus group resources at the right time. Technical competence in the job to be done is less important than political sensitivity, or similar skills. Leaders that focus too much on traditional managerial goals of tight control will fall short of attainable high-quality performance and can expect failure, even destruction.

Quality improvement is a long-term, values-changing process. Attaining high quality requires total employee involvement at all levels within the organization. It is a matter of cultural change to give high priority to quality values. It requires effort by everyone: workers, middle managers (Fairholm 2001), and those at the top. Each needs to play a role in changing the culture to value quality and performing to attain it. Producing high-quality products or services also implies quality of worklife factors that are difficult to attain. Excellence leaders need to create a culture that meets the needs of all stakeholders, both inside and outside the organization. They need to give employees something meaningful to commit to before they will obligate themselves to achieving quality goals (Pascerella 1984). Ludeman (1989) suggests, and rightly so in this perspective, that we need to replace the old Protestant work ethic with a "worth ethic."

High quality will come only as we move from a situation where workers work because they fear economic deprivation to a situation where they work because they want to improve themselves and make a difference in the world. It is an empowerment idea that involves several kinds of leader skills, including self-development, the ability to help stakeholders, and the capacity to build an organizational surround that facilitates excellent performance. Perhaps the most critical feature of the leadership excellence approach is in the behavior exhibited by individual leaders. As they incorporate excellent principles into their lives, they change. And as the leader's behavior toward others changes, the organization changes. Techniques leaders use to change are many and varied, but they all center on an overriding concern for the development of others so that both leader and led can do a better job in accomplishing the organization's work. The most significant characteristics of leader behavior are summed up in the idea that leaders care for and respect their stakeholders. This caring behavior is demonstrated in courtesy, listening to understand, and otherwise showing respect for and acceptance of the ideas, actions, and opinions of all coworkers.

Excellence leaders have a penchant for close interaction with coworkers. As the leader seeks to motivate workers to want to perform excellently, critical relationships with employees are forged. Two technologies among several that might be identified in this connection are crucial: coaching and empowerment. Excellent leaders also work to change corporate culture to value quality. This model of leadership is concerned with behaviors that link performance expectations to such compensations as productivity improvement, motivation, inspiration, commitment to doing right things, accomplishment, ethics, participation, and expectation. Excellence leaders devolve worker responsibility (e.g., QCs or self-directed work teams). Excellence leaders build a culture committed to development and concern for workers. It is results-oriented, not merely activity-oriented. In sum, excellence managers focus on (in order of priority) quality, vision, service, follower transformation, and productivity improvement (Fairholm 1991). This perspective transcends traditional management because it suggests a human values orientation to leadership.

Leadership as Excellence Management: Tools, Behaviors, and Approaches to Followers

This second perspective in the LPM suggests that leadership is limited to the few excellent practitioners of management. Popularized by Peters and Waterman (1982), this perspective concentrates on systemic quality improvements with a focus on the people involved in the processes, the processes themselves, and the quality built into the products produced. The leadership task here is to foster high quality in an environment of honest concern for all stakeholders.

The general framework of Leadership as Excellence Management revolves around an organizational cultural change based on a philosophy of meeting customer requirements through continuous improvement of people, process, and product. Elements of manager-cum-leader behavior in this perspective abstracted from the factor analysis include fostering an atmosphere of continuous process improvement for increased service and productivity levels, transforming the environment and the perceptions of followers to encourage innovation, providing high-quality products and excellent services, focusing on process improvement, listening actively, being accessible (managing by walking around and open-door policies), motivating, engaging people in problem definition and solution, and expressing common courtesy and respect. The mechanisms to achieve success in this perspective include training, communications, recognition systems, teamwork, and customer satisfaction programs. The following brief elaborations of the leadership elements found in Table 4 and shown in Fig. 4 help describe this perspective of the LPM.

Encouraging High-Quality Products and Services

Contrary to popular myth, corporate customers do not often provide useful information about what they need and the level of quality they require. Often customers do not know what is possible or what options may be open to them respecting new

Table 4 Key excellence management leadership elements

Leadership perspective	Leadership elements	Illustrative citations
Excellence Management	Foster continuous process improvement environment for increased service and productivity levels	Deming 1986; Juran 1989; Ross 1993
	Transform the environment and perceptions of followers to encourage innovation, high-quality products, and excellent services	Deming 1986; Juran 1989; Peters and Waterman 1982; Rago 1996
	Focusing on process improvement	Davis and Luthans 1984; Deming 1986; Ross 1993
	Listening actively	Fairholm 1991; Hefitz and Laurie 1998
	Being accessible (to include such things as managing by walking around, open-door policies)	Deming 1986; Hefitz and Laurie 1998
	Motivation	Deming 1986; Herzberg 1987; Herzberg et al. 1959; Hughes et al. 1993; Juran 1989; McGregor et al. 1966; Roethlisberger 1956

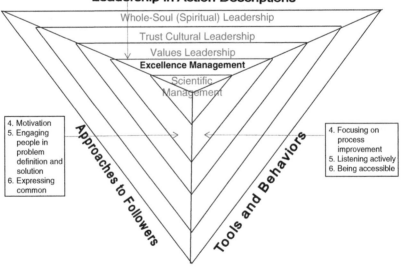

Fig. 4 Leadership Perspectives Model – leadership as excellence management

or higher quality products or services. However, leaders do. A central task of excellence leadership is to cultivate in customers and workers the idea that "best-practices" are most often guided by knowledge developed though the actions of leaders. Unfortunately, traditional definitions of quality, including automation, computerization, close inspection, zero defects, Management by Objectives, and quality control ignore the responsibility of leaders and place responsibility on workers, equipment, suppliers, or third-party quality control experts. Leaders create quality, shape control programs, and give these programs meaning. Surely this is the case with one such successful program: quality circles (QC). Consisting of small groups of about ten people, including a unit leader, a QC meets regularly to identify, analyze, and solve problems they experience on the job. In effect, a QC program makes the members minileaders, each with the same goal of improving current performance by creating improvement programs, selling them to higher management, and ensuring their implementation.

Ultimately, the success of quality improvement is a function of workers' willingness to take personal ownership of their part of the organization. Along with other techniques, QCs help workers improve productivity, raise employee morale, sharpen interpersonal problem-solving skills, and improve the level of customer service – all functions and goals sought by leaders. To be effective, quality values must be an integral part of the organization's management philosophy. Leadership as excellence targets productivity improvement by changing the way people work together, what they value, and their problem-solving and goal accomplishment skills. Excellence managers ask organizations to treat employees as adults: to trust them, respect them, and help them become their best selves. Attaining high quality requires group members to be involved in the quest for quality (Peters and Waterman 1982). More than just discrete programs of action, it is a philosophy of worker self-governance.

Process Improvement

A critical element in leadership excellence is the leader's ability to direct attention toward established priorities. We all pay attention to something(s). The problem is to select and consistently focus on what the corporation needs and wants. Paying attention is focusing on one thing as opposed to all other – often good – things. Focusing helps the leader communicate a consistent message to all stakeholders and to the larger communities within which the corporation has place. Focusing tells members of the group and the world what the leader thinks is important.

The leadership excellence literature describes a new kind of leader, one markedly different from the traditional managerial model. The old model is not wrong; it is just incomplete. While it specified elements of style, the style espoused was sterile. While it included elements of interpersonal relationships, the relationships defined lacked passion, emotion, and commitment. The old management model is founded on one value: efficiency. The Leadership as Excellence Management Perspective is supported on several development-of-others values in addition to efficiency. The practice of leadership is active, enthusiastic, dynamic, and personal. Excellence values honor people, innovation, and high-quality service. The leader's ability to inculcate these ideals and demonstrate them in his or her relationships with stakeholders and through the corporate culture is the measure of leadership success.

The essence of this philosophy is much more than just statistical control: it is a leadership paradigm involving a new iteration of the role of the executive. It involves the use of prediction techniques and scientific methods, but it adds to the leader's work the essential elements of building relationships, encouraging communication, and inculcating pride for and rewarding quality work. The role and functions of leadership in this perspective emphasize quality and productivity process improvement rather than just product and people over either product or process, and, furthermore, this perspective requires the management of values, attitudes, and organizational aims within a framework of quality improvement. Some of the key elements of this perspective include being sensitive to the human relations needs of workers along with the productivity demands on them, improving work processes, having a concern for performance excellence and quality, and focusing on stakeholder development and interaction. Certainly as leadership pertains to fostering quality improvement, Davis and Luthans (1984) are right in concluding that it exists as a causal variable in subordinate behavior and organizational performance by evaluating the impact of specific process improvements.

Listening Actively

Heifitz (1994) emphasizes the importance of listening and accessibility in managerial roles, and Fairholm (2001) mentions that leaders need to listen naively – as if they had not heard the worker's ideas before. Deming (1986) also makes a point that quality initiatives must place significant emphasis on the individual and on individual expression. Study respondents likewise emphasized the tools and behaviors referenced in the research regarding excellence management. Several of their comments elaborate this element's scope. They expressed that leaders should "listen, not necessarily agree, but listen"; "Give ideas, give feedback"; "Go to [the] group and ask, include, share." Overall, participants indicated that leadership "is about involving other people, including others in the work done, and helping them feel good about it." You must be a good listener. Some of the best changes have come from ideas generated by interactive conversation.

Being Accessible

Excellence leadership is done at the work sight. Excellent leaders cultivate people critical to their success, as well as other stakeholders, including ordinary workers. In this connection, surveyed executives noted that "because of leaders, some organizations are progressive and come up with, and allow for, new products and services. Leaders are enabled to redefine the work place to make it more comfortable, productive, people-focused, employee friendly, customer friendly, diverse, etc." They noted that Management by Wandering Around, a name for an extensive network of informal, open communications with all stakeholders, is often used by excellent leaders. The purpose of this technique is to tap information sources and get mutual understanding of what is going on, what is needed, and how to go about closing the gap. It involves staying in regular, informal contact with stakeholders at their work sites, not just in formal conference rooms. Good leaders wander around in all of the corporation's workstations (Peters and Waterman 1982). Wandering puts leaders literally in touch with workers and their work and with customers and their concerns. It balances book knowledge about leadership with working knowledge of the work being done.

Motivation

Study respondents confirm that motivation is a key descriptor of the Leadership as Excellence Management Perspective. One commented that "leadership is a process of organizing to get work accomplished. The task is to motivate others and get others involved. Lead the ship; give guidance. Help others see the same vision." Two techniques were highlighted by this research: Empowerment and Authentic Coaching. Empowerment assumes that the leader values workers as the best parts of the corporate machine. Study respondents urged leaders to "involve people in process" and to "[e]ncourage ownership of the work, of the process."

Former theory believed the opposite: while they may be important to success, the employee was viewed essentially as a bundle of skills, knowledge, and abilities useful to the manager in the production process. However, times and people have changed. Workers no longer will accept this limited view of themselves and their level of contribution to the collective enterprise. Today's workers are better educated and far more independent than ever before, and they are more wanting. Pfeffer (1977) argues that people want to achieve feelings of control over their environment. Workers want to make a difference, and leaders will attract followers if they allow them to make this difference.

Conger and Kanungo (1988) define empowerment in terms of motivation. For them, it is enabling, rather than simply delegating. Being empowered enlarges employees' perception and gets them to explore possibilities. It raises their capacity to perform. It releases the power in others through collaboration. It endows employees with the power required to perform a given act, and it grants them the practical autonomy to step out and contribute directly, in their unique ways, to the job. Empowered people respond to work and to crises at work with commitment; powerless people do not. It is moving people from *believing* to *doing* to *becoming*.

Excellent leaders respect their coworkers. They expend large amounts of time and resources in seeking, developing, and expanding the capacities of those around them who are engaged in the common work. Leadership excellence reflects this kind of caring in the same way that craftsmen feel about their craft (Tolley 2003). Real craftsmanship, regardless of the skill involved, reflects authentic caring, and real caring reflects our attitudes about ourselves, our fellows, and about life itself.

Sharing Problem Definition and Solution

Vroom and Jago (1988) advocate the engagement of followers in defining problems and solving those problems in a context of participation throughout the organization. Typical of this is the comment of one surveyed executive: "Leadership is change. It is providing tools that others need. You need to be able to see what change is necessary." Hughes et al. (1993) confirm this when they state that many people think the key attribute of a leader is being able to help others to complete group projects. Roethlisberger et al. (1941) emphasize the impact of human influences in personal and organizational motivation. McGregor et al. (1966) summarize various perspectives and research findings concerning the managerial imperative of motivation. Herzberg et al. (1959) also emphasize the role of motivation in organizations and unpack the meaning and tools of motivation.

Surveyed executives confirm this aspect of excellence leadership by observing that "followers need to feel that their input is valid and appreciated. Having an open door policy is good and you need to be approachable. You must never seem that there is a disconnect." Another adjured leaders to "get more people involved in decision-making to tackle whatever issues pop up. Involvement is essential. If you can change the level of involvement, you can change the quality of outcomes." These responses support and specify the nature and scope of excellent leadership action.

Expressing Common Courtesy

Deceptively simple is the technique of showing courtesy to others' works. Leaders can increase quality commitment in their employees through the simple act of being courteous in their relationships with them. Excellent leaders respect the talent, feelings, and concerns of their stakeholders, including customers. This often uncommon behavior works, but only if the relationship is authentic. This was confirmed by specific comments from study subjects. One said: "Treat everyone with respect; respect their skills, point of view, perspectives (professional, cultural, etc.)." Another remarked: "You need to be respectful to their opinions, whether you agree or not. You need to value them as people; as a person. At times, you have to call them on inappropriate behavior, but you don't get respect easily by bossing them around." These findings reinforce the idea that excellence management elements are useful in distinguishing this leadership perspective from the other five. They consistently focus on change and improvement, listening and accessibility, motivation, respect, and engaging others in the work of solving problems as key distinguishing characteristics of this perspective.

Summary and Conclusions

Survey and interview respondents who described themselves as holding the Excellence Management Perspective see leadership as a function of a few superlative qualities, concentrated around quality performance and excellence, which a manager possesses. The perspective differs from scientific management in that respondents referenced the Approaches to Followers elements most often in describing this perspective. Motivational elements in their Approach to Followers make up 32% of their descriptions here. All tolled, 48% of the references to this perspective deals with how individuals relate to and interact with followers. Data confirm that this perspective is more heavily weighted toward recognizing the importance of followers in the leadership phenomenon than is the previous perspective (only 22% of comments deal with Tools and Behaviors). The Leadership in Action category makes up 31% of the elements, suggesting that the perspective is reasonably well-defined and generally recognizable by surveyed respondents.

These data reveal that the main elements in this perspective deal with motivation, highlighting high quality, focusing on continual process improvement, and engaging others in responding to problems. The emphasis is on continuous improvement and follower involvement. Typical of this emphasis is the comment of one respondent: "Leadership is… a state of constant education. Not only of oneself but also of a process, the act of changing or trying to improve a system or process is one that needs to be a focus point of a leader. There is nothing worse than hearing 'it's the way we have always done it.' …" Another said: "The leader must facilitate continuous improvement in staff performance and continued input from staff and customers to keep the vision relevant as it moves along." Innovation and improvement are central to these quotations and to the perspective as a whole.

Leadership excellence is partly about transforming the leader's perspective, partly about changing follower perceptions, and partly about transforming the common culture. And in the attainment of these results, all three parts are improved, developed, matured. Leadership excellence is a change process affecting all stakeholders and the institution itself. This leadership mindset changes each into something more than it was before. This transformation takes place in a consciously created and managed culture that prioritizes quality excellence. As such, the Leadership as Excellence Management Perspective provides the bridging structure supporting the leadership tree that now is defined in terms of values, culture, and the spiritual center of both leader and led.

Chapter 5
The Values Leadership Perspective

Applying past management models beyond their legitimate bounds only complicates the process of creating a viable leadership theory appropriate to today's tasks. Fortunately, there is a new philosophy, a new way to think about leadership that is people-focused, values-based, and future-oriented. The key to this model is to re-envision leadership as centered on personal values.

This third perspective in the LPM suggests that leadership is essentially a values-based relationship between leader and follower that allows for group objectives to be achieved without recourse to managerial direction and control. Our past reluctance to deal directly with individual values ignores a vital element of reality and limits our collective capacity to lead. Therefore, a central feature of the Values Leadership Perspective is its emphasis on a few values mutually held by group members. These values are encapsulated in a vision of what the group and its members are and can become.

Values leadership reconsiders leadership to include the values-rich interplay between leaders and led. This perspective confirms that the constrictive nature of scientific management and the stylized process improvement techniques of excellence management are insufficient to describe the leadership phenomenon or engage followers. Rethinking leadership can define it in philosophical terms as a shared-values relationship in which the leader helps the led achieve shared goals by accommodating collective values and aspirations.

Defining Values-Based Leadership

Values leadership is the name of the process through which leaders use their beliefs and values to inspire others to behave and grow in certain ways (see Greenleaf 1977; DePree 1989; Fairholm 1991; Covey 1992; Bass and Avolio 1994; O'Toole 1996). At their worst, past management-oriented models divert our thinking from real leadership principles. At best, they are only precursors to values leadership theory. They contain parts of the principles central to values-based leadership, but not its essential whole.

M.R. Fairholm and G.W. Fairholm, *Understanding Leadership Perspectives,*
DOI: 10.1007/978-0-387-84902-7_5, © Springer Science + Business Media, LLC 2009

For example, defining leadership in terms of headship – the person at the top of the organization chart – does not make him or her a leader. Some high office holders are chief managers or mere figureheads. High status, however, is not irrelevant to leadership (Gardner 1990). There are positions that carry with them symbolic values and traditions that enhance the possibilities of leadership. An obvious example is the President of the United States of America. Nevertheless, position alone does not make a leader, nor does the capacity to impose rewards or punishments. Relationships, not consequences, are a reliable measure of leadership. Management connotes controlling; leadership connotes unleashing follower power.

Values Leadership subscribes to a different reality than management. It is building followers, freeing them, and allowing them to grow (Peters and Austin 1985). Leaders think differently, value things differently, relate to others differently, have different expectations for followers, and seek different results from individuals and from the group. They impact group members in a volitional way, not through formal authority. Leaders are forever innovating and moving outside the constraints of structure or tradition. In sum, leadership and management are separate technologies with different agendas, motivations, histories, and thought processes. What is needed is a theory that focuses fully on leadership as a discrete technology with separate systems of behaviors and techniques (O'Toole 1996; Vaill 1998; Mitroff and Denton 1999; Bolman and Deal 2001). Such a theory can be found in the Values Leadership Perspective promulgated in the LPM.

Review of Values-Based Leadership Theory

There is growing consensus of the value of Values Leadership. Values-based leadership deals with leader actions to create a specifically defined value construct within which to practice leadership and a unique technology with definable techniques. Several writers have considered aspects of this new leadership mind-set. Review of their work can crystallize the underlying philosophy supporting this new leadership perspective. They help illustrate the ways leaders apply their skills in shaping group values, goals, and action (see Biberman 2003; Cook-Greuter 2002; Delbecq 1999). This point of view is not concerned with leader personality traits, behavioral patterns, or critical situational contingencies. Rather, it centers on the relationships engaged in, the attitudes supporting those relationships, and the philosophical "reality" adopted by the leader. Its core orientation is on what leaders think about and value (see Kegan 1982; Fairholm 1991; Fowler 1995; Mitroff and Denton 1999).

Peters and Waterman (1982) conclude that leaders introduce values and a culture supportive of innovation, service, quality, and caring for all stakeholders. Values leadership builds on the notion of values and culture, but is mainly focused on independent personal and professional growth. The worker emerges fully functional and capable of self-directed, organizationally helpful action. Given this kind of leader-follower relationship, workers see themselves as part of the larger whole with responsibility for affecting that whole (Palmer 1998). This conclusion, as well as a growing body of similar research, supports this values-based new leadership theory directed at both producing needed work effort and, importantly, aimed at developing stakeholders (see Fairholm 1991; Jernigan 1997; Colvin 1996; Martin 1996). The Leadership Perspectives Model (LPM) adds to this type of theory building in terms of the Values Leadership Perspective.

Indeed, the centerpiece of values theory is the adoption of a specific mind-set that facilitates realization of certain values-based processes and outcome desires. This mind-set asks the leader to create a values-vision for the corporation and then enroll members in that vision. This is a transformational model: indeed, the Values Leadership Perspective of the LPM reflects a theme of change and transformation resulting from leader actions toward their coworkers. Values leaders take responsibility for vitalizing or revitalizing the corporation. They define the need for change, create new values-visions, mobilize commitment to those visions, and ultimately transform organizations.

An Example: The Values-Based Leadership Model

To help apply the ideas of Values Leadership, we present this model in Fig. 5 as an example of a values leadership process. Consistent with the Values Leadership Perspective, it includes elements of designing, creating, and working within a culture that fosters the values and technologies implicit in a developmental environment.

The view of leadership modeled in Fig. 5 sees leadership as involved with several essential functions leading to (E) self-led, productive followers. These functions are (B) creation and maintenance of a cultural context supportive of excellent follower performance and (C) teaching and sitting in council with others to facilitate independent, high quality, innovative follower performance. The leader's virtual environment (A) is one of caring and development. The (D)

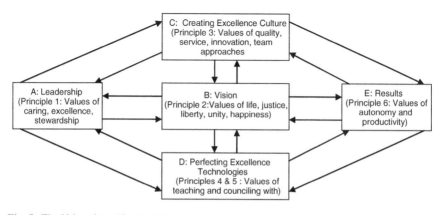

Fig. 5 The Values-based Leadership Model

vitalizing vision integrates the culture and technologies and establishes the value needed to let members increase their capacities for self-direction. To help think about this philosophy of leadership, Fig. 5 places the components of this model in relationship to each other.

There are some foundational notions that ground the model and make its application more real. These foundations ultimately distinguish this activity from management and also point to subsequent perspectives. Success in implementing values-based leadership is based on helping others become their best selves. Values leaders come to see the organization, its people, and resources in steward-ship terms – a jointly held, but transitory service responsibility. As stewards, leaders take responsibility to care for and develop the people they work with and the team they represent. Creating and maintaining a culture conducive to accomplishment of personal and group goals is a characteristic of this perspective. Values leaders define the working context or culture and use it as a vehicle for communicating and enforcing desired values. Leaders create a culture supportive of such values. Leaders do that by creating a vision of their people's present and future potential and then enrolling them in that vision. The vision provides the basis for both the leader's action to inspire stakeholders and his or her self-directed action. This task affects all other tasks the leader performs. Visioning emphasizes the central values and possibilities that define the group and constitute its niche in society. The vision activates deeply held beliefs about what the individual and the society are all about. It is an invisible force binding leader and followers in common purpose.

In this model, the vision harkens back to the core values that established American society and ideals about what organized group action should entail: respect for life, liberty or freedom of choice, justice, unity, and happiness (see Fairholm 1991). These founding values define deeply held beliefs about how groups should act. They provide the values-context within which the group's work is done. While one may be spotlighted, all five should be respected, at least implicitly, in the culture supporting any vision. While acceptable bottom-line performance is a given in any corporate relationship, Values Leadership has the dual goal of producing both high performance *and* highly developed, self-led followers. Values leaders maximize follower talents for the sake of both accomplishing the goal and the fulfillment of the individual's values.

Principles of Values-Based Leadership Model

The true essence of leadership is not procedures; it is setting and teaching values to followers. Relating leadership behavior to program, policies, or other organizational factors is risky. As they change, and they always do, the requirements for leadership action must also change. We risk being misled or misleading others as we over-rely on these "technical" aspects of leadership in the organization. Organizations, programs, procedures, and policies can and do change, while values and principles are more enduring. Hence, the power and usefulness of a values-based conception of leadership.

Values leadership asks the leader to formulate and then teach certain principles so followers can lead themselves. These foundational principles of leader-follower relationships are not responsive to fleeting situational vagaries. The leader's role becomes one of internalizing these value principles and teaching them to followers who can, in turn, internalize them in their independent action. It is one of learning and then teaching principles so followers can lead themselves. As followers do this, they develop a loyalty toward the leader and the institution that cannot come in any other way. The core principles of the Values Leadership Perspective include:

One: The Leader's Role is Stakeholder Development

Values leaders are enthusiastic supporters of their people (Tolley 2003). They love, encourage, enthuse, and inspire employees and others to attain the organization's vision. They foster innovation and they celebrate individual successes. They inspire coworkers by words, ideas, and deeds that convey a sense of connection, excitement, and shared commitment to group goals and methods. Values leadership is a philosophy of (1) personal change toward high quality, (2) education of followers toward their potential for self-directed action, and (3) creation of an environment conducive to team member improvement. In this model, the leader must be taught, trained, and committed to the values constellation that is at play. Then the leader's role is one of transforming self, each follower, and the group to achieve the vision by allowing followers to lead themselves within the constraints of the shared vision and their own understanding of the values at play which the leader has taught and exemplified at all times. This kind of leadership is empowering. It seeks to expand the scope of personal control that followers enjoy in working collectively. It seeks to change people's lives for the better.

Two: Values Leaders Focus Attention on the Small Cluster of Followers in Their Immediate Team

Mostly leaders work closely with a small core of immediate followers – the deputies, assistants, and other officers or workers – making up their "leadership cluster." It is impossible for a leader to lead all the people in most large-scale organizations. The work of leadership is more intimate. For example, unit directors interact most often and most intimately with their few deputies, assistants, a secretary, and perhaps one or two others, and a deputy interacts most often with a few supervisors and a few technicians. Each of these individuals presides over a specific program staff or a group of technical people in a chain down to the first-line workers. It is with these small clusters of people that leaders practice their leadership. It is within this cluster that the leader has the best opportunity to impact, change, and assist in their development.

Three: Values Leaders Strive for and Develop Follower Trust and Commitment

Leaders and followers are interdependent: the unifying factor is mutual trust. Without trust there is no basis for a relationship. Unless both have trust in the other, our organized relations will dissolve when confronted with difficulty. Getting this deeply committed trust and insuring effective self-governance is based on three interrelated elements or conditions: The first is mutual agreement, a reciprocal understanding and commitment regarding what is expected. Second is responsibility. As an agreement is reached, leaders have the responsibility to pull back from direct performance of the delegated task and let followers do the job. Leaders become a source of help, not a judge or a controller. This is a reversal of the traditional, supervisory relationship in which the subordinate is subject to the leader's wishes in all things. Rather, the values leader becomes a concerned, caring agent of support. The leader, in effect, goes to work for the follower. The third element of a trust interrelationship is accountability. It includes follower self-evaluation and self-judging in addition to the leader's evaluation. Accountability is an event and a process. Followers periodically report on their progress, but, in a sense, they are always reporting to themselves. They are continually measuring their performance against their understanding of the group's vision, of what they need to do to be true to it, and of their individual capacities and talents to meet that need.

Four: The Leader's Role is to Create a Vision

The principle mechanism for implementing desired values and purposes is the vision. The vision provides the basis for the leader's work to inspire stakeholders to self-directed action in order to realize the vision. The impact of this essential element is powerful. It pervades all else the leader does. It is the force binding leader and followers in a common purpose. In their behavior toward followers and others, leaders reflect these vision values. Vision values are seen in leader actions such as goal setting, prioritizing activity, selection and promotion of staff, and all other decisions and conduct.

Five: Leaders Create a Culture Supportive of Core Values

Culture includes experiences, expectations for the future, and values that condition behavior. Coherent, cooperative action is impossible where commitment to common values is missing, even if only implicitly. Creating and maintaining a culture conducive to attainment of personal and group goals is, therefore, a hallmark of leadership. Values-based leaders establish and maintain a culture that fosters this core-values vision and the other purposes the leader has. Creating a culture is a values displacement activity. It is setting standards of conduct and performance that implement cultural values and behaviors. All of the leader's actions must be congruent with these values.

Six: The Leader's Personal Preparation is for One-on-One Relationships with Followers

True leadership is personal and intimate. It is many small acts involving the leader and followers individually. Leadership over large groups is possible. However, if it is effective, individual group members must see it as a personal relationship. They must see a melding of their personal values, purposes, and methods with the leader's. Preparation in this model is essentially preparation to succeed in individual one-on-one relationships with followers. Leadership is, in essence, learning to sit in council with all stakeholders to insure understanding and acceptance of common values, work processes, and goals. The sitting-in-council-with-followers relationship puts the leader and follower together in an equal, sharing relationship. Both leader and follower may propose the agenda, contribute ideas and methods to solve group problems, and/or suggest new or altered program plans. Sitting in council with others is democratic and egalitarian. Counseling is unilateral action taken by the counselor toward the other person in the relationship. Counseling is telling. Counciling-with, a coined phrase meaning leader action in conferring with followers on mostly equal terms, is finding out together what is right, proper, and needed. Values leaders use followers as informal advisors to collaborate on policy, strategic decisions, and overall program guidelines. The leader seeks opportunities and creates opportunities to share planning, decision making, and work methods determinations with coworkers.

Seven: Values-Based Leadership Asks the Leader to be a Teacher

Leaders are primarily teachers of followers because followers are invariably volunteers. Their role is to communicate with, inform, and persuade followers to cooperative action. In all their behavior toward others, leaders teach the vision, its values and goals, and specific techniques to operationalize the vision, values, and results. Many see this teaching role as coaching: that is, one-on-one interaction with employees to teach, train, and aid in the development of their skills, values, and capacities. It is empowering of the individual. Teaching/coaching encourages independent action of employees. It focuses on the individual's strengths. While the principle of teaching emphasizes coaching, other techniques support this leadership approach. Internalizing principles of leadership is the only way that followers can develop a loyalty toward the corporation.

Eight: The Values Leader Has the Dual Goal of Producing High Performance and Self-led Followers

This model captures much of the conception of the Values Leadership Perspective in its unique emphasis on improving the individual follower's capacity for self-directed action to accomplish group goals. Both the context and technologies of this model move the follower toward this result as well as to performance improvement. Success is attaining both results. Failing this, the leader must alter or improve either the contextual culture or the technology. Values-based leaders intend to create more leaders imbued with the same values and ideals who can work to realize envisioned goals and methods.

The model described earlier and its various principles illustrate the philosophical base for values leadership. They define the essential elements of this leadership mind-set. The result is to have independent followers capable of and desiring to apply commonly held values in all their work relationships. The task is one of learning and then teaching values so followers can lead themselves.

Values Leadership: Tools, Behaviors, and Approaches to Followers

Earlier leadership perspectives sought improved follower performance measured in outcome terms. They each argued that their brand of leadership would result in enhanced productivity. The worker remained in each of these models as a labor slave of the corporation and leader, essentially casting workers as tools to help achieve the leader's corporate or personal goals. The Values Leadership Perspective rejects this focus, concentrating instead on developing mutually satisfying relationships.

Values leadership is a relatively new approach, but one recent, informative study shows productivity improvements when values-leaders, not managers, are present in line organizations. Jernigan (1997) studied approximately 200 first-line laborers, their supervisors, and top departmental executives in a medium-sized public works organization. He found that leader-led work crews produced more work per unit of output than their manager-led counterparts. Jernigan identified work crew supervisors as either managers or leaders based on worker and supervisor perceptions of their bosses' success in developing trust and insuring values congruence. He then measured productivity of all work crews over a 3-year time span. Invariably, leader-led crews outperformed their manager counterparts. The percentage improvement ranged from 3% to 479%. This study is a powerful argument that leadership based on shared values can and does make both human and financial sense.

Other research clarifies a number of elements of this leadership perspective. These studies are identified in Table 5, which capsulates some of the intellectual sources of the specific leadership elements associated with this perspective. Figure 6 illustrates the elements of the LPM for this perspective. The Values Leadership Perspective is the most well-balanced perspective of the five in terms of the three operational categories of the LPM. The Leadership in Action category is most useful in delimiting this perspective, receiving 28% of the mentions in the authors' research. Tools and Behaviors received 42%, and Approaches to Followers received 30% of total elements mentioned by respondents. Consistent with the overall findings in this research, the leading element in the Values Leadership Perspective is

Table 5 Key values leadership elements

Leadership perspective	Leadership elements	Illustrative citations
Values leadership	Help individual become proactive contributors to group action based on shared values and agreed upon goals	Barnard (1938a), Fairholm (1991), Kouzes and Posner (1990), Sullivan and Harper (1996)
	Encourage high organizational performance and self-led followers	Bennis and Nanus (1985), Fairholm (1991), Kotter (1996), Manz and Sims (1989), Rosenbach and Taylor (1989), Rost (1991)
	Setting and enforcing values	Conger (1991), Covey (1992), Fairholm (1991), Frost and Egri (1990), Nirenberg (1998), O'Toole (1996)
	Visioning	Barker (1992), Collins and Porras (1997), Kouzes and Posner (1990), Nanus (1992), Sashkin (1989), Thornberry (1997), Cleveland (1972)
	Focusing communication around the vision	Felton (1995), Kouzes and Posner (1990), Sashkin (1989), Sashkin and Rosenbach (1998)
	Values prioritization	Bennis (1982), Burns (1978), Covey (1992), Fairholm (1998b), Kidder (1995)
	Teaching/coaching	Fairholm (1991), Rost (1991), Tichy (1997)
	Empowering (fostering ownership)	McFarland et al. (1993), O'Toole (1996), Rost (1991), Sullivan and Harper (1996)

found in the Tools and Behavior category. That element is visioning. Teaching and Coaching followers received the second most mention, and even though this element is found in the Approaches to Followers category, this perspective seems best distinguishable in terms of its Tools and Behaviors.

Illustrative of this are the following comments made by surveyed respondents: The goal is to lead…to lead as opposed to manage. People want to have someone to look up to and to follow. Leaders have to stand for something…" Another executive said: "Leadership is the capacity to influence people with a vision tempered in reality." A third commented: "You need to sell and tell everyone the vision, then coach and guide them along. Sometimes you just have to do things, despite the followers' reticence or complacency, to keep the change going…." Certainly, in these comments are found a distinction from management and the notion that the leader engages with others rather than merely exerting power over them.

This third perspective in the Leadership Perspectives Model (LPM) suggests that leadership is essentially a relationship between leader and follower that allows for critical corporate values to be achieved in ways different from prediction and control. This is a key idea. Fairholm(1998b) suggests that premodern leadership models reflect a penchant for control and accounting and that management developed to allow for predictability and stability to counter the previous organizational

Fig. 6 Leadership Perspectives Model – leadership as values leadership

structures based on personality, traits, charisma, and shamanism (e.g., leadership) that yielded unpredictability in organizational systems. For Fairholm, leadership is persuasion, not control.

Other researchers, like Sashkin and Rosenbach (1998), are also rethinking leadership as they highlight the work of Burns (1978) and Bass (1985) in applying transactional leadership and transformational leadership. The former has come to be known as management and the latter has been known to better describe the unique leadership phenomenon. Sashkin and Rosenbach describe elements of transactional leadership to include contingent-reward dynamics and management by exception. Transformational leadership, on the other hand, points to the less measurable elements of charisma (noting that charisma is the result of transformation leadership, not the cause), inspiration, individualized consideration, and intellectual stimulation (see also Ready and Conger 2003; Thompson 2000; Wilber 2000).

Sashkin's Visionary Leadership Theory (see Sashkin and Rosenbach 1998) states that leaders take everyday managerial tasks – a committee meeting for example – as opportunities to inculcate values. Leaders "overlay" value-inculcating actions on ordinary bureaucratic management activities. This third leadership perspective, then, separates the management technologies from those of leadership. Within the five perspectives in the LPM, this perspective marks the dividing line that says the skill sets and functions of leadership differ from those of scientific or excellence management.

Understanding values leadership necessitates understanding of the leadership elements defining this perspective, which are: (1) helping individual workers be proactive contributors to group action, (2) encouraging high organizational performance and self-led followers, (3) setting and enforcing values, (4) visioning, (5) focusing communication around the vision, (6) prioritizing values, (7) teaching/coaching, and (8) empowering or fostering ownership. The objectives of this leadership construct are to encourage high organizational performance and, equally, self-led followers. The foundation for such action is the values of the people involved and of the organization. The tools and behaviors they use include setting and enforcing values, visioning around those values, and broadly communicating that vision. Their approach to followers is via values. They help others prioritize their values, they teach and coach others, and they empower others, even fostering in followers ownership of the work, the group, or the product. Each of the key leadership descriptive elements in this perspective is elaborated as follows.

Help Each Worker Be a Proactive Contributor to Group Action

Values leaders help individuals become proactive contributors to group work based on shared values and agreed upon goals. Proactivity can be nothing more than taking action and seeking permission afterward. It is often seen as a *fait accompli*, a situation in which the values leader presents the group with a completed decision or action and seeks support and endorsement after the fact. Proactivity is a unifying and coalescing idea essential to any successful working relationship. It tends to bypass official system constraints as well as psychological resistance, aggression, or hostility. Proactive workers reorder internal relationships by changing the environment. Proactivity is also seen when either leaders or their followers promulgate actions in situations where no other solutions are readily identifiable – that is, suggesting ideas in a vacuum.

Reinforcing the approach of developing proactive, self-led followers, a studied executive wrote, "Workers need to be seen as mature, desirous of being productive, wanting to identify with the job and contribute to its success, and willing to accomplish the organizational goals." Both McMurray (1973) and Merrell (1979) propound the virtues of proactive behavior for, in the one case, the maverick executive, and, in the other, the successful huddler. Merrell describes the proactive individual in terms of assertiveness. Those with assertive authority, he contends, assume a dynamic posture, one involving initiation of action to cause something to happen.

Encourage High-Performing and Self-led Followers

Bennis and Nanus (1985) describe a leader as one who commits people to action, who converts followers into leaders, and who may convert leaders into agents of change. Manz and Sims (1989) say the most appropriate leader is one who can lead others to lead themselves. They call this "superleadership" and suggest that leaders become "super" because they can possess the strength and wisdom of many persons by helping to unleash the abilities of the "followers" (co-leaders) who surround them. Rost (1991) argues for a paradigm of leadership that includes the interplay between leaders and followers. Fairholm (1991) focuses on the social interactions within organizations and a reliance on values that allows the leader to not only evoke desired results from the organization, but also, more importantly, develop individual followers into leaders in their own right. Sullivan and Harper (1996) provide new thought on the meaning of leadership as a commitment to shared values, the ability to identify objectives and maintain a long-term vision, the knowledge of when to challenge the status quo, and the understanding of how to invest in and nurture employees.

Setting and Enforcing Values

Leadership is a values-displacement activity. The Values Leadership Perspective describes the integration of group behavior with shared values as a result of the leader setting values and teaching those values to followers through an articulated vision that leads to excellent products and service, mutual growth, and enhanced self-determination. A key element of this perspective is that values leaders know the power of individuals' values in dictating behavior. Burns (1978) says that values are standards that can be used to establish choices made, determine equity, and balance policies and practices. Thayer (1980) says that values are operationally similar to objectives, goals, ends, purposes, or policies. Fairholm (1998b) suggests that values are statements of "oughts" – that is, broad general beliefs about the way people should behave or some end-state that they should attain. Covey (1992) describes a perspective of leadership that emphasizes a reliance on principles.

Study respondents echo these sentiments. One participant noted, "I call myself a leader and am trying to think it through. Leadership is different from managing people. Relating to people in a way that they follow through a mutual embrace of values, ideals, goals . . . that is leadership. In the end a leader must have followers." This links nicely to what Conger (1991) suggests is essential to leadership: the melding of individual values into the values of the organization and vice versa.

Which values to highlight is a concern in this approach. Kidder (1995) conducted interviews all over the world and concludes that there are some common values held by people regardless of culture or nationality. These include love, truthfulness, fairness, freedom, unity, tolerance, responsibility, and respect for life. Others mentioned include courage, wisdom, hospitality, peace, and stability. These values,

Kidder says, present us with a way of setting global goals and strategies. They also give us a starting point from which to begin values leadership.

Focusing on shared values may be the most valuable intellectual exercises of our time. Values serve to unite us into communities by providing an area of mutual understanding and agreement. Fairholm (1991) espouses a philosophical conception of leadership that is grounded in specific values for American executives embodied in the Constitution and Declaration of Independence. Frost and Egri (1990) say there is a need for leadership perspectives large enough to embrace the fact that we are living, valuing beings and to place that value-centric fact at the core of our studying the leadership question. Nirenberg (1998) concludes that in the last analysis diversity of thinking will usher in a renewed concern for exploring shared – not individualistic – values and the impact of serious values-based differences in organizations because, ultimately, leadership is the expression of common values. And, finally, Bennis (1982) holds that leadership is concerned with organizations' basic purposes and general directions centering on doing the right things, not merely doing things right.

As a concluding comment on this leadership element, note the words of another surveyed executive: "You must understand who the people are – their skills sets, the knowledge they bring. Leadership has a personal component to it. . . . I really did this once (tried to understand my workers as individuals) and it worked in the unit, but it is hard to do. Early in this job, I didn't do that and I found myself in a rough place. Understanding values and skill sets – that is the beginning of [leadership] the relationship." Indeed it is.

Visioning and Focusing Communication About the Vision

The main leadership elements in this perspective deal with visioning, teaching and coaching, and helping others to be proactive as the leader communicates ideas about the vision. One quotation from the group of executives is illustrative of this perspective's focus on creating and communicating visions: "The person in a leadership position first and foremost has the capacity to 'see' a future – however that future is defined for that organization. People in leadership positions therefore try to determine what the future direction of an organization should be. They typically express their vision in conceptual form, that is, as ideas, because their concern is not with planning and how to get to the future, but with painting a picture of what the future will be." Such a description of the role of vision is poignant and helpful.

Visioning involves activating the emotions as well as the mind. It is more than rational. It involves the leader in setting a future vision for the group, promoting that vision, and planning strategically to attain it. The vision statement is a primary tool for explaining the purpose of the work to bosses – higher management, clients, customers, citizens. The leader's vision carries the powerful message that the future is vital and will be different. We cannot predict it, but we can create it (Brassier 1985). Though some essentially short-change the power of vision by simply borrowing common phrases found in other organizations' vision statements, as if from a "vision warehouse," the power of a sincerely articulated vision forms the foundation of leadership activities (Thornberry 1997). Collins and Porras (1997) describe vision as a vivid description with an artistic and emotional component. The vision serves to make explicit the organizational purpose or *raison d'être* and inspires organizational members in their work. Barker (1992) describes vision as dreams in action that are leader-initiated and then taught to followers.

Kouzes and Posner(1990) suggest that leaders challenge the process, inspire a shared vision, enable others to act, model the way, and encourage the heart. To Bennis (1982), how organizations translate intention into reality and sustain it is the central question, answered mainly by communicating a direction and vision. Nanus (1992) suggests that a key function of leadership is creating a compelling sense of direction by visioning

Respondents made the following comments in elaborating this element:

Articulate in talking about the vision and what an organization is and isn't striving to be.

Provides vision, articulates vision, doesn't deviate from vision – everyone is on one path among all the priorities possible.

Visionary, the leader is there because he or she wants to be and feels they can have an impact . . . Leadership makes things tangible and is the capacity to be influential and persuasive. Need to be able to develop a team that buys his dream/vision and sees it to fruition. Therefore, he must be influentially persuasive.

Be able to communicate effectively things like expectation and motivations

A leader is someone who has a vision and is able to move someone to the vision. Instills confidence in the vision and instills confidence in others to carry out the vision.

[a] Visionary . . . has a vision of the future for the organization and for the employees.

One respondent went further: "always start with vision. Inspire a vision that [becomes] the goal and task. Inspire a vision to get the work accomplished; [leaders] use a vision to develop rapport and relationship with people that gets work done together. I've learned it is important to communicate a clear vision and direct. You need to know what people value and their strengths and abilities and through that knowledge motivate them by a vision. Really have to learn a lot about people." Vision is neither rhetoric nor platitude; it provides direction and guidance and aligns people.

Teaching/Coaching

Tichy (1997) says teaching is what leaders do and proposes that teaching is leading (see also Fairholm 1998b). McFarland et al. (1993) discuss the idea of bringing out the best in others in terms of developmental coaching and empowerment activities. Sullivan and Harper (1996) discuss how to invest in and nurture employees. O'Toole (1996) posits that the most difficult challenge of leadership is bringing about change without imposing one's will on others and suggests a strategy of empowerment and teaching based on legitimate values.

Coaching is a new conception of the leader's role. Few writers, with the exception of Levinson (1968), prior to the 1980s related leadership to teaching. They saw coaching as face-to-face leadership. Its purpose is to bring out the best in individuals by building on their strengths. At its heart, coaching is the power of personal attention that can be communicated in only one way: personal presence.

Survey respondents support these ideas. One wrote that, "a good leader should be a coach for his or her staff and recognize and develop the potential of each person on the team." Another said, "Leaders aren't always at the top. Wherever you are, you are a leader . . . if you are a leader. You have to be what you want your followers to be. Need to demonstrate and model behavior. There will be values differences, but you bring them together through core mission and shared values." And, finally, one other surveyed executive said: "You need to relate to them personally. People need to know their leader. The leader has to be really visible. You need to know them, talk to them. We are not in an ivory tower giving commands. You should be out and about and lead by example and participation." Being in a position to teach and model that which the leader and the organization view as important is central to this perspective.

Empowering (Fostering Ownership)

Empowerment is exercising control based on results, not just activity, events, or methods. Empowerment is endowing others with the power required to perform a given act. It is granting another the practical autonomy to step out and contribute directly to his or her job. It does not mean that leaders give away their power. Rather, it involves adding to the power of coworkers. No one is powerless. Empowerment is sensitizing coworkers to this fact. It is intellectually connected with several leadership ideas like team or participative management, transformational leadership, personal change, and McGregor's (1960) Theory Y.

One studied executive noted that leadership asks the leader to: " . . . establish the goal, communicate it, and empower followers by giving them knowledge and an understanding of their roles to be played out. They need to figure out how to meet follower needs, have an individual focus, get into them as people. Leaders help or allow followers to lead themselves. Leaders must be clear on mission so followers know the direction and you can't allow followers to stray off course. But you need to have respect and kindness."

Summary and Conclusions

Leadership based on values suggests that leadership is or can be a part of the routine actions of many people in the organization, not just the preserve of a few at the top. It has little, if anything, to do with managerial orientations. Intellectually, it may be hard to classify. Operationally, we see it in all our organizations, often continuously. Leadership models and theories that ignore values, as past models do, because values "contaminate" the process fail to understand the true function, the true nature of leadership.

Leadership subscribes to values and principles of life as well as to operational action. Therefore, it is a question of philosophy, of the principles of reality, and of human nature and conduct. The philosopher deals with analysis and with moral values (Burns 1978). So, too, do leaders. On the other hand, a theorist (as opposed to a philosopher) deals with analytical ideas and data (Hofstadter 1955). The theorist tries to order, adjust, manipulate, and examine. The theorist mind-set relates most accurately to ideas about management; the philosopher mind-set to leadership. We cannot see philosophical principles; they are not tangible or observable, like a production line. We cannot count, measure, or control them. Yet, these philosophical leadership principles are essential to understanding the relationships within which we live and work.

Today's world asks its "chief" people, indeed all people, to understand the relationships, more than just the action, of team members. For, in truth, relationships constitute the very idea of organization. Thus, philosophical questions are basic. They clarify our understanding of our world and ourselves. While often times the philosophical questions are general, they are nonetheless real-world concerns (Honderich and Burnyeat 1979).

The leader's task is to integrate behavior with values. If we are to improve our organizations, leaders must consider the character and attitudes they inculcate in group members, and they must model acceptable member behavior. This is, at heart, a philosophical task. It makes leadership philosophical and its operational environment value-laden and relationship-oriented.

The great leaders in art, science, and literature lift their companions to new levels of beauty, craftsmanship, appreciation, understanding, and skill. The qualities of leaders in all fields are the same: leaders are the ones who set the highest examples. They open the way to greater light and knowledge. They break the mold. Leaders are inspiring because they are inspired, caught up in a higher purpose.

Leadership places a higher emphasis on values, creativity, intelligence, integrity, and sobriety. These are the traits managers seek to screen out in interviews in favor of loyalty and conformity. These qualities are needed today. Our corporations and workers cry out for interesting, exciting, challenging work and leaders who can make the work of the world seem worth personal time and identity. Notwithstanding the silence of past leadership theory, these topics, these philosophical values and capacities, are present in the practice of leadership. They are seen in most of our corporations. They are essential to understanding our work relationships, which constitute organization. Something more personal than efficient action is needed to understand how to lead business corporations.

Two points of view on the place of values in corporate life are applicable here. In one, the individual's values are preeminent and organizations are formed to serve these values. The other idea suggests that organizations themselves have values that supersede those of individual members. Whether or not they emanate from the individual member or from the group, values shape group action, dictate reward systems, and are the measures of individual and group success.

Several researchers have recognized the place of shared values in group life. Scott and Hart (1979) describe a generic corporate value system that they say prioritizes the value of corporate health. Values which support this overarching value are those of rationality, efficiency, loyalty to the group, and adaptability. As corporation members accept a particular set of values and act upon them, they become the truth for them. Values that strengthen and perpetuate the corporation and not the individual may be the source of much of the pressure some see in corporate life. For Burns (1978) values are standards that can be used to establish choices made, determine equity, and balance policies and practices. In his seminal work on leadership, Burns also suggests that values can be a source of vital change in people and organizations. The central task is to manage values conflict in favor of a shared value system. Leaders appeal to widely held "ends values," which unite leader and follower and provide a shared ideal.

Chapter 6
Trust Culture Leadership

A crucial leadership task is building a culture within which leader and follower can relate in a trusting way in accomplishing mutually valued goals using agreed-upon processes. The reason trust is critical is because the leader-follower relationship is essentially voluntary. This becomes clearer as we realize that leadership is understood to be based on values and the choices people make to adopt and apply certain values. Followers need not respond to leadership in the same way that employees obey their manager's orders. Leaders cannot use force or coercion to attain their ends, nor do they want to. To gain the use of follower talent, time, and imagination, leaders must create initiative (Wagner-Marsh and Conley 1999): no one can force creativity or commitment.

This fourth perspective in the LPM, Trust Culture Leadership, refines the focus from values generally to the specific value of trust and the specific phenomenon of facilitating certain kinds of interaction between the leader and the led. This perspective acknowledges that followers have an influential role in the leadership relationship situation. The focus on the follower is important in this perspective because of the emphasis on teams, culture building, and fostering mutual trust between leader and led.

Trust leadership is a process of building a trust culture within which leader and follower can amicably relate in accomplishing mutually valued goals using agreed-upon processes. In this sense, leadership is a sharing, not a starring, role. The leader's role is to create unity, a team, out of different individuals. This activity is not a function of amalgamation but of aligning individual concerns with the core values and purposes of the group.

Cultures: Definitions and the Need for Unity

Culture is said to be a manifestation of commonly held beliefs, behaviors, and language. Building cultures that maintain and encourage trust is the thrust of this leadership perspective. This implies, of course, that the culture is one of unity and cohesion. However, much leadership literature is still devoted to an emphasis upon supposed organizational gains of encouraging multiple cultures within the system.

M.R. Fairholm and G.W. Fairholm, *Understanding Leadership Perspectives*,
DOI: 10.1007/978-0-387-84902-7_6, © Springer Science + Business Media, LLC 2009

Such multiculturalism works against the needed internal unity and cohesion. It stretches our collective imagination to suggest that a leader can, by dint of personality or even authority delegated by the organization, get diverse individuals or groups to cooperate long enough to consistently produce anything. The task is simply beyond the capacity of any one leader. This is especially true when the leader's effort is also directed to respect, honor, and preserve largely intact each cultural subset's unique values, customs, and traditions. Hence, while recognizing that the vitality of diversity is both natural and perhaps even inevitable, the goal in this view of leadership is to bring such diversity into a harmonious union of purpose.

Again, unity from diversity is the goal. Such unity in diversity has been taught throughout the ages by such notables as Gandhi and Lao Tzu. Of course, unity is not uniformity and that warning is important. A unifying culture based on shared values and accepted norms of group member behavior is the gist of trust leadership and its central purpose. It allows for people to retain their individuality, but commit to unifying principles.

Of all the pressing problems leaders face day to day, one stands out: the problem of the integration of worker and organization so the system meets the needs of both without destroying either. Shaping a culture in which group members can trust each other enough to work together lets leaders create the mental and physical context within which they can lead, followers can find reason for full commitment, and both can achieve their potential. In this context, a harmonious culture is the basis of leadership. Lasting leadership is a result of specific, planned actions to create a culture characterized by internal harmony around values and ideals the leader and follower have come to share.

Leadership is an expression of community. Leaders are successful only when they unite individuals in collaborative action without losing too much of the individual freedom they and their followers want. Only in this kind of unified, harmonious culture characterized by mutual trust can leadership take place (see Konz and Ryan 1999; Fairholm and Fairholm 2000). It is a culture where both leaders and followers can be free to trust the purposes, actions, and intent of others. Leadership is a culture-building task, but it is a special kind of culture-building based on mutual, interactive trust.

Defining Culture

We can define culture simply as that character of commitment and order in a social team that allows people to trust each other enough to work together. Most people's definition of organizational or corporate culture includes elements like shared values, beliefs, assumptions, patterns of relationships, and behaviors. Uttal (1983) defines it as a system of shared values and beliefs that engage team members, corporate structures, and control systems to produce cooperative behavior, trust, and security. Seen in this way, the organization's culture is founded in core values and beliefs that have evolved in a team over time (Nadler and Tushman 1990). These core values are imbedded in generally known and understood statements about what is good or not good in and about an organization. Corporate culture refers to the pattern of basic assumptions about which team or group members agree. Culture is real, if often assumed and implicit rather than explicit. It defines the nature and character of the organization.

We can look at culture from two viewpoints. First, culture is the overarching system of settled beliefs that define the person or institution initially and give direction to daily life. Culture prescribes the general ways people relate to each other, whether in trusting or distrusting ways. This is a strategic, global perspective which proceeds from both internal and external guiding beliefs. Second, culture is about the daily routine of a given organization. Culture defines the accepted system of meanings that give direction to specific routine acts we perform daily.

We can make several assumptions about culture. First, it exists. Every organization and group that endures for even a modestly short time develops a culture, and each culture is unique. Second, it provides members with a method of understanding events, symbols, and messages formed within the group and unique to it. Third, culture is a kind of lever for directing group behavior. Fourth, it is a control mechanism for approving or prohibiting some behaviors and shaping others. Without general agreement on appropriate behavior and the value context within which we will operate, team members are free to follow divergent paths. Indeed, no coherent, cooperative action is possible where at least implicit common agreement in a core culture is missing.

Organizations are about culture. They are about how much members trust each other, if indeed they trust others at all. They are about attitudes and emotions and their impact on team performance. Of course, there is value in looking at corporations from the perspective of physical facilities, structure, systems of workflow, and the tools and equipment used. But the work group is mostly about people in interaction. It is about the collective values people hold concerning the common enterprise.

The leader's task, therefore, is to create a culture that integrates all individuals into a natural unity so individual actions can strengthen the results of the whole (Howard 2002). When the prevailing culture is incompatible with the leader's vision, the task is to change the culture to insure that it promotes needed integration and harmony. Of course, a given corporate culture may contain several subcultures. Each can differ, in some respects, from each other and from the parent culture. Knowing the parameters of the larger culture, though, helps in defining and analyzing the details of the subcultures making up the larger body. In this sense, leadership is about finding or unleashing the natural unity and order in the apparent chaos of large scale organizations (Wheatley 1999). This idea is especially important as leaders begin to lead in cultures peopled by widely diverse individuals. Again, making these culturally diverse people a part of a harmonious whole has always been the prime task of leaders.

Successful cultures are characterized by enough mutual trust and respect to let members be free to make choices, which empower them to meet at least some of their needs. Command and control systems and structures typical of past industrial

age business and government bureaucracies seldom provide that trust or that freedom, except, perhaps, at the very top levels. This argues against traditional tight
managerial control. What we need today are trained, focused, and committed workers whom leaders can trust to respond appropriately in rapidly changing situations
where top-level oversight is not desirable or even possible. Such a new culture is
one that focuses more on results than on process. Leadership in this changing social
and cultural environment must change too.

The dimension of this cultural change is as broad and comprehensive as the
corporation itself. Some critical dimensions of corporate life which have practical
cultural implications include: communication as the nerve system of the organization; cooperation (see Barnard 1962); conflict creation and resolution mechanisms;
commitment; cohesiveness and member ownership of organizational aims; levels of
acceptable caring and concern for others; and ultimately, trust. These operating
processes interact to form the social aspects of the organization.

Other factors are also present in any corporate culture and may change behavior
and ultimate success. Indeed, any aspect of the corporate relationship or external
factors impinging on team performance can shape or modify corporate culture.
Thus, professionalism, personal or professional biases, and social or corporate politics can be features of culture. Similarly, task or system complexity, changing work
values, training and development, task design, and task assignments systems are
also cultural determinants. Collectively, these cultural factors influence how people
respond to the requirements of the work system employed and constitute the work
culture.

The Impact of Culture on Leadership

Obviously, then, leadership and culture are intertwined. Values establish the foundation for more specific operational and interpersonal work standards used by the
group. Selznick (1957) asserts that the function of the institutional leader is to help
shape the environment in which the institution operates to define new institutional
directions infusing the organization with values. And Barker (1992) states that
strong cultures act as intellectual and emotional paradigms. Schein (1992) suggests
that culture and leadership must be understood together. If we want to distinguish
leadership from management we can argue that leaders create and change cultures
while managers live within them. Schein convincingly argues that organizational
cultures are created by leaders, and one of the most decisive functions of leadership
is the creation, and sometimes even the destruction, of organizational cultures. In
this sense, leadership and culture are conceptually intertwined. Culture determines
a large part of what leaders do and how they do it. It also determines corporate
practice and confirms that practice. In actuality, leadership is a consequence of
corporate culture and culture is a result of leadership (Wildavsky 1984). The two
are inextricably intertwined.

Trust and Its Impact on Leadership

The Trust Culture Leadership Perspective assumes that follower development, team success, and effective cultures depend upon trust. Fairholm (1998b) states that common values build trust and that trust is the foundation of cooperative action. The kind of leadership that grows out of shared values only flourishes in a climate within which individuals can accept the uniqueness of others without sanctioning all of their behavior. Without trust, he warns, cultural values can become strictures, impeding individual and group progress.

Sashkin and Sashkin (1994) suggest five strategies for leaders to create a successful team culture, which are (1) value-based staffing, (2) using conflict constructively, (3) modeling values in action, (4) telling stories about heroes and heroines, and (5) creating traditions, ceremonies, and rituals. Dreilinger (1998) states that one leadership role is to overcome organizational cynicism by building cultures through accountability and high ethics and eliminating causes of mistrust. Kouzes and Posner (1993) suggest that people want leaders who are credible. Credibility includes being honest, competent, and inspiring and doing what you say you will do. They say that the leaders we admire do not place themselves at the center; they place others there. This reinforces the notion of follower participation in the leadership phenomenon. Fairholm and Fairholm (2000) outline individual, organizational, and societal forces that hinder the development of trust, which when overcome encourage cultures of trust.

The cultural environment leaders create may produce a trust situation where we can trust certain actions to produce certain results. It may also prescribe our willingness to trust. One culture may allow us to trust others more or less than another, but without the restraints imposed by cultural features we could not exercise trust at all. Being trusted by followers allows leaders to lead. Low trust cultures reduce the willingness of members to volunteer to follow. Low trust cultures necessitate use of control mechanisms to secure member compliance. Consequently, low trust cultures force us to manage, not lead.

Trust places obligation on both the truster and the person in whom we place our trust. It is the foundation of success in leadership or any interpersonal relationship. With trust we can act in an otherwise unknown, ambiguous, or even risky, situation. Without trust, the individual has no power in relationships, especially those outside the leader's immediate sphere of influence. Trust is central to ideas of empowerment, expectation, and predictability.

We build our lives on trust relationships. All aspects of human interactivity are based on trust of others – superiors, peers, subordinates, customers, and other stakeholders. Trust or its lack is at the heart of many of the problems society presents to the thoughtful observer. Much of social culture today is fragmented and conflict ridden. Leadership in this kind of environment requires adherence to ethical principles that highlight trust (Maccoby 1981).

Sadly, people appear to have lost confidence in their leaders and in the programs that they lead. We have lost the sense of community that former cultures provided:

groups of individuals have replaced communities. Many of our business organizations and even some of our families lack the cohesion that mutual trust provides. As a result, many people suffer from isolation, anomie, and anxiety. Unless workers trust both leaders' motives and their ability to lead, they will not follow (Hitt 1988). Past reliance on structural form or workflow processes has improved efficiency. Unfortunately, this focus alone largely ignores the sociopsychological dimensions of corporate life, and it is in this dimension of team interrelationships that we can find the solution for many contemporary problems. It is trust, more than either power or hierarchy, that makes a team function effectively (Barnes 1981).

Trust leaders are aware of both the existence and the potential significance of trust in established cultural beliefs and norms systems. They learn to identify and alter those cultural norms that act to limit trust. Once shaped, cultural values and norms provide the base against which we can measure changes in organizational activities and assess potential changes to determine the level of interactive trust present.

The Trust-Truth Model

Trust is, in essence, based on the truth. The information we use to base our trusting behaviors must eventually prove accurate if we are to expect success now and in the future. Our leap of faith to trust another must pay off in reality or we lose interest in and sever our association.

Trust and an eventually proved reality are inseparable. Properly placed trust empowers us. Misplaced trust precedes defeat. Trust is effective only as we use it in terms of an ultimate reality – a reality that eventually will be proved-out in practice. To trust, one must have some evidence, some clue, or an assumption, at least, about what the truth is. The expectations and assumptions members hold about how much risk they can or should accept in working with others in situations where full knowledge is not present shapes our relationships. Whether placed in people or organizations, our trust is a belief that what we hope is in fact inevitable. To trust another person or thing means that we have confidence that we will eventually confirm that that which we see or hope for in or about that person or thing is actually the truth about them. It is a hope in their reality based on factors in the person, the situational context, or their behavior. Thus, trust is or can be a logical, thoughtful expectation. It need not be blind.

Trust, as a word and as an idea, connotes feelings of security, confidence, self-reliance, intimacy, and integrity in the absence of hard proof. To be trustworthy is to be dependable, deserving of confidence, a reliable person, one who is faithful, believable, or who others see as having a firm belief in honesty and justice (Wagner-Marsh and Conley 1999). Our trust continues and is sustained and enlarged only as future experiences confirm that early perception to be, in fact, correct. That is, trust builds as experience proves the essential truth of our initial perceptions. Trust diminishes by the reverse: as people or things are proved less than or different from our initial perceptions, we withdraw out trust.

Trust is an interactive, interdependent process of taking a risk to trust, gaining experience, and then enlarging or diminishing trust as that experience proves our initial perception truthful or not. Having defined trusting relationships as we have, we are all continually engaged in trusting. Farmers plant seed without total assurance that a harvest will result. We marry without really knowing the full truth about our partner. We delegate work to subordinates or accept our leader's guidance without knowing their full importance or relevance to our personal concerns or responsibilities. We exercise faith in a Supreme Being without visual or tactile contact. Yet we engage in these relationships and countless others daily, trusting that most of the time we will not misplace our trust: we trust that the person or thing trusted will prove to be true.

The Impact of Trust on Leadership

Creating the kind of physical and psychological environment necessary to create a following taxes the leader's ability on all levels. The task of creating a corporate culture that engages both the emotions and the best efforts of members and coordinates them into a unity is difficult. At its core, it is a problem of developing trust. Once given, trust opens opportunities for us to gain experiences. That is, we increase trust by the acquisition of more true knowledge about a subject. We diminish it by the same process: acquisition of information that belies our initial perception of the truth about the person that formed the basis of our initial trust actions. Yamigichi and Yamigichi (1994) suggest that specific and interpersonal trust may be understood better by suggesting that the issue is one of caution. As specific interactions prove to be true or good, one's sense of caution diminishes. The opposite, of course, is true if the trust-truth model provides no validation of the trust. A sense of caution rises. In this sense, leadership can be thought of as a process of lowering people's sense of caution in our relationships.

The process of gaining trust relies first on having or securing some accurate, real, or true knowledge of the person, thing, or situation. Gaining this intimate knowledge is a necessary prelude to a lasting trust. It is encouraged by a culture that values trust per se, that honors the individual, and that fosters cooperative interaction, but it is also encouraged by interaction and communication with others. In a climate of trust, individuals can give open, candid reactions to what they see as right or wrong. In trust cultures, there is little manipulation, few hidden agendas, no unreasonable controls or saccharine sweetness which discounts real problems. Instead, there is a congruency in concepts, conduct, and concern and a unity appropriate to group membership that does not risk individuality.

Without trust, values can become strictures, impeding leadership and individual and group progress. It accomplishes very little, for instance, to develop elaborate corporate work flow charts if the people who inhabit the real world symbolized by these charts do not trust each other. Striving to achieve goals is futile if leaders allow themselves to be too much at the mercy of their moods so followers see them as ambivalent administrators whom they find unpredictable or capricious.

Table 6   Key trust leadership elements

Leadership perspective	Leadership elements	Illustrative citations
Trust Cultural Leadership	Ensure cultures conducive to mutual trust and unified collective action	Dreilinger (1998), Fairholm (1998b), Kouzes and Posner (1993), Schein (1992), Malmberg (1999), Mitchell (1993)
	Prioritization of mutual cultural values and organizational conduct in terms of those values	Hofstede (1993), Hollander (1997), Schein (1992), Selznick (1957)
	Creating and maintaining culture through visioning	Collins and Porras (1997), Schein (1992)
	Sharing governance	Fairholm (1994), Gardner (1990), Kaufman (1969), Rosenbach and Taylor (1989), Rost (1991)
	Measuring/appraising/rewarding group performance	Fairholm (1994), Fraser (1978), Gardner (1990), Luke (1998)
	Trust	Fairholm (1994, 1998a), Kouzes and Posner (1993), Fairholm and Fairholm (2000)
	Team building	Luke (1998), Sashkin and Sashkin (1994), Tuckman (1965), Fairholm (1998a), Nolan and Harty (1984)
	Fostering a shared culture	Conger (1991), Quinn and McGrath (1985), Schein (1992), Wildavsky (1984), Nolan and Harty (1984)

In sum, this perspective places two obligations on leaders: first, to create a common culture where all members can trust one another to do their part to attain agreed-upon results and second, to insure that the trust culturethat is created allows individual members to grow toward their personal self-development goals. Low trust cultures force us to manage, not lead. Table 6 summarizes the intellectual foundations of these ideas.

Trust Culture Leadership: Tools, Behaviors, and Approaches to Followers

Trust Culture Leadership is practiced in ways that ensure created cultures are conducive to mutual interactive trust and unified collective action consistent with shared values which ensure that member conduct is conditioned by those values. In sum, this perspective places two obligations on leaders: first, to create a common culture where all members can trust one another to do their part to attain agreed-upon results and second, to insure that the trust culture that is created allows individual members to grow toward their personal self-development goals. Low trust cultures force us to manage, not lead. Table 6 summarizes the intellectual foundations of these ideas and Fig. 7 illustrates the LPM elements.

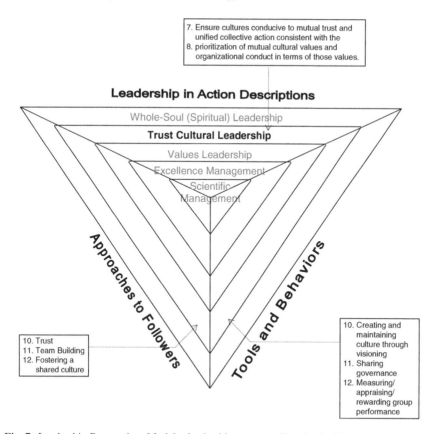

Fig. 7 Leadership Perspectives Model – leadership as trust culture leadership

The specific leadership elements abstracted from the research are: (1) ensuring that the culture is conducive to mutual trust and unified collective action, (2) prioritizing mutual cultural values and organizational conduct in terms of those values, (3) creating and maintaining culture through visioning, (4) sharing governance, (5) measuring, appraising, and rewarding group performance, (6) trusting, (7) building teams, and (8) fostering a shared culture.

The Trust Culture Leadership Perspective is most distinguishable in terms of its Approach to Followers. Respondents identified team building as the leading element. It encompasses 32% of all comments describing this perspective. Together with trust and fostering a shared culture, the operational category Approaches to Followers received 50% of respondent mentions. The Leadership in Action operational category received only 13% of mentions, the lowest of any operational category for any of the five perspectives.

This perspective relies mostly on its Approaches to Followers to differentiate it from other perspectives in the LPM. Data reveal that the main elements in this perspective deal with team building, measuring and rewarding group success, and creating a culture through visioning. The focus on teamwork rather than individual performance is emphasized in the unedited comments of surveyed executives. One said, "The team that brought you to today's mishap or failure will be the team that has to bring you to tomorrow's success." Another offered that a leader must "...reinforce the concept that everyone on the team is a contributor to the end product and that all work as all recognition is a group effort." Trying to develop and maintain work teams that grow and develop is an important focus in this perspective.

The value of creating a mutually trusting culture where purpose and action are agreed upon is evident in this comment from one manager: "Within this process the leader will elicit input and feedback to mold the group members into an invested and participatory team to define respective roles, responsibilities, and objectives which each part must play in accomplishing the goals and the purpose previously defined." Such is a task in this perspective.

The following sections encapsulate the elements of this fourth LPM perspective.

Ensuring Cultures of Trust

Leadership success is increasingly dependent on achieving positive, trusting relations with others. Mitchell (1993) argues that trustworthy leadership involves reliable stewardship and social responsibility. As outlined earlier, Kouzes and Posner (1993), Schein (1992), and Fairholm (1998a) also express a needed focus on trustworthiness, credibility, and cultures of trust. Fairholm (1994) holds that culture affects and influences the leadership of a group and, therefore, leaders should cultivate a culture of trust. Trust leadership resolves itself into a process of building trust cultures within which leader and follower voluntarily relate in order to accomplish mutually valued goals and behaviors. Malmberg (1999) suggests the ability to attain desired outcomes is driven by workers' job satisfaction and maintenance of an ethical correlation between their feelings and their sense of what is correct versus what is expedient.

Studied executives' comments also reflect these same factors:

Leadership is having the courage to lead with your heart. It is the only way you can sleep at night. I said five years ago I would have had different thoughts. That's because in my current job I am really focused on and committed to a real culture change here in the organization. I want to change the way of running this organization in the future, with or without me here.

Leadership is having the ability to develop a network of professionals as well as friends that have the same mission and goal. This means getting away from the idea that there is one person who has to lead out front. Leadership shifts within the network, depending upon situation, yes, but more dependent upon balance in work and life. I have learned that community and team are not necessarily the same thing. Community is what we should be after...network and balance.

Prioritizing Cultural Values and Values-Related Conduct

A culture is a self-contained environment that members see as conventional. Conventions are rule bound, internally complete, and values laden. Conventions separate, distinguish, and isolate this culture from other cultures, and they value some things as opposed to others. Organizational actors can define personal success in organizations in terms of our fit with the prevailing cultural values. We realize a fit when our behavior conforms to dominant cultural values, when it becomes conventional. Ultimately, all culture is convention. It is applying design and shape onto the group's environment. It begins in the mind.

Our individual or corporate values are part of a set of variously rated values that guide our life and actions and that make that action predictable. Most peoples' values are similar to those of the people around them, those in their cultural surround. Values constitute a network of known and shared understandings and norms that we take for granted. They provide a base of commonality in community life. In the group, values represent those truths all or most members of a community share and know they should seek after, whether they do or not. We accept group values because they are good for us and we feel they will result in greater material, moral, or spiritual development. Commonly shared values are the foundation of trust between individuals and form the basis for interactive trust between nations, social communities, work cultures, or any other group.

Corporate trust and the culture that gives it context is based in shared values that leaders set, maintain, and change as needed to keep them constantly relevant to present action and plans. Trust is both an individual and a collective, cultural human phenomenon. Leaders understand and use trust to ensure member commitment. Trust is neither a new program nor a result of a series of "new programs." People will not continue to offer their commitment to leaders who continually present new programs that are really rehashes of the same basic paradigm to accomplish the same task. Rather, programs that implicitly or explicitly prioritize joint values and are conducted consistently in terms of those values best indicate a trust culture.

Creating and Maintaining Culture Via Visioning

Values define both what ought to be and what is in our lives (Schein 1992; Sathe 1983). These values often find voice in a vision statement or narrative around which the corporation and its leaders interact. The vision that trust-leaders create inspire group members to consistent directed action. To inspire means to enliven, excite, or animate another person. Going beyond motivation, inspiration appeals to the human need to be part of and engaged with others in lofty enterprise. The task of inspiring workers asks that the leader appeal to them on a different level than mere motive or internal drive. Leaders inspire us when they take us outside and beyond our routine ways of thinking and behaving and lead us to another, higher, reality.

Visions become inspiring because leaders have touched powerful inner emotions and desires shared by others in the organization. Visions provide meaning, direction, and social energy that move the firm into productive action, mediocrity, or destruction, if it becomes a counterpoint to formal corporate policy and structure.

Sharing Governance

Fairholm (1994) suggests that sharing governance fosters mutual trust within groups and helps effective teams and team leaders to emerge. Gardner (1990) confirms that the leader should share leadership tasks with followers. When leadership is dispersed throughout the group, it produces greater vitality in top leadership. Luke (1998) outlines a similarly dispersed model of catalytic leadership that respects and rewards the interactive trust found in organizational life. Nolan and Harty (1984) focus on the followership aspects of the leader's trust relationships and describe behaviors that bring leaders and followers together.

Measuring, Appraising, and Rewarding Group Performance

Peoples' desire for association with others is based on more than just the bottom line economic rewards possible through group work. They need to be free to innovate, to alter their work processes, to do the organization's work in different ways, or even to do other work because in so doing they receive the rewards of personal growth and development. People work in groups because it is within groups that they can most effectively attain *their own* personal and work goals. In developing, rewarding, and recognizing those around them, leaders are allowing the human assets with which they work to increase in value. The leader's actions to empower followers involve sensitizing coworkers to recognize their power and capacities and training them in their full use. In this relationship, the leader promotes alignment by providing fair extrinsic rewards and appealing to the intrinsic motivation of the collaborators (Cober et al. 1998). They also promote uniformity by providing positive or negative extrinsic rewards to the collaborators that reflects the team's values and cultural traditions.

Trust

Developing trust is difficult. Haney (1973) says to trust is to take a chance on the other person. It is a risk relationship; it increases our vulnerability (Zand 1972). Trust and distrust is cyclical. The more one trusts, the more trusting the relationship. And, alternatively, the more one distrusts others, the more distrust results.

People cannot demand trust of another or in themselves: it must be earned, and it is a process. While leaders can ask others for their trust, they cannot enforce that demand simply because they have the authority to hire and fire. Trust is a gift, given freely by others because it is based on their confidence, respect, and even admiration for those they trust. Trust is a range of observable behaviors and feelings that encompasses predictability (Rossiter and Pearch 1975). Trust behavior shows a willingness to be vulnerable to another.

Trust is reflected in an attitude of faith or confidence in another person. This faith is such that we believe the other person will behave in ways that will not produce negative results to the trusting person. Trust implies more than confidence (Gibb 1978). It is an unquestioned belief. Confidence implies trust based on good reasons, evidence, or experience, but real trust is based on open, nondefensive interpersonal communications with others. Trust begets trust. We have to trust to become trusted. People base their trust of others on expectations developed from past contacts with individuals or with groups or things generally (Good 1988). Sometimes we give our trust to another in novel situations. This is fragile and not necessarily mutual trust. A more durable, full, and mutual trust is contingent upon full communications, need-satisfaction, and experience with others over time.

Several factors are critical in understanding how we develop, nurture, and expand trust. Among them are ideas of integrity, patience, altruism, vulnerability, action, friendship, character, competence, and judgment (Fairholm 1994). We trust people who persistently demonstrate these qualities more than those who do not. These factors define the individual. They are also characteristics of corporate culture that make it suitable for mutual trusting interaction. When leaders understand and appreciate a follower's efforts, they are bestowing trust on that follower (Culbert and McDonough 1985). This kind of respect for individual differences is the key to the trust relationship, for trust comes and is developed out of the context of shared acceptance of difference, not of dependency. At least four approaches to developing trust are helpful. Each has something to offer in our overall understanding of trust, its development, its maturation, and the ways people apply and use it in formal and informal relationships.

Trust through participation. Trust is encouraged and fostered by shared experiences, ideas, or philosophies. One surveyed executive said the leader "must have a process orientation with mechanisms for change in place, communicate based on service, values, and sound arguments, receive feedback, get information." Such techniques encourage trust. Also needed are methods of shared decision making, encouragement of expression of feelings, and informal corporate structures and relationships engaged in by the leader to increase support and commitment to corporate policies and goals.

Trust through the helping relationship. We can summarize the main elements of the helping relationship as one in which we look at other people in terms of their potential. It is evaluation-free. Leaders who are judgmental find few opportunities to provide real, needed help to followers. And they find that, in judging, they trade-off trust. Trust leaders accept others as they are. These leaders display attitudes of warmth, caring, liking, respect, and interest in followers. They try to see things as the other person sees them.

Developing trust through active listening. Active listening is a process that asks the listener to get inside the speaker and understand his or her point of view. It is listening for total meaning and involves listening for feelings, not just content. It is a kind of naive listening

(Fairholm 1991) in which the listener listens as if he or she has never heard the communicated information before.

Developing trust through a consistent leadership approach. Leaders can adopt any approach to leadership to encourage trust, but the essential need is for consistency. As followers come to rely on the leader to behave in a consistent and predictable way, they can be free to extend their trust to that leader. When leader behavior is erratic, there is no true basis upon which to develop trust.

The surveyed executives' responses regarding Trust Leadership include confirming comments like the following:

Soft skill sets come into play. You need to develop or create a 'leaderful' (sic) organization. Ego is key. You've got to understand the role of ego and check it, so that it is more humble than it might be…. Leading with your heart gets the 80% who will work and takes ego out of play.

Follow, be a steward, team, be respectful, be truthful.

Interpersonal skills – you have to have people on board. If not, people will sabotage and resist… Most effective leaders must instill trust and confidence in others – must be an authentic person.

As noted, trust is central to any continuing relationship. Martin (1996) develops the idea that leadership is a function of trust. Her findings show a high correlation between follower's perceptions of leader action to set a vision and develop a trust culture and their willingness to respond as the leader desires. While both evolving a vision and fostering trust are important in leader success and in getting followers to behave as leaders desire, developing trust is statistically more significant. When both are present in the culture, the correlation with follower behaviors is strongest. Martin's work, which uses over 4,500 practicing executives, concludes that basing leadership on either or both trust and vision results in follower behavior congruent with the leader's desires. Conversely, undesirable results can be expected if trust is lacking or the vision is ambiguous. She found her results to be consistent even when correlated with demographic factors of age, sex, or length of service as a leader.

Team Building

Chaleff (1997) noted that followers' skills are learned informally, but they are essential for effective organizational leadership. This is especially important as we conceive of leadership in terms of teams and shared culture. Followers play a key role in the success of teams and coproduce the shared culture that is essential for leadership to be present. Data gathered from interviewees reflect a focus on trust and team building: "[A leader] can instill trust"; "I consider myself a follower, but I guess I'm both. I need those below me to be able to be above. Leaders have a greater perspective, so they must share information, goals, and issues with others . . . . Leadership is a fluid thing with leadership flowing back and forth in the group. Leaders are followers and vice versa . . . Leaders need to trust others and have faith in them. That is a challenge. But they need to try to focus on followers' strengths. People will rise to the occasion if they trust you. Leaders must role model trust, integrity, ethics every day. You have to have your own life in order to help others and to stay focused." Another respondent said: "Followership is how you create community. Leader and follower shifts depending upon the situation. This happens only when you have respect, both professional and personal, for each other. As you develop a team, you need to have that synergy between everyone and if you do, then, necessarily, leadership will shift. It goes beyond the situation; it is about synergy. That synergy is created by respect, actions that cause respect, and through modeling behavior that is right for the community. A lot is dependent upon a relationship based on unconditional love." These comments summarize important concepts and techniques about team building and group interaction.

A team is a group of people who share a common purpose and work in a coordinated and interdependent relationship. Teams help members create a positive culture, one identified by high trust levels. These relationships allow members to align with the culture and the team's purposes. They lead to synergy. Team participation engages leader's and follower's mental and emotional involvement, which includes the member's egos as well as their physical and mental capacities. Teaming also asks members to increase their personal sense of responsibility through involvement. Team members need to recognize that the corporation wants their total involvement; when given, this involvement increases the member's sense of responsibility and ownership for the corporation and its results.

Adair (1986) says that team work is the by-product of leadership. Team leaders are members of teams: they are not outside the team. Teams do not emphasize normal rules of authority and hierarchy, though the leader may legally have the last word. Rather, consultation in which leaders have a high degree of self-confidence is part of leading teams. Team leadership requires different skills of the leader, not the least of which is the ability to share power. Communications are also critical in team leadership as is skill in value displacement. Choosing the right people to be on the team is critical to team success. Members need to be technically competent, have an ability to work with others, and have desirable personal attitudes. Team building is a slow process. It consumes much of the leader's energy. Becoming familiar with team members and their way of thinking and behaving may make it easier to set and meet high standards.

Fostering a Shared Culture

Culture evolves through the accumulation of actions and events the members of a team experience. Leaders play an essential role in this maturation process. They, more than any other participant, are pivotal in structuring experiences for team members that point them toward desired action. Leaders emphasize some experiences over others and in this way further focus the cultural integration process. It is a process of changing the way people thing about their work, their coworkers, and their joint purposes. Creating a corporate culture involves leaders in several important mind-changing tasks. Among these tasks are setting the value base for mutual interaction and thinking strategically about the team and its future. This perspective involves systematically shaping a desired culture within which members can trust others and expect others to trust them (Howard 2002).

Several techniques for culture creation can be identified, including communication because intended meaning is only done between people who share a common mind-set about essential values and behaviors; shaping the types of office politics techniques that are allowed (see Lasswell and Kaplin 1950; Fairholm 1993); letting members know what to value and how to feel about certain actions or events (see Ott 1989; Steers 1985); influencing attitudes (see Howard 2002); changing values and circumstances that can eventually change people's minds and hearts; and strategic planning (see Eadie 1983; Card 1997).

Research by Colvin (1996) suggests that leader actions to build cultures can be very effective in influencing followers in desired ways. He found a strong positive correlation between leader culture building and maintaining behavior and attaining desired follower responses. Colvin concludes that building and maintaining a cultural environment consistent with vision values results in leader success. He also couples the leader's culture-focused action with actions focusing on the individual-in-the-group, e.g., teaching, coaching, mentoring, and empowering workers. Leader actions that focus on culture-building concerns achieve dramatic results from followers. Those directed to his or her individual-focused behavior were even more statistically significant. Either leader approach is effective. Individual-focused actions are, statistically, a little more significant. But when leaders exhibit both behaviors simultaneously, their expectations for desired follower responses are mostly assured.

Summary and Conclusions

Leadership is a culture-building, value-infusing, behavior-changing, trust-causing activity. Culture dictates acceptable behavior and measures its fidelity to group expectations. Establishing shared values is the most crucial culture-setting leadership task. The values thus set become the basis for a corporate mind-set that guides subsequent individual and group trust and interaction. While leaders shape values, they are made manifest in the culture though attitudes fostered and rites, rituals, myths, strategies, and goals assumed.

A common set of values binds people together. Conflicting values disrupt and may even destroy a corporation or other work team. Quinn and McGrath (1985) present a conceptual values framework designed to provide consistency and structure to the study of human values while at the same time clarifying the fundamental tensions and paradoxes that often exist among values. They exemplify their model by using it to map leadership as a framework of competing values and by showing how different types of organizational forms must be congruent with their cultural surroundings if leadership is to be effective.

Rosenbach and Taylor (1989) conducted research that suggests the qualities we find in good leaders are the same we find in good followers. Pittman et al. (1998)

note further that the fundamental dimensions of followership are performance initiative, which include the ability to do the job, work with others, use self as a resource, embrace change identify with the leader, build trust, engage in courageous communication, and negotiate differences. Nolan and Harty (1984) agree that followership and leadership share many of the same characteristics and argue that little attention has been paid to the nature and power of this trust-based relationship.

Trust Culture Leaders engage in action to explicitly alter specific values and common behaviors. They form and maintain the group. When someone joins an organization, that organization's values eventually take precedence over the individual's values. These new values prescribe their subsequent behavior in that group. For this reason, management of corporate culture is a critical tool for the leader. If he or she does not shape the culture, someone else, who may have different motives and desire different results, will.

Hence, the leader's task is one of continually building unified work groups within which leadership can take place. This task is even more important in these times of multiple changes. Diversity in our workplaces is a fact. And this fact places increased pressure on leaders. Different people have different needs. Leaders must accommodate each if they are to increase excellent performance, and create and maintain a corporate culture conducive of high trust.

It is not an easy task. The character of our work force has become more diverse and less harmonious. The people coming into our organizations enter with different values, mores, and customs. These cultural differences in the people making up the American corporation pose major problems in developing a trust culture. Indeed, diversity itself makes the task of developing leadership more difficult. The leader's role is to build unity, a team, out of diverse individuals. Indeed, we distinguish leaders by the fact that they provide the values and vision focus around which a voluntary group consensus can be sought. Leaders can lead only united, compatible, colleagues who, in essence, volunteer to accept the leader's cultural vision and values.

Cultural relativists reject the idea that any culture is better than another. The effect of this mind-set is to accept all people's values and their resultant behavior, whether or not they thwart needed group action like productivity or quality service delivery. Leadership, on the other hand, is an integrative activity that proposes one value system, or culture, around which many people can gather to accomplish socially useful results. Of course, all cultures include some attractive features, but the fact is there are too many cultures that condoned slavery, the subjugation of women and children, or human degradation to let us conclude that all cultures are equally good. Leaders must accept "the good" and reject values and behavior that are unproductive in reaching group goals. All of us should be open to new values and alternative ways to behave. The task is to unify disparate coworkers holding mismatched cultural values.

Each culture represented in the work force and that of the larger community reflects cultural values that, while often including values appropriate to the leader's vision, attach different levels of importance to each value. So the goals for the leaders are still the same: to define the common values and customs and to integrate and acculturate workers into the team, its value systems, and operating practices.

Leading in a diverse culture complicates these tasks. This cultural factionalism in the team costs leaders time and resources. Dealing with special interests and advocacy groups and responding to charges of bias or favoritism can take considerable time and resources. Organizational factionalism also contributes to lost time in directing a diverse work force that does not respond equally to an instruction, order, or policy. Poor morale is also a frequent result that contributes to a loss of productivity. Unfettered corporate factionalism, which some say reduces bias, may, in fact, generate more conflict based on bigotry. As we allow members of corporate subcultures to behave in nonconforming ways or receive different treatment, we can expect those not similarly treated to react in nonhelpful ways. High trust cannot exist in this kind of situation, nor can high-quality, productivity, or long-term corporate excellence.

Leading culturally diverse workers is not an exercise in mere acceptance: it is an exercise in creativity. The leader's task is to create a new culture and new values to which we can induce diverse people to align for their individual benefit and the benefit of the organization. Leaders who are more culturally sensitive will be better able to understand and serve their customers and all stakeholders. Trust leaders develop skill in accepting and capitalizing on different people and methods to add to the organization's capacity to survive in a growing and increasingly complex world. They overcome their feelings of fear and antagonism and increase their capacity to accept difference.

Trust allows the leader to provide professional and psychological direction, a values base for relationships, and a system for balancing competing ideas, values, and systems in the culture. Creating and maintaining a trust culture facilitates co-ownership in the full team. Leaders who foster feelings of co-ownership decentralize to the maximum extent possible – to the limit of their trust, their authority, and their good sense. Such leaders create other leaders out of followers at all levels in the organization. They create a climate of personal satisfaction, individual dignity, challenge, and opportunity to be successful. Allowing others to share ownership feelings about the group's work and products provides all with a stake in the outcome. It creates a sense of individual and corporate worth.

Leadership in today's world is changing. Successful leaders are willing to engage in a continuing program of personal, mental, attitudinal, and behavior change to develop those capacities and those values that both honor people and high-qualityperformance. They assimilate these values into their personal and professional lives, in all their decisions and actions. They ignite an equal concern in workers for their own growth and transformation so they will want to use more of their innate talent and intelligence in doing the organization's work. In essence, follower growth is the core of the leader-follower relationship. Trust Culture Leadership is a process of educating people to take control over their work lives and assume personal responsibility (while trusting in the personal responsibility of others) for the organization's goals and work process by including the people in decisions that affect their actions.

Chapter 7
The Spiritual Heart of Leadership

Our inner self has a powerful life of its own. It controls both individual and collective action. As we advance in our understanding of the nature of work, workers, and leadership, it is necessary that we also advance in our understanding of the spiritual facet of these ideas. It is clearly necessary to invent corporate forms appropriate to our multicultural, electronic, global age. But we doom such efforts to failure if they do not respond to something deeper: the widely held core values of participants. Our understanding of leadership develops now toward the final perspective. The center of attention is to the core nature of the individual: the spiritual nature of both leader and led. This perspective asks leaders to see each worker as a whole person with a variety of capacities and attributes that invariably go beyond the narrow confines of job needs or position descriptions.

Spirituality is a new notion in leadership research, one that has been ignored for most of the history of modern leadership theory; it has not even been mentioned in most contemporary textbooks. Yet throughout all of social history, we have listed inner moral – spiritual – standards as the primary influence on human action. Our sense of spirit defines us, determines our guiding values, is central to philosophy, and directs our intimate and important choices and actions. To leave it out of our thinking about leadership is to diminish, perhaps to irrelevance, extant theory and unnecessarily constrain our potential success.

The Place of Spirit in Our Work Lives

Present attention on the spiritual self in leadership is, in part, a reflection of the increased prioritization of work in most people's lives. Work has become the center of our lives. Inevitably, work is becoming the source of values in our society and the site of our most worthwhile contributions. The work-community is becoming our most significant community and the setting where most of us find our sense of full meaning. It is hard for many of us to separate our work from the rest of our life. Obviously it is central to economic wellbeing. It is also central to personal and group happiness. Marko's (2002) research finds that workers desire more from their work-community than just economic reward. Given the dominance of our work lives, personal, professional, or other life changes will most likely take place at work. For after all, life is about spirit and we humans have only one spirit that must manifest itself in both our personal and professional lives.

Our spirit self is finding outlet in the secular workplace. People in all kinds of occupations are voicing a cry for spiritual foundation in a chaotic world. They display their spiritual values as they create a culture that fosters spiritual expression in the workplace and nurtures the whole person (Krishnakumar and Neck 2002). We are redefining work to include satisfaction of our inner needs for spiritual identity and satisfaction. Jacobsen's (1994) survey of national leaders and Fairholm's (1997) survey of midlevel managers confirm a growing need for workplace cultures, leadership, and work processes that celebrate the whole person with needs, desires, values, and a "wanting" spirit self. These and other studies provide verification of the presence today, and always, of spiritual forces in the workplace.

It is no longer, if it ever was the case, that production alone defines successful leadership. Leaders bring their whole self to work and so do their followers. They must include their knowledge of the spiritual dimension of life that, perhaps more powerfully than any other force, shapes human action over the long term. Spirit is about what we are. Our behavior is guided by who we are and why we think we are here in life. Our spiritual dimension conditions our relationships with others and their relationships with us. The idea of spirit is central to life and to any activity, like leadership, which purports to order and direct our human condition.

The shift to give attention to the Spiritual (Whole-Soul) Leadership Perspective in the LPM is only now taking place. It introduces another powerful drive, which is coming not just from the few people at the top of the business hierarchy but also from ordinary workers. It is a drive to become all that we can become within the confines of the work unit. Spiritual leadership is a reflection of a rising worker demand for opportunity to use and sharpen more skills and abilities than just those used on the assembly line or prescribed by restrictive position descriptions.

The reasons for this reoriented leadership mind-set are many. They reflect major changes in our social undergirding and have been abundantly addressed in recent years. Among these changes is the rise of an increasingly diverse labor pool made up of workers, each with different kinds of experiences and striving to honor different core values systems seems particularly cogent. Changes in the way we do work are also significant. Today most workers are knowledge workers: people who use words and numbers as both the raw material and the outcomes of their work effort. The rise of knowledge work has changed the nature of the workplace. Today's workers want and expect the firm to provide them with the kinds of work and satisfactions that former generations of workers expected to receive only after years of work and promotion to supervisory ranks (Myers 1970).

All of these ideas belie that notion that a spiritual core lies at the heart of all human life. This spiritual core expresses itself in beauty, esthetics, and in our relationships with others. Our spirituality includes our thoughts and feelings. It is a part of our overall perception of the world. Spirituality has some religious overtones, but it has to do primarily with our inner or private being, our "life-force," whether or not we see it in religious terms. Some perceive spirituality to include a much broader range of experience while they see religion and faith as limiting the discussion to experiences that arise in traditional institutions or ways of thinking (Vaill 1989). And clearly, leadership partakes of philosophy, the study of core life questions.

Our spirituality is manifested in emotional or intellectual activities or thoughts that transcend normal physical and biological wants or needs. Following Fairholm (1997), we can define spirituality in terms of its several conceptual components. For some people spirituality is an inner certainty, a conviction that certain principles or beliefs are intangible and may not rest on logical proof yet are trustworthy and valuable. It is belief in a higher spiritual power with whom they have a relationship. This idea has strong religious overtones but also describes spirituality in terms of universal values that some people believe guide their everyday actions and by which others should judge their actions.

Others see spirituality as the capacity that separates human beings from all other creatures. Spirituality is an inner awareness that makes possible the integration of self and the world. Jacobsen (1994) concludes that the secular and spiritual do not have to be separate and leaders do not separate their inner self from the role they play. Instead, they are indivisible. This is a holistic view of leadership action, one more responsive to both our needs and our objective experience. Others define spirituality also in personal terms, but in less metaphysical ways. Human beings have values and principles, and from them we select qualities and influences that are exhibited in our behavior and interactions with other human beings. For these people, spirituality is the part of us that we use or rely upon for comfort, strength, and happiness. It is a source of contentment both off the job and at work.

Still others see spirituality as the source of personal meaning, values, and/or life purposes. They define spirituality as any philosophy that lifts people and gives meaning to their lives. It is the side of us searching for meaning and life purpose. It is the ethics we follow and the degree to which we seek to do things for the common good and to be a better person. In this dimension, spirituality is a relationship with something intangible, beyond the self. These people define spirituality as being true to one's beliefs and internal values. It is a goodness of mind and spirit. Spirituality is also seen by some as an emotional level of awareness, and, for a few, spirituality is transcendent. It is acting out in thought and deeds the experience of the transcendent in human life.

In sum, spirituality is the process of reconciling the fact that our hearts and minds and not just our bodies are critical to our work relationships. For life is about spirit and we humans carry only one spirit that manifests itself in both life and livelihood.

The work we do, the people we interact with, and the kind of skills we use all challenge or reinforce our sense of self: they have a spiritual dimension. Leaders who accept the challenge to relate to followers in terms of a shared reverence for spiritual things can add another tool in their professional stock. Their spirituality helps leaders understand self and others better. As they recognize their workers' spirituality it helps the leader motivate and inspire them. Spirituality is another source of strength for the leader. Spirit-centered interaction helps leaders and led work more fully together.

The Spiritual Leadership Perspective integrates a variety of implicit ideas recently made explicit by a few people. These ideas include issues of optimism, balance, capacity, and continuous improvement. Spiritual leaders are moral engineers who liberate the best in others. These leaders expand work-life concerns to include "soft" ideas of meaning, fidelity, and caring; they communicate their inner strength to others; they create bonds that fulfill people's needs; they help followers find the sacred everywhere. They are stewards of virtues. They create oneness in the group.

Acting out of our spirituality is difficult. It asks the leader to use previously untapped energies and forces. Leaders gather strength from their inner conviction that their vision values are correct, right for their followers, and true for them and the group. Added strength comes from the support of their followers as they come to share the leader's values, accept the constraints defined by those values, and participate actively in accomplishing the joint vision (Fairholm 1997). Other spiritually renewing sources are the other people we interact with, the spiritual activities we engage in, and the community and social groups we are part of. These sources of personal spiritual renewal are useful because they confirm and revitalize our values, ethics, and beliefs. They provide a source for restoring the spirit self, something not as difficult to do in times past.

For most of human history, no one had to search for the sacred. At the core of every culture was a "cult," with sacred times and places set aside for public rituals. For most of our history, religion was the core force that created our sense of morality, of right and wrong. Religious principles defined moral conduct. They defined good and evil and provided the context for human interactivity. Today, it is otherwise. Now we move in secular time and space. We have moved away from our religious, moral roots. In a drive for so-called sophistication, many people have dropped their dedication to a specific religious orthodoxy. Instead, many of us are looking for the sacred in what we do every day: our work. Work is the place where we spend most of our time and to which we devote most of our true selves. It is logical that we should seek a secular substitute for our lost morality in our work, the place where we occupy ourselves most fully and through which we define ourselves. But the quest is difficult as our core values of humanity often lead us to religious conventions. Whether we rely on the religious or secular, our spirit cries out to understand our core.

Today, analysts are searching everywhere for insight into the nature of personal spirit and its relationship to work. Some have examined recent and ancient history (Kaltman 1998). Others have perused literature (Clemens and Mayer 1999) and film (Dunphy and Aupperle 2000) in their search for this insight. Still others focus on scriptural accounts (Friedman 2004) to fill in the dearth of knowledge about spiritual leadership. Spirituality is the essence of who we are. Separate from the body, it is about our inner self. Often it has some religious overtones, which is significant. While it is important, the religious nature of spirituality is not considered here. This aspect of spirituality is better accommodated in doctrinaire religions and their social institutions, rather than being introduced into the workplace. And yet the workplace itself has a spiritual component (see Vaill 1989).

Few may accept his argument, but Boyce (1995) says that what is most needed today is not more intellect, but more soul. Neglect of our spiritual nature helps explain the whole range of workplace problems we now face – the persistence of hopelessness, worker anomie, lowered productivity, and substance abuse (Raspberry 1995). Efforts aimed at improving people's lives that do not have moral and spiritual dimension are literally a waste of time. A sense of spirituality is the anchor for most people's work ethic and social morality.

The idea of spirit at work is in reality a shift in our mind-set. In the past it was easy to compartmentalize our mind so that each part of our life competed for its own self-interests in relationship to all others. The tendency now is to view life and its living as a vast number of cooperative relationships with other independent units. In terms of our work, this is nothing less than a total reinvention of the workplace, a redefinition of work as not merely an economic site, but a prime philosophical locus of life. Nevertheless, most current efforts to reinvent work ignore this human element (Krishnakumar and Neck 2002).

Leadership is coming to mean the task of creating an arena in which competing interests come together and through negotiation strike a deal with workers, as long as that deal does not intrude on what the corporation stands for. The challenge to leaders is to find a new language of the spirit, one which gives point and meaning to our lives, and then use that language to shape the corporation, our leadership of it, and our concept of leadership itself because the organization, reshaped though it will be, will remain the lynchpin of our lives (Handy 1994).

Badaracco and Ellsworth's (1992) research with the chief executives of several large firms confirms what many suspect. They found that leaders are motivated by self-interest and by a search for power and wealth in the face of self-interested behavior by others. However, they also confirmed that these forces fail to explain fully the motivation of high-caliber individuals sought after for their corporations. They found an acute need for people in leadership positions to exemplify the highest moral principles as they lead the several business, social and governmental organizations, or activities. Thus, it is important that leaders not only have the right goals for their relationships with their followers, but also that they employ spiritually based forces in these relationships.

Pressures That Focus Our Spirit Self at Work

The nature of work is changing. No longer do we need machine-like bureaucratic procedures. The movement taking place is from unskilled work to knowledge work, from individual work to teamwork. We are replacing meaningless, repetitive tasks, with innovative ones (Marko 2002). Now we ask our workers, and they ask leaders, to move from a system that requires single-skilled expertise to one requiring multi-skills (Pinchot and Pinchot 1994). Power is moving away from supervisors and toward workers and customers. We are replacing coordination from above with cooperation among peers.

Workers today are asking the company to weave personal, spiritual, social, and environmental dimensions into the fabric of work life. Business is, after all, simply another form of human activity, and workers are saying that we should not expect less from it than we do other social institutions. We are also changing demographically. The more highly educated people coming to work in our social institutions today want to focus on self-fulfillment values. It is logical that these values be carried into the workplace when these young people enter the job market. They see work as merely another extension of their lives, another venue to practice their own style of relationships, an additional arena where they can receive the mental, emotional, and spiritual stimulation they want. Changes in family structure, work cultures, and society all combine to move larger cultures toward different work-related goals and methods of interpersonal relations.

And finally, we now work under a new psychological work contract. The abandonment of the traditional psychological contract connecting workers to a life-long career with the company has effectively destroyed the security and tranquility of the workplace (Cappelli 1995). People need something else to repair the damage. For a growing cadre of people spirituality is the answer. Workers are voicing their yearning to include inner spiritual as well as economic and production needs in the work experience. They expect more from their work than just a pay check. They are asking that their values be not only recognized but also reflected in work cultures. In so doing, they are transforming their lives, the workplace, and the larger society.

The Power of Spirit

People are much more than a bundle of skills and knowledge, as many managers assume. People also come to work armed with a spirit, a life-giving principle that is concerned also with higher moral qualities. Today's workers come to work wanting to take responsibility, accept challenging work, and make a contribution to corporate success from the foundation of their whole self, not the few skills, knowledge, and abilities delineated in a sterile position description. They want meaningful work and to make a legitimate contribution to the betterment of themselves, others, and their community. Success in today's global market demands innovation, creativity, commitment, and vision from all levels of work and leadership. We cannot easily reduce these capacities to a position description. Yet they are essential to the kind of employee every leader or manager wants and our textbooks advocate: people who work hard, are innovative, exciting, curious, highly ethical, constantly learning, a joy to be with, seek growth, and make money.

Of course leaders should build into any corporate culture a distinction between corporate rights and personal rights to the private enjoyment of religious convictions. But there should also be mechanisms present to allow workers to see the larger societal purposes and results of their work. There should be opportunity to make personal, individual contributions in response to worker's highest-order spiritual goals in addition to the routine of day-to-day work. Spiritually tuned workers want to achieve, and they feel guilty if they fall short.

A sense of our spiritual self has always been a part of the dynamic of leader-follower relationships (Tolley 2003). That it is only receiving popular – and some academic and practitioner – attention now does not take anything away from its pervasive power and utility as an important tool for leaders. Our spiritual capacities are a vital part of our true self and a powerful force in shaping our actions at work and elsewhere. And it has always been so. The current discussion of spirituality as an issue for serious debate by business leaders is not propelled by their concerns about personal faith or religious traditions (Terry 1994). Rather, it arises out of the disconnection many workers feel. Spirituality provides the basis for a new connection between workers' and the leaders who want to guide their professional lives.

Spirituality in the workplace is moving workers and leaders away from ideas of us-against-them and, even, from the idea of taking ownership toward ideas of a unifying stewardship. The spiritual standard of moral conduct we adopt as our guide cannot help but shape our behaviors on the job, whether or not this standard is formally included in theory and practice. It increases and focuses caring behaviors; it changes the character of internal communications systems; it is the source of our most powerful and personal values; it increases effective team membership; it creates a dynamic, appealing, and creative culture.

Defining the Spiritual and Its Impact on Leadership

The spiritual in us describes the animating or life-giving principle within human beings or in an event or thing (Wharff 2003). We can define the idea of the spiritual as the essential human values from around the world and across time that teach us how humanity belongs within the greater scheme of circumstance and how we can realize harmony in life and work (Heerman 1995). Our spirituality is a source guide for personal values and meaning making. It is an inner awareness, a way of understanding our own world, and a means of integration of the self with the world (Jacobsen 1994). Spirituality is another word for personal awareness. It involves accepting universal values that we come to believe guide our everyday actions and by which we judge our actions (Wharff 2003). Spirituality in the workplace refers to the inner values of the leader and the followers – the mature principles, qualities, and influences that we implicitly exhibit in our behavior and interactions with other people.

Secular and spiritual concepts are not opposed because we need not limit the spiritual only to a religious context. Traditional religion is still a prime repository of moral history and present practice. For many of us, religion is the context within which moral virtues are defined and the standard of the moral life. Nothing said here is intended to diminish this idea: the attempt is only to underline the importance of moral values in directing our total life and to suggest that, as society or individuals move away from traditional religion, they still must find outlet for these moral drives. For a growing number of people, that outlet is in the work they do. Integrating the many components of our work and personal life into a comprehensive system for dealing with the workplace defines the holistic or spiritual leadership approach.

The Spiritual (Whole-Soul) Leadership Perspective compels a holistic, integrated approach. Autry (1992) finds that a holistic leadership approach includes organizational services and programs that address both the professional and the personal lives of stakeholders. Herzberg (1984) explains that leaders and organizations earn loyalty from their members when they help unify beliefs that fit into the underlying "mystery systems" of their cultures. Greenleaf's (1998) writings suggest that organization members routinely concern themselves with matters of the spirit, which informs their leadership. Through their personal efforts, leaders assure that the team's value system is integrated and holistic in nature so they do not have to sacrifice values (Cound 1987). A holistic approach includes services and programs that address both the professional and the personal lives of stakeholders. This new approach will help companies realize a multitude of significant benefits. By using a comprehensive holistic approach, they can focus their investments of people, money, time, and resources to get the maximum return possible (Kuritz 1992).

Spiritual leadership is both new and old. Like all new ideas, it challenges, by its very presence in the leadership arena of ideas, all old ideas and practices. It is new in the sense that to date researchers have not considered the spiritual orientation in people as a factor in their theories of leadership, management, or organization. It is also new in that many people's professional intellectual environments have excluded any sense of the unique self from their preconceptions of work, workers, managers, and leaders. They have ignored its force in shaping the interactions in which these corporate actors engage. As such, introduction of spirit to the workplace is new, and even foreign, to many.

Spirituality, however, is also old. Individuals have always been aware of and responsive to their spiritual center. They have fostered its growth and have often let it dominate their lives, both on and off the job. However, they have not found a receptive community for exercising individual and team spiritual values at work. As a result, many people compartmentalize their lives into work, family, religion, and social spheres and relate spirit only to religion. Nevertheless, people are the sum of their life experiences, whether physical, mental, or spiritual. To try to compartmentalize our inner self and core values into a complex of disparate external relationships is to invite stress, tension, and dysfunction. Such a bifurcated life contributes to the social maladies that characterize contemporary American life. A reintegration of the whole person into our leadership theory is necessary.

Whole-Soul, spiritual leadership focuses on transformation of self, others, and the team. It involves the heart and mind, spiritual values, intellectual skills, inner certainty, the essence of self, and the basis of comfort, strength, and happiness. Spirituality is the source of personal meaning, values, life purposes, and personal belief systems, and it reflects transcendent experiences (see Fairholm 1997; Miller and Cook-Greuter 1999). Vaill (1989) concludes that in a typical western organization leaders can adopt a spiritual life at work, be it public or private, profit or nonprofit, large or small, successful or not successful. In fact, he says, organizations are inherently spiritual places, where all members invite a spiritual life.

The Spiritual Leadership Perspective allows the spiritual component of work to be made explicit and valid. There is really no place to hide from spirituality, no extraorganizational place to be more spiritual than seems to be possible in everyday organizations (see Weinberg 1996; Wheatley and Kellner-Rogers 1998; Dent et al. 2005). It is because organizations are valuing systems that leadership of the whole soul is credible and perhaps the most inclusive perspective. Vaill (1989) outlines five dimensions of organizations as valuing systems and highlights the spiritual connotations of each, including the economic, technical, adaptive, communal, and the transcendent factors.

The idea of spirituality as a major area of leadership study makes sense intellectually. However, as we attempt to apply it we may encounter problems. Prime among these concerns is the fact that spiritual matters have never found a place as a major part of past theory. As a result, there is little concrete ideological support for this perception of the leader's role, and professionals are not exposed to ideas of spirit in their professional training. Indeed, they are taught to "objectify," not personalize their professional lives. Business success has always been defined in objective terms. Spiritual satisfaction and professional success are seen as separate goals, not attainable by the same effort. Career and material acquisition, not spiritual peace or maturation, is the goal in today's work world. For many, and for all textbook authors, material goals are considered more important than individual longings for harmony, peace, and satisfaction, even given the fact that these goals are sought by all people, whether at home, in church, or in the office.

Spirit as the nucleus of leadership theory is a radical notion and contrary to accepted theoretical principles. The classical model of the business firm is highly structured and focused on control of tangible objects: products, services, and people. The environment within which most people work is a bureaucratic one. While good at ensuring high productivity, in yielding repeatable products, it is not geared toward meeting individual human needs. Hence, introducing one's spiritual sense into the discussion of leadership is foreign to many.

Nevertheless, our spiritual self is our most accurate self-definition. It shapes who we are and what we do. It has to be a part of our work situation and the goals we seek from our work. But acceptance of the spiritual side of both leader and led can be difficult given the history of separation between work and worker spirit. Some of the problems spiritual leaders encounter in introducing spirit into leadership thought and action are discussed below. The intent is to present some of the limits on spiritual leadership in the workplace arising from traditional theory and practice.

Spirit and professionalism. Some suggest that attention to our spiritual side discourages education and professionalism. They believe that the purpose of professional training is to drive out the mists and shadows of religion and free the human mind from error and delusion. Like day and night, were either of them to gain the ascendancy the reign of the other must necessarily cease. Rather, the purpose of education is the expansion of the soul to the fullness of its capacity. Education increases our faculties and disciplines and develops them. Education is the full and uniform development of the mental, physical, moral, and spiritual faculties. Education of the spirit, that is, exploration of the spiritual side of self, is a part of the daily experiences of mankind.

Spirit and success ambition. Americans work hard. We may live well, but we no longer live nobly. Workaholism and its handmaidens, careerism and materialism, are not only social issues, they are spiritual issues dealing with the essence of the individual. Spiritual leadership requires a seminal mind shift. It lets leaders and led see that they are made for rest and holiness as surely as they are made for work and ambition. We are moving from career dependence to career self-reliance by placing work in its proper context. We are judging ourselves and forcing others to judge us not by what we do, but by how and for what reasons we work. No matter what the work we do is, it can be done better with heart and spirit.

Spirit and self-overcoming. Getting in touch with our inner spiritual being lets us inventory and use our best qualities like confidence, quickness, alertness, dedication, courage, perseverance, charm, thriftiness, trust, commitment, faith, hope, and love. We can also define our spirit by our less-than-positive traits. There is a hidden part of our spirit, an aspect of our personality, that we do not like to acknowledge or that society discourages us from showing. It too is part of what makes us human. Thinking about our negative inclinations and forming strategies to counter them is also part of sensitivity to our spiritual side along with emphasizing our positive qualities.

Again, the Spiritual (Whole-Soul) Leadership Perspective is the integration of the components of the work done and the self into a comprehensive system that fosters continuous growth, improvement, self-awareness, and self-leadership. These leaders see each worker as a whole person with a variety of skills, knowledge, and abilities that invariably go beyond the narrow confines of job needs. Successful corporate leaders model their leadership on a comprehensive mental picture of humankind which respects all the dimensions of being and which rank material and instinctive dimensions as less important than interior spiritual ones. It is union of spirit and work through a reaffirmation of the moral point of view in all decision making (Delbecq 1999).

Most people accept the possibility of spirituality in the workplace, but some question its desirability. They see it as a dangerous intrusion on worker privacy and an invitation to inefficiency and unaccountability. Nevertheless, the key questions for today's leaders are no longer issues of task and structure but are questions of spirit (Hawley 1993).

Our soul is integrated with all parts of our life. We respond to the force of our moral and ethical values perhaps more than we guide our actions in terms of organization-set standards. Seen this way, spirituality is an essential foundation for the quality of the decisions we make. It moderates and conditions our day-to-day life challenges and helps us make "right or wrong" choices. It subliminally shapes the opinions that we see as viable. As people understand the distinction between religion and spirituality, then spirituality can take its place in theory as an important determinant of all individual and group action because we draw on our core values in dealing with people every day. Our moralcompass determines our career path and all that we do along that path.

Present business practices that dehumanize the workplace, treat workers as economic objects, and value corporate profit above humanness run counter to the intuitive forces within all of us. Workers are searching for a deeper meaning in their work life, thus integrating their spiritual identity with a professional work persona

(Giacalone and Jurkiewicz 2003). Operationally, spirituality implies a means of personal and group integration. In this context, spirituality has place in our work lives.

Spiritual leaders live by a higher moral standard of conduct in their relationships that affects all we do and become at economic work levels as well as at social levels of existence. Successful corporate operations are those that respect individual rights and dignity. Often without explicitly recognizing it, spirituality is at the heart of much of the values leadership literature popular today. Leadership based on core values counters the secular tendency toward fragmentation of our spirit (Senge 1998), the common description of our present and past work cultures.

We can connect spirituality at work to ideas about employee ownership, attitudes of cooperation, and attempts to honor diversity while also confirming a sense of corporate community. Spirit makes use of the values of creative work, work with a deeper sense of life purpose. It defines work that lets people feel they are making a difference, creating meaning, being fully alive, living with integrity, and developing sacredness in their relationships. It involves turning the corporation into a learning community where everyone can grow (Howard 2002). These corporate values draw heavily on principles from Judeo-Christian teachings (Erteszek 1983). They reflect core American values (Fairholm 1991) and, Kidder (1995) argues, of most nations of the world. They reinforce our traditional beliefs in the dignity of all people. They define corporate leaders as the trustees or stewards of life and resources. They reflect ideals of what is good for individuals and for groups. They are convictions about what will promote the faith or protect the country or build companies or transform our schools. Spiritual leaders link our interior world of moral reflection and the outer world of work and social relationships.

Foundations of Spiritual Leadership

A working definition of spiritual leadership today must center on ideas of teaching our followers correct principles and on the application of techniques that enable self-governance. Spiritual leadership creates cultures where followers can function freely with the leader and within their work group, subject only to broad accountability. It is redefining the leader's role in servant and steward terms. It asks leaders to provide environments that both recognize and feed the spirit in us all while we are directing work activity.

This perspective of the LPM sees transformation of self, others, and the team as important and even critical. This transformation is toward service. This perspective values the education, inspiration, and development of others. To function in this way, leaders need a change of heart and of spirit, not just technique. It asks leaders to put those they serve first and let other obligations resolve themselves. Leaders are first servants to those they lead. They are teachers, sources of information and knowledge, and standard setters more than givers of direction or disciplinarians.

This leadership environment is radically different from the earlier, nonleadership managerial perspectives, and, on the surface at least, it is counter to conventional wisdom. The difference is not one of quantity, but of quality. It represents a mind-shift. Spirituality stretches the leader's mind toward vision: toward reality, courage, and ethics. Although it accepts the context of values-based leadership, the spiritual leadership perspective lets us add timeless philosophical questions of the spirit to the formula for leadership success. Popular culture celebrates the material and largely ignores the ephemeral spirit, but competition and compassion need not be mutually exclusive. Indeed, the goal of work may essentially be to become more deeply people of quality. Spiritual leadership involves trying to teach followers about this spiritual core and to convince them of its utility for them and for the group.

Spiritual leadership is inevitably shaped by the leader's heart-felt values, by his or her soul, which drives what he or she is and does. When leaders respond to their heart values, others will truly know what they are about and can more freely choose to follow. Only then can the team's collective needs be fully met because, a leader's core philosophy about life and leadership is given substance, and meaning by the internal system of spiritual values focused on. Together, the heart and mind, our spiritual values and our intellectual skills (our heart-thoughts), shape our behavior, our decisions, our actions, and our relationships.

A Spiritual Leadership Model

One way to see how spiritual leadership ideas are applied is to consider the spiritual leadership model developed by Fairholm (1997). The model accepts the fact that people come to work owning all of their human qualities, not just the few skills, knowledge, and abilities needed at a given time by the employing corporation. Workers today, and perhaps, always, come to work armed with and ready to use their total life experience. They have and want to use all of their skills (McGregor 1960). The infrastructure of spiritual leadership is based on an idea of moral service, and the ethic of spiritual leadership is love. Spiritual leadership rejects coercion to secure desired goals. It is noninterfering of human freedom and choices, though these choices may entail some painful decisions and shifts in priorities. Spiritual leaders understand that all people have the inalienable right of free moral choice, and they know that the irrevocable law of the harvest– restore good for good, evil for evil – operates in our lives. Figure 8 pictures the dynamics and interrelationship patterns of this new leadership approach, which are further explained as follows.

The Leadership Tasks

The three spiritual leadership tasks are (1) task competence, (2) vision setting, and (3) servanthood. Task competence in teaching, trust, and in the particular work the group does are essential in leadership. Competence in these spiritual leadership techniques is a critical part of spiritual leadership (Maccoby 1976; Burns 1978; Fairholm 1994). Vision Setting requires a spiritual leader to create and then share

Fig. 8 Model of the spiritual leadership process

meaning and intentions via a vision which comes from the leader's individual sense of spirituality. Spiritual leaders develop vision statements, or better yet vision stories, that foster development of cooperation, mutual caring, and dedication to work. Finally, servanthood means that leaders lead because they choose to serve others. They serve by making available to followers information, time, attention, material, and other resources and higher corporate purposes that give context to the work. Spiritual leadership asks leaders to create and facilitate a culture of self-leadership.

The Process Technologies

The four spiritual leadership processes include a sense of personal spiritual wholeness in both leader and led, the setting and honoring of high moral standards, the notion of stewardship, and service and building community within the group.

Wholeness

Wholeness denotes the Spiritual leader's concern with the whole person, not just the specific skills they have that are useful to the current work being done. Relationships with followers, therefore, are about what the individual can now do, what they want to do, and what their capacity is to prepare for this more inclusive work. There is peculiar power in this new leadership perspective, which embraces a holistic conception of the corporation both as an economic enterprise and as a human system. This holistic approach addresses the personal as well as the professional lives of workers. The challenge is to achieve and maintain a renewing balance between work and family and between personal and professional areas of life.

Morality

Spiritual leaders set and live by a higher moral standard and ask others to share that standard, thus communicating the leader's intentions about raising the level of human conduct. Including a moral dimension in our choices and actions helps us think and act beyond narrowly defined business or political interests. Such leadership will give meaning and purpose to our working lives. Spiritual leaders set moral standards and defend them on the theory that they simply cannot compromise some ideals: they must defend them. Spiritual leaders prefer to compete with some opposing ideas rather than accommodate them, and they affirm the perspective of the spiritual over other leadership models.

While traditional functions and roles may be similar, spiritual leaders apply them in overtly moral ways. We can define moral leadership as a process both of asking questions about what is right and wrong and as a mode of conduct: setting an example for others about the rightness or wrongness of particular actions. Essential, then, to this leadership model is a sensitivity to inner promptings that creates an ethical base for a common understanding of the nature of the group. Also important is self-discipline and the fostering of appropriate social networks that reinforce the core values at play. Freedom from certain situational constraints that may hamper growth toward full moral effectiveness is also important. In real ways, spiritual leaders engage the heart to help transform themselves, others, and the organization to create a new scale of meaning within which followers can see their lives in terms of the larger community.

The spiritual leader's role is to change the lives of followers and of institutions in ways that are mutually enhancing. They convert followers into leaders because they know that our spiritual values, whether we are aware of it or not, are always with us. They are an activating mechanism of our moral character. They are part of our self-analysis as we observe and reflect on our actions and judgments of events. Spiritual leaders understand all people have the inalienable right of free moral choice and recognize their role is in part to set the moral climate and the norms of accountability and responsibility. In doing so they remember the irrevocable law of the harvest – restore good for good, evil for evil – operates in our lives. Hence, operationally, morality involves following ethical standards and patiently sticking to one's purpose. It is feeling good about one's self and reflecting on the ideals of current business questions, but also thinking about our actions in terms of our inner standards of right and wrong.

Stewardship

It is significant, too, that spiritual leaders understand their leadership is held in trust for a temporary period and may not always be with them. Therefore, they function as stewards over the group's resources as they propose plans and programs, allowing followers an opportunity to consent before the actions taken are finally adopted. Hence, a stewardship role, which forms a shared responsibility team, is central to this perspective (Bradford and Cohen 1984). Different from an ownership view which connotes possession and control, which lower order perspectives might and do adopt, stewardship connotes holding work resources in trust for a temporary period. In a stewardship team, power is inherent in each steward to help accomplish the stewardship team's – ends, not just the steward's own ends. Every steward has the same rights and is subject to identical limitations in the exercise of self-direction, and every team process and procedure enhances such shared governance and unity of purpose. It is a relationship system based on mutual accountability, but that accountability occurs only after the steward is allowed to fulfill the responsibilities and expend the resources allotted in his or her own way. Stewardship includes the exercise of team work *and* individual free choice.

The stewardship team is critical in discussions of stewardship. As members come to identify with the stewardship team, they are participating at a level beyond consensus and compromise. A member does not merely accept another member's position. Instead, it becomes a course of action all members accept, support, and foster. Membership in a stewardship team asks spiritual leaders to lead the team but also to play a role as a member of the team community. The basic entities of the stewardship team are the individual stewards and the stewardship leader who form a council of the team and are subject to a higher-level council made up of team leaders. All stewards are coequal with all others in the stewardship team, and the loss of the contribution of any one diminishes the team and jeopardizes its success. Each steward has the right to exercise power in forming the particulars of his stewardship within the team. However, the steward-leader retains the power of counsel and consent. The steward-leader's role, then, is that of servant rather than master. By assisting stewards to achieve their potential, steward-leaders multiply the contribution they otherwise could make.

Community

Community building denotes the creation of harmony from often diverse, sometimes opposing, organizational, human systems and program factions. It is a job of making one from many. It involves generalizing deeply held values, beliefs, and principles of action in ways that all stakeholders will find acceptable and energizing. Spiritual leadership recognizes the simultaneous need we all have to be free to act in terms of our own reality and to be part of a similarly focused group.

Bureaucracies are not communities. They so segment responsibilities that humanity becomes a departmental rather than a universal responsibility. The task for leadership is to transform work organizations into viable, enticing communities capable of attracting workers with needed skills and talents. A sense of community invigorates workers' lives with a sense of purpose and a feeling of belonging to an integrated group doing something worthwhile. Community is from the root word meaning "with unity," and such unity comes out of collective vision, beliefs, and values. Leaders build workplace communities by providing this common vision because no community or society can function well unless most members voluntarily heed their moral commitments and social responsibilities the majority of the time.

Leaders build group relationships, not just membership. The communities in which we have membership act as emotional environments that can block the acceptance of alternative cultures while embracing community values. They can also unite individuals into strong coalitions of mutually interdependent teams.

The key to attaining this latter result is the strength of community, which the leader builds. The corporation is defined by ideas of authority, power, bureaucracy, competition, and profit. Adding the idea of community, however, adds factors of consistency, democracy, cooperation, interdependence, and mutual benefit. Free individuals require a community that backs them up against encroachment on their sense of independence by society's formal institutions, including economic ones. The resurgence of the idea of community is a reaction against controlled social processes that rob people of their sense of self and substitutes a senseless conformity to a barren, abstract, and spiritless system. We have come to know again that the important, meaningful outcomes in life cannot be attained alone. We recognize that many of us live much of our productive lives in workplace communities (Brown 1992), and, therefore, we need to gather information on making productive communities, for this is the place we make ourselves.

The Prime Leadership Goal: An Old/New Definition of Success

The Spiritual Leadership model has one single goal: continuous improvement. Spiritual leaders seek to provide high-quality services and products. Spiritual leaders also seek to liberate the best in people. This task involves an education of the heart more than training of the head or hand. The spiritual leadership approach can adapt to and respond to worker disconnection by making concern about the worker's and leader's spiritual needs a part of the team vision. A focus on spiritual needs lets leaders and led unite on common ground at a metaphysical, not a just transaction, level. Spirituality enlarges our soul and gives it purpose, and, as Covey (1992) says, people are determinedly seeking spiritual and moral anchors in their lives and their work. They are feeling the need for values that do not change. Spiritual leaders see spirit as the basis for everything. They cannot imagine looking at the world in any other way (Magaziner 1994). They are people who feel safe outside what they know and who are passionate about what they have never tried. Recognition of the spirit of work and of workers endows the corporation with soul, or at least it recognizes the soul of the corporation, which we have previously ignored.

Hence, there are some important general indicators of success in a spiritual leadership process. Spiritual leaders facilitate creativity (Freshman 1999), honesty and trust (Wagner-Marsh and Conley 1999), personal fulfillment (Burack 1999), and commitment to goals (Delbecq 1999). Furthermore, they develop a healthy organization. Healthy companies have and radiate a certain vitality and spirit, a deeply held feeling of shared values (Rosen 1992) that anchors the community. The first duty of spiritual leadership is to insure that the corporate community is healthy. Success for spiritual leadership also entails creating a sense of spirituality and moral rightness. Such leaders change context, not just content, in our organizations. Content deals with the surface issues that we can see, hear, touch, and smell. Context, on the other hand, concerns the things we cannot touch; it is about the things we feel. Context shifts within the corporation will not occur unless those who are influential in the system go through their own personal transformation and raise their own consciousness level. The real goal of enterprise is the mental and spiritual enrichment of those who take part in it.

When such context is changed, a more intelligent organization often develops, characterized by independent decision making and a work environment that aids freedom to choose, learn, and grow. Intelligent organizations will be communities that develop their people within the freedom of responsible communities. In fact, they recognize that leadership success is enabling followers to be and do their best, adding to the capability of the team by developing follower capacities for action.

Basically, spiritual leadership is a matter of values and ethics. Being ethical cannot be measured only by productivity, profitability, or product sales. Being ethical is creating a climate of ethical expectation. Being values based is creating a climate where first things come first and the core of the human soul is acknowledged and embraced as important and enhanced through mutual interaction. The results and measures of success in this model of spiritual leadership, then, include the achievement of corporate goals at high levels of quality but transcend those measures as well to include the development and support of individuals who are, and who see themselves, at high levels of quality.

Spiritual (Whole-Soul) Leadership: Tools, Behaviors, and Approaches to Followers

The fifth perspective builds on the ideas of values and trust culture maintenance, but it focuses full attention on the whole-soul nature of both leader and led. The Spiritual (Whole-Soul) Leadership Perspective assumes that people have only one spirit that manifests itself in both our professional and personal lives and that leadership engages individuals at this level. Spirit in the workplace has no real relationship to religion in the workplace. The elements of spirituality as understood in this perspective define who the person *is*, not just what his or her moral stance is or the religious doctrines he or she espouses. Applying this perspective may pose difficulties in contemporary work organizations. Spiritual matters have not been a part of leadership or management theory, and there are limits placed on unrestrained reference to spirituality in the workplace arising from traditional theory and practice as well as legal injunctions. However, leaders in the modern organization can and do link their interior world of moral reflection and their outer world of work and social relationships (see Fairholm 1998b): we take our whole self with us everywhere we go.

Some key elements of this final leadership perspective include (1) showing concern for and integration of the whole-soul of leader and led, (2) liberating people to grow continually, (3) enabling individual wholeness in the context of a community, (4) fostering an intelligent organization, (5) setting moral standards, (6) inspiring, (7) freeing followers to build stewardship communities, and (8) modeling a service orientation. These leadership elements have been researched and analyzed by a large and growing group of experts whose work is abstracted later. Table 7 summarizes some of the intellectual foundations of the Spiritual Leadership perspective's eight leadership elements and Fig. 9 illustrates this perspective of the LPM.

Whole-Soul Leadership is most distinguishable in terms of the Tools and Behaviors identified in the LPM. That category was mentioned in 46% of the comments about this perspective and, within that category, the leadership element Setting Moral Standards received the most mentions at 23%. However, not far behind is the element Inspiration found in the Approaches to Followers category. One executive wrote, "A leader is an individual that possesses certain qualities that inspire individuals to achieve and accomplish goals in life that seem insurmountable." Inspiration constituted 21% of elements and notably outweighs every other element except Setting Moral Standards. Twenty percent of the elements in the Whole-Soul Leadership perspective are found in the Leadership in Action category, illustrating that the tasks involved in implementing this perspective operationally are fairly well understood as a discrete leadership construct.

Data also reveal that the main elements in this perspective deal with Setting Moral Standards, Inspiring Others, Fostering Continual Learning, Having a Concern for the Whole Person, and Servanthood. Significantly, leaders in this perspective are expected to lift others to higher levels of thought and action. One executive wrote, "A leader is a trendsetter. He sets the standards and motivates others to live up to those standards. He leads by example and encourages those around him to always reach to a higher level." This perspective also evinces an abiding respect for personal growth and for

Table 7 Key spiritual (whole-soul) leadership elements

Leadership perspective	Leadership elements	Illustrative citations
Spiritual (Whole-Soul) Leadership	Relate to individuals such that concern for the whole person is paramount in raising each other to higher levels of awareness and action	Argyris (1957), Burns (1978), Cound (1987), DePree (1989), Herzberg (1984), Levit (1992), Fairholm (1998a)
	Best in people is liberated in a context of continuous improvement of self, culture, and service delivery	Autry (1992), Jacobsen (1994), Manz and Sims (1989), Nelson (1997), Senge (1998)
	Developing and enabling individual wholeness in a community (team) context	Barnard (1938b), Cound (1987), Drath and Palus (1994), Herzberg (1984), Vaill (1989), Greenleaf (1998)
	Fostering an intelligent organization	Senge (1990, 1998), Vaill (1996)
	Setting moral standards	Barnard (1938a), Burns (1978), Covey (1992), Gini (1997), Prince (1995)
	Inspiration	Berry (1997), Burns (1978), Fairholm (1997), Greenleaf (1977), Wheatley (1999)
	Liberating followers to build community and promote stewardship	Block (1993), DePree (1992), Fairholm (1997), Vaill (1989), Wheatley and Kellner-Rogers (1998)
	Modeling a service orientation	Greenleaf (1977, 1998)

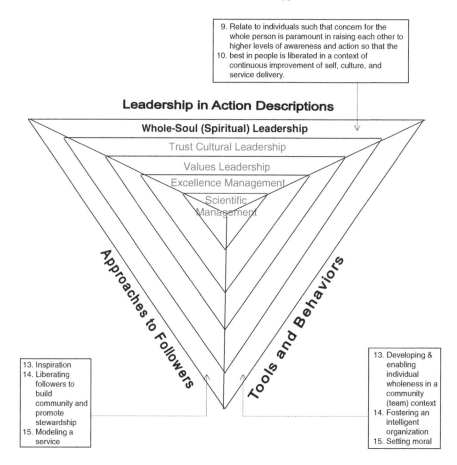

Fig. 9 Leadership Perspectives Model – leadership as Spiritual (whole-soul) leadership

bringing people into a community that respects individual capacities and mutual purpose. Another respondent said leadership is "allowing your employees the freedom to make a mistake yet learn from [those mistakes].... [It] is better for them and the organization in the long run." Another suggested, "The most important aspect of leadership is the ability of individuals and groups to build the capacity of an organization or a community." Further details for each leadership elements follow.

Concern for the Integration of the Whole-Soul of Leader and Led

There are, of course, obvious risks in trying to act authentically in terms of values formerly relegated to creed. Few will argue that the typical workplace resembles the average house of worship or that typical workers act like the average believer. But religious believers are on the job 8–12 hours a day, and they want to relate the best of themselves to the activity in which they spend the bulk of their time: their work. Nonreligious believers at work do the same. This integration process may be helped as leaders try to understand self and others better. It is facilitated as the leader trusts others, since trust motivates people. Spirituality is another source of strength for leaders; it helps them know their coworkers better.

Some elements of a model for applying spiritual concepts on the job are becoming visible. One element is process thinking, which is reconceptualizing the corporation as a circular process of complex interactivity. Another is self-esteem. When seen from the perspective of the soul, motivation takes on a different nature. It becomes a task to inspire and encourage others to be their best selves through innovation, intuition, spontaneity, compassion, openness, receptivity to new ideas, honesty, caring, dignity, and respect for people.

One executive summed his thoughts on this as follows: "I always think of different settings – work, family, religion – when I think of leadership. A common denominator is that in my life my leaders have given me a chance to lead. They compel me to work harder based on getting to my sense of wanting to achieve, wanting more. They allow me to lead, therefore they become stronger leaders." Covey's (1992) work is sympathetic to this stated point of view and is another leadership standard that helps resolve several dilemmas encountered in applying spiritual leadership. His principle-centered leadership focuses on the whole person of the leader. It is an approach that calls into play the soul of the leader in defining him or herself to the team.

Leading others today asks us to employ the whole person (Hawley 1993). Leaders need to use their head, thinking linearly. They must also engage their heart. They need to make use of their spirit, the deep inner self, striving for inner peace, happiness, contentment, meaning, and purpose. Both the spiritual and the worldly coexist as an overlapping whole. They are two parts of the same force that also activates work life. Leadership arouses and channels this human energy. Belief is power thinking, a force that shapes all human affairs. It is focusing thoughts to produce actions and is something we are as much as it is something we believe. It is the foundation for doing anything; not the actual doing.

Liberating People to Grow Continually

Argyris (1957) suggests that attention to the worker's spirit is a very necessary link between individual personality and the organization's dynamics and success. Herzberg (1984) suggests that the leader does much for individuals to help us understand "mystery systems": those elements of life that give meaning and self-efficacy. Levit (1992) hypothesizes that the motive force behind the influence of a leader is meaning and purpose making, and that if leaders are to clarify meaning and purpose for others, they must have a definite sense of these concepts themselves. Jacobsen (1994) points out in his research that spirituality plays a vital role in the personal and professional activity of the participants in organizations. Burns

(1978) reminds us that the purpose of transforming leadershipis to raise followers and leaders to high levels of existence.

Nelson (1997) states that to be effective, present-day leaders have to produce work environments that support and influence, but do not command, certain behaviors and results. Autry (1992) feels that love and caring for people as individuals is central to leadership. A perceptive study respondent commented that he views leadership as "[b]ring[ing] calm to chaos. The ability to identify the real questions involved in organizational life, not necessarily what may seem to be the obvious questions. Leadership is getting to identify the real issue and then lead to appropriate answers. Share information as much as you can. Be compassionate (I'm growing in this area)." And another said: "You measure leadership by seeing what happens when you leave an organization.... It is developmental in nature, helping guide others to the next level of work and as a person. Therefore, interpersonal skills are imperative. You need to know yourself and help others know who they are. When you get the inward issues taken care of, then you can handle the outward issues. I ask my staff to look in the mirror and ask the question, 'Who am I? Where am I? Am I the person I thought I am?' ..." These respondents reveal that the liberation of the best in others and the desire to guide others to better themselves are key elements of this view of leadership.

Enabling Individual Wholeness in the Context of a Community

Facilitating individual feelings of wholeness and completeness is a part of spiritual leadership that has strong research support. Barnard (1938b) claims an individual is always the basic factor in organizations and that the goal of the executive is to combine sentiment and rationality within the organization. Drath and Palus (1994) argue that leadership is a sense-making activity, but that meaning creation is leadership only when it is found in a community of practice. Block (1993) suggests that the stewardship concept defining leadership as service overcomes self-interest in organizational and social life. DePree (1992) states that while leadership is a serious meddling in people's lives, the active pursuit of common good gives us the right to ask leaders and managers of all kinds to be not only successful, but faithful to certain core, fundamental values. Wheatley and Kellner-Rogers (1998) suggest, as a basic principle of leadership, that in order to create better health in a living system, leader and followers need to connect more in terms of core values, self-awareness, and holistic perspectives.

The comments of several study respondents echo these academic injunctions. For example:

> To get the job done through other people was my initial reaction. But more recently, I am aware that you must incorporate other goals like help staff feel secure, being aware of and in control of your area, sharing information while admitting you don't have all the answers.

> Very few things come to my mind as sadder than a leader that is unactualized (sic). Leadership is about actualizing other leaders.

> The goal of leadership is to try to make the organization the best it can be, especially the people, meaning you develop them, help them... You try to build on their strengths. This approach promotes ownership; then they tend to work harder for the organization. Ownership means having say in the goals and tasks, and being accountable for them. Ownership and accountability go hand in hand. Basically, leadership is making the organization the best it can be. Develop people. Pull together the best groups possible. Develop and promote ownership and accountability.

Without a view that individual wholeness is a concern for leaders, these comments would not make much sense. But with such a view, spiritual leadership helps explain how individuals become complete, significant actors within community life.

Fostering an Intelligent Organization

Wholeness is fostered in an intelligent organization. Senge (1990) advises that only leaders who can learn to work within a learning organization will be successful in group relations. He suggests four core disciplines – personal mastery, mental models, shared vision, and team learning – that are reminiscent of spiritual leadership. Vaill (1996) recommends that managers actively and continually learn to be able to cope with the complexities and rapidity of change in today's organizations. One respondent explains Whole-Soul leadership this way: "[you need] ability to learn yourself; ability to learn about people in the organization, so that you can help them develop. Leaders develop people by having conversations with people, seeing strengths and areas for improvement. You ask, 'If you could be doing anything in the organization, what would it be and how can we get there.' You need to be able to know what their interests are, point them to them and expose them to opportunities." Another interviewee states that you must be "courageous, doing the right thing even if it is not popular," pointing to the idea of setting moral standards. Another says that leaders must "have trust, honesty, integrity, respectfulness, compassion – values you look up to." And a third executive stated that "a leader believes in continuous learning and strongly encourages it." The significance of such institutionalized learning is obvious to these respondents.

Setting Moral Standards

This perspective focuses on setting high moral standards, inspiring others around those standards, visioning, encouraging learning and growth, and focusing on individuals so that their best is liberated. The authors' research confirms these findings. The work we do has a moral dimension. Most individuals want to do good work and to contribute to the success of the team. Unfortunately, in too many work situations we have been led to believe that there is one standard for private morality and another for public or business morality and conduct (Nair 1994). Not so. Morality argues for one constant standard, applicable in personal, social, economic, and all other aspects of life. Barnard (1938b) makes explicit reference to the executives' moral responsibilities, as do DePree (1992), Covey (1992), Gini (1997), and Fairholm (1997). Prince (1995) summarizes this leadership element when he states that, in essence, the leader can influence the moral conduct of others by demonstrating the desired behavior, rewarding ethical behavior, and punishing unethical conduct.

Inspiration

Speaking of creativity and empowerment, Berry (1997) suggests that managers cannot order people to be commercial; they hope to motivate them to be creative and give extra attention to the customer. Greenleaf (1977), Burns (1978), and Fairholm (1997) focus attention on the inspirational aspects of leadership. Wheatley (1997) says the culture most people were raised in taught that management was telling people what to do and then following up to make sure the task was completed. It encouraged the notion that we could make people do perfect work. But people cannot be forced into perfection; leaders can only involve them so that they want to have perfect results. The task is not telling, but selling. As one surveyed executive said: "Understand that the leader does nothing without willing followers. Leaders are agents of change and as such they motivate those predisposed to change to liberate them. They bring out the best in others by developing leaders who are already leaders. Negotiation is involved. You educate them about their own leadership and enable or create an atmosphere of excellent to become a leader. It is a cascading of leadership."

Other executives repeated this sentiment in their responses to study questions:

[Leadership is] [s]taying in touch, being attentive. We tend to think about building on previous skills to get where we are and to progress. At times leadership has more to do with listening to people to know their priorities more than you knowing what your priorities are. Try to address them. Help them know who they are and where they can go or what they can become. Walk around, talk, let others express their ideas, feelings, and thoughts.

Everyone can be leaders… I don't like the word 'follower.' Leaders need to be modeling behavior, what you want from people you must model. If you want to have a certain type of communication from others you must communicate that way. If you want people to develop people, you must develop people. You must model the work ethic; do what is required to help. I believe in having respect for the position one holds, but I also believe in equality. You need to work to build a community.

You need to try to relate to the follower (have empathy, sympathy, a real awareness) so that they feel valued. There is a genuineness about it.

These responses highlight the significant place followers and their wellbeing have in the thinking and practice of spiritual leaders.

Freeing Followers to Build Stewardship Communities

The idea of adding a stewardship orientation to corporate governance is new. Many leaders have no operational experience with this concept and, therefore, cannot immediately visualize either their steward-leader role in the corporation or their part in building stewardship teams. While the idea may be appealing, many do not know how stewardship works in practice. As one executive said, "At a certain point the skills, tools, and techniques are not enough. What you need is to comfort, assist, and be concerned about others and love them." Building community becomes, therefore, a critical spiritual leadership task. We need to focus on interactive communities of enabled, moral leaders and followers. We need to engage the people, constructing these communities through meaningful work which ennobles them and their colleagues and customers. The workplace is a community in which many of us live much of our productive lives. Therefore, we need to know how to make work communities not only productive but personally liberating as well.

Modeling a Service Orientation

Spiritual leadership is operating in-service-to rather than in-control-of those around us. It is less prescriptive. It has more to do with being accountable than it does with being responsible for what the group creates or with defining, prescribing, and telling others what to do. Spiritual leadership asks us to reject past models of human leadership that focused on values of self interest. The energy driving these earlier models was implicit values focusing on power, wealth, and prestige. Rather, the transcendent values of spiritual leaders include a rejection of self-interest and a focus on servanthood. They focus on core ethical values including integrity, independence, freedom, justice, family, and caring. The critical focus, however, is on service.

The spiritual leader is a servant committed to principles of spiritual relationships defined earlier. The leader's job is to prepare followers to provide high-quality, excellent service to clients, customers, and citizens. Rather than attempt to dominate followers, spiritual leaders go to work for them, providing all things necessary for follower success. Greenleaf (1977) suggests that more servants should emerge as leaders and, more dramatically, that we should follow only servant-leaders. His models and theories have brought service to the forefront of much of the leadership literature.

Summary and Conclusions

Many people struggle to respond directly to their inner voice and still meet the demands for compromise placed on them by external sources. Because we spend so much time there, the workplace has become the site where much of this struggle takes place. Workers are coming to recognize that many of the failings of our society are due to our past disregard for core values and a willingness to let a minority of the world lead us astray, contrary to our core values. Leaders who cannot or will not see the power of spirit in what they do will fail to attract tomorrow's workers.

The movement today is from the age of production to an age of thought (Marquardt and Reynolds 1994) with results and organizational measures of success coming more from the heart than from the mind. Tomorrow's organizations will engage the mind, body, and heart or soul of all stakeholders (Pinchot and Pinchot 1994). It assumes workers are thinking contributors, not just physical extensions of the manager's capacities, ideas, and creativity. We need radically new organizational structures and systems to meet these challenges of a more complex and turbulent business world. The test is to build cohesive teams which include workers and leaders. It is to create and communicate effectively a strategic vision, institute strong intracompany support systems, and organize a participative structure recognizing worker's innate needs and desires as well as those of the organization.

The leadership famine in our social, business, and civic communities stems in part from the fact that many would-be leaders focus more on special groups and not the larger encompassing community. The leadership gap also has been deepened because too few would-be leaders have been willing to forego tight control of their group members to become orchestrators of followers' independent actions and spiritual wholeness.

Spiritual leaders are sensitive to others' needs to grow, change, and mature. They vary their responses according to the person in-the-situation. These leaders believe that their real success is in the successes of the people they lead. This new breed of spirit leader understands that as people feel cared about they will go to extremes to help those who help them. Spiritual leaders seek to create a climate in which both leader and led bring forward their best. They set standards and values so others can increase their own capabilities. For the individual, this can result in closing the gap between what he or she is and what he or she might become. Leaders do not place themselves at the center; they place other people there, and usually those other people are better than they were before.

Chapter 8
Further Issues to Consider

Leadership continues to be an idea in motion. As a result, it is almost impossible to find the kernel of truth in the welter of ideas, models, perceptions, and perspectives that characterize leadership studies. However, as business, government, and all other social organizations continue to include discussions of leadership more explicitly in their activities, we are certain that this book will help produce men and women who are competently and confidently prepared to both understand and do leadership. The overall conclusion we make is that the five-perspective approach to understanding leadership in the Leadership Perspectives Model (LPM) is a credible and valid way to better think about how people do and can operate together in this diverse, complex, yet intensely personal world.

In terms of the leadership phenomenon, the perspectives approach contends that individuals hold alternative conceptions of what leadership actually is and use these conceptions to measure their own leadership activities and the relative success of others. The mention of leadership causes individuals immediately to draw upon their conceptions to internalize the conversation, define leadership for him or her self, and judge whether or not others are exercising leadership. The variety of conceptions that individuals hold regarding leadership leads to much frustration and confusion surrounding the definition and discussion of the phenomenon. Judging which alternative perspectives are right is a significant question.

While much has been done to flesh out the parameters of leadership in the past few years, ample research opportunities remain. The five perspectives presented in this book make headway in explaining the apparent confusion about definitions that are present in offices, classrooms, board rooms, and academia. However, the overall sense of this book is that leadership is and always has been one thing: an endeavor to liberate in ourselves and others the best in life, values, community, and spirit; a relationship of values, culture and spirit.

Summarizing the discussions of the theoretical, philosophical, and operational aspects of values-based leadership as they are perceived in each of the five perspectives is difficult. While new light has been thrown on the subject of leadership and new, more useful definitions and distinctions have been presented, the work of fully delineating the nature and scope of leadership is not complete. Indeed, as with all seminal ideas, full understanding of leadership is still very much a "work in progress." Gratefully, much of the mists and shadows created by a lingering bias

M.R. Fairholm and G.W. Fairholm, *Understanding Leadership Perspectives*,
DOI: 10.1007/978-0-387-84902-7_8, © Springer Science+Business Media, LLC 2009

that tends to force our understanding of leadership to coincide with management are being dispelled as contemporary writers are shaping a new theory on the nature of leadership as a new technology, or set of technologies, focused on ideas of values, trust, inspiration, and stewardship.

The LPM helps this effort as it both describes and prescribes leadership alternatives. It is descriptive in the sense of defining or exploring how individuals may view leadership and positioning that perspective into an overarching leadership model. It is also prescriptive in the sense of explaining what activities, tools, approaches, and philosophies would be required to be effective or successful within each of the five perspectives.

The five perspectives of leadership posited herein are legitimate constructs to understanding how different people may view leadership. In fact, an understanding of leadership is dependent upon one's perspective. The data reflect a distinct progression of leadership perspectives, though, depending upon the individual's level of the organization. This lends credibility to the idea that leadership, as a phenomenon, is understood best by understanding its hierarchical nature. But leadership is more than the simple aggregation of those perspectives. Importantly, data illustrate that successive perspectives encompass and transcend previous perspectives. Furthermore, the tools and behaviors of a "lower order" perspective may be the building blocks for the tools and behaviors of succeeding perspectives, but they are not adopted unchanged from one perspective to another. As one moves up the hierarchy of leadership perspectives, the tools and behaviors and approaches one uses are themselves encompassed and transcended and can at certain levels be totally subsumed into other tools and behaviors so as to be obsolete or even antithetical to the activities of a higher order perspective.

As one interviewee suggested, the things she did and believed as a first-line manager are totally different than the things she does and believes now as a senior executive. The skills and perceptions that got her to her current position were no longer effective in that position. As she progressed through different levels of the organization, she also progressed through different perspectives of the practice and meaning of leadership.

The Holarchical Nature of Leadership Perspectives

A potential caution with the perspectival approach to leadership theory is an almost emotional reaction against the idea of a hierarchy of perspectives. Koestler (1970) observes that when one refers to hierarchy there is often a strong emotional resistance because it conjures up wrong impressions of rigid, authoritarian structure or is wrongly used to refer to simple, linear orders of rank. He suggests that the "almost universal applicability of the hierarchical model may arouse suspicion that it is logically empty; and this may be a further factor in the resistance against it. It usually takes the form of what one may call the 'so what' reaction: 'all this is old hat, it is self-evident' – followed by the non sequitor 'and anyway, where is your evidence?'" (p. 195). However, he argues that not only is hierarchy pervasive in the biological world, it is also pervasive in the social world, though it is, he admits, not well understood. He states, "All complex structures and processes of a relatively stable character display hierarchic organization, and this applies regardless whether we are considering inanimate systems, living organisms, social organizations, or patterns of behaviour" (p. 193). He then begins his explanation of the autonomous holon and how it better explains the pervasiveness of what he prefers to call holarchyrather than the misunderstood term "hierarchy."

The question relevant to this study and future explorations of the leadership perspectives is whether or not the leadership perspectives are themselves holons related in holarchical, rather than hierarchical, ways. Koestler defines a holon as "any stable sub-whole in an organismic, cognitive, or social hierarchy which displays rule-governed behaviour and/or structural Gestalt constancy" (p. 197). He also suggests that holons within an organismic or social hierarchy are "Janus-faced entities: facing upward, toward the apex, they function as dependent parts of a larger whole; facing downward, as autonomous wholes in their own right" (p. 207). Furthermore, "holons on successively higher levels of the hierarchy show increasingly complex, more flexible and less predictable patterns of activity, while in successive lower levels we find increasingly mechanized, stereotyped and predictable patterns" (p. 215). The nature of holons has interesting parallels to the notions of leadership perspectives that on their own are the reality for those adhering to them and together make up a more complete description of the leadership phenomenon.

Each perspective may appropriately be considered a holon in Koestler's typology. Each displays rule-governed behavior in that there are certain descriptions, tools, behaviors, and approaches that define each perspective, and each perspective is whole unto itself. In other words, each can stand on its own, without reference to the other perspectives. Like Koestler's description, each perspective is in some sense Janus-faced. Looking downward, each perspective serves as an encompassing whole. Looking upward, each perspective serves to point toward larger, more encompassing ways of engaging in leadership. Also, each successively higher perspective encompasses more flexible, less predictable (and some may say more touchy-feely) patterns of interaction. Each successively lower order perspective illustrates more mechanistic, predictable, and in terms of the vocabulary of the industrial model, more stereotypical patterns of behavior and structure.

Making a more direct link between the ideas of holons and holarchyand leadership perspectives may serve to be an interesting course of future research. If, indeed, holons and holarchies exist in the social world and in patterns of behavior, as they are observed to do in nature, this research track may reveal significant additions to the distinctive, yet related, nature of the leadership perspectives explored in this study. Such research may yield a better understanding of leadership as a social and personal phenomenon and help clarify the vocabulary needed to better implement leadership in our personal, professional, and social lives.

Two More Tracks

The LPM also suggests that Values Leadership, Trust Culture Leadership, and Whole-Soul Leadership technologies currently are not fully understood as being three distinct perspectives. Future research into the leadership phenomenon sprouting from this study may include at least two tracks: the first track might be called a trans-leadership track. The second track may be defined as a unit of analysis track.

Trans-Leadership

The first track begins with the observation that the Leadership Perspectives Model may suggest that Values Leadership, Trust Culture Leadership, and Whole-Soul Leadership are simply three elements of an overall conception of leadership as values based and interpersonal: that the three are one conception in three parts, perhaps three parts of an overarching Values Leadership Perspective. The LPM's Values Leadership Perspective introduces the notion that defining, refining, and reprioritizing values are essential leadership endeavors. But it does not indicate which values should be used. It is neutral as to which values should be the focus in a leadership endeavor.

Values selection is a task for the leader, followers, or both. While this seems liberating, it also allows for immoral values to rule and gives us the quandary of having to define a Hitler, for example, as a leader while at the same time wishing we did not have to. Trust Culture Leadership helps us marginally. While still a values-based perspectives, Trust Culture Leadership tells us that of all the values a leader may use, trust is the best. Trust becomes the "ubervalue," the key to success, and the glue that holds organizations and people together. Along with values such as teamwork, courageous followership, and sharing of governance, this perspective takes a stand on which values should predominate in a leadership endeavor. Whole-Soul Spiritual Leadership goes even farther. It suggests that there are core human values, even spiritual values, which are the key to leadership. Far from being values-neutral, this perspective asks all leaders to carefully determine which values are actually and eternally true, good, and beautiful and to apply them in self-consistent ways.

Hence, these three perspectives may yield more profound understanding of the leadership phenomenon as a values-laden activity, even further enhancing Burns' theory of moral leadership, which may have started the whole leadership studies movement. These three perspectives of one main idea shed light on Burns' notion of transforming leadership, while at the same time, quite frankly, possibly rendering it passé. But the LPM also seems to encompass other "trans-leadership" notions: transactional leadership, also from Burns, and transformational leadership, popularized by Bernard Bass (Fairholm 2007).

Indeed, much of the literature on leadership can be compiled under three headings: transactional leadership, transformational leadership, and transforming leadership. The prefix *trans* – meaning across, through, or by – is a useful common denominator. As the LPM shows, different people believe that leadership can be done across, through, or by very different goals, purposes, and means. Therefore, figuring out through or by what means leadership is done is a helpful way to connect contemporary leadership and the Leadership Perspectives Model.

Leadership Through Actions

Transactional leadership, as Burns defines it, is that kind of leadership that induces *action* based on values of mutual, though typically temporary, importance to leader and led. Relying mainly on utility power derived from an exchange of valued things (see Covey 1992), the object of change in this leadership activity is focused on people's actions, on general behaviors, or on the activity itself. It is easy to see, therefore, that this type of leadership is often associated with traditional management theories – our Leadership-as-Management and Excellence Management perspectives. The goal is to use transactions of valued things to cause others to behave or act in accordance to the leader's wishes and demands.

Leadership Through Formations

Transformational leadership is often confused with Burns' counterpart of transactional leadership: transforming leadership. However, it was actually Bass (1985) and subsequent researchers (see Bass and Avolio 1994), who popularized transformational leadership theory and along the way almost overshadowed Burns' work on transforming leadership. Couto (1993) describes the transformation or overshadowing of transforming leadership. He suggests that Bass' transformational leadership downplays the two-way change process Burns envisioned with a one-way process where (1) a leader changes the follower and (2) the follower is found only in organizational contexts. Couto further suggests that transformational leadership emerges from management goals, and any change in an organization is likely to come from formal systems and causal factors that transformational leaders create and control. In essence, transformational leadership takes the more intimate, personal, and individual notions of transforming leadership and adapts them to aggregate issues of the organization writ large, essentially creating a bridge from transactional to transforming.

Transformational leadership focuses on changing *formations* and structures and the actors within those structures. Simply put, transformational leadership has to do with change at an organizational level. This is where "the leadership" of an organization exercises leadership that envisions certain corporate missions, structures, designs, and associated performance levels for an organization. Such leadership expends energy on pursuits like reorganizing to efficiently line up the functions and hierarchy of the collective with the intended business or mission, realigning with agreed upon collective values and visions of a future state, and steering the organization to specific measures of performance. This leadership approach understands the role of culture and performance and the need for the organization to have clear values, goals, and objectives (see Collins and Porras 1997; Schein 1992). In many ways, this leadership is the ideal taught in most business and leadership schools as a way of maximizing performance through transactional leadership aligned with, and grounded by, a useful culture (Nirenberg 1998). In sum, like the LPM perspectives of Values and Trust Leadership, this type of leadership changes the formations of an organization hoping to establish the structure, culture, or performance levels and metrics that will motivate employees to adopt the organization's stance in society and perform in the best possible way as defined by agreed upon values, goals, and objectives.

Leadership Through Forming

Day (2000) quotes Drucker as saying, "in the traditional organization – the organization of the last one hundred years – the skeleton or internal structure, was a combination of rank and power. In the emerging organization, it has to be mutual understanding and responsibility." While this may require a transformation of an organization's formations, mutual understanding and responsibility will also require a change in the way some people see themselves, see others, and see their mutual interactions. That is, people may have to change the way they "form" themselves.

Transforming leadership(read, Spiritual Leadership) is the ultimate leadership philosophy identified by Burns. Rather than a specific focus on organizational performance and change, this leadership is at its heart a moral endeavor and is, therefore, ultimately intimate and personal in the relationships created between leader and led. The intimacy is centered on the mutual values, aspirations, even wants and needs that the leader and led agree or come to agree on through the interactions of leadership and the mutually ennobling results that such leadership delivers. The change is focused on the leader and led better understanding themselves as individuals and as social beings in line with mutually agreed upon values that make up their core selves, the values that form who they really are, and how they work together. This leadership is, at its heart, inspirational because it deals with the spirit of the people involved and it is moral because the values at play are central to living life in relation to others in the hopes of raising each other to higher levels of morality. This leadership also envisions changing the leader as much as the led, thus effectively distinguishing this type of leadership from other more authoritarian or positionally based leadership described earlier.

Transforming leadership is about identifying higher levels of values, showing by examples what those values may mean in the living of life, creating a sense of good versus ineffective behavior, and ultimately serving others with a sense of stewardship rather than authority in order to help them achieve their own higher potential. This activity may require some sacrifice on the part of the leader, which in itself reinforces the values that have caused such selfless service in the first place. Such leadership involves change, but it is very different from changing actions and behaviors, culture, and mission. It is about changing who we are at our core, spiritual self. It is about changing us for the better so that we will necessarily act and behave and perform in the ways that are valued because we value them ourselves; they are not forced, induced, incentivized, motivated, or trained. Rather, they are inculcated through inspiration, reason, and freedom of choice.

Transforming leadership theory is the kind of theory that Graen and Uhl-Bien (1995) say helps move the discussion of leadership beyond a levels or formations perspective toward a thought process of leadership in broad relational contexts, contexts that help form people themselves and their interactions. It helps shape organizations and the people within them, who then reshape the organizations in which they participate. This transforming leadership flows naturally from Wheatley's (1997) view of organizations and is akin to what Fairholm (1991) alludes to when he suggests leaders focus on the social interactions within organizations and a reliance on values that allows the leader to not only evoke excellent results from the organization, but also, more importantly, develop individual followers into leaders in their own right. Table 8 serves to link the LPM with some interesting concepts of the three "trans-leaderships."

Table 8 Three trans-leadership notions

Prefix "trans" = through, by, across	Focus	Explanation	Leadership values and approaches	LPM perspective link
Transactional leadership	Organizational	Leadership through helping to get and change certain actions done by others; ensuring certain behaviors	• Utility/efficiency • Predictable behavior • Incentivization	Leadership as Scientific Management
Transformational leadership	Organizational	Leadership through helping to change/shape organizational formations in terms of structure and corporate values	• Culture change • Innovation/organization design • Motivation	Leadership as Excellence Management Values Leadership
Transforming leadership	Personal	Leadership through helping to how people form themselves as individuals; liberating the best in others	• Change/enhance individual core values • Change institutions • Inspiration	Values Leadership Trust Culture Leadership Whole-Soul (Spiritual) Leadership

Unit of Analysis: Organizational Leadership and Intimate Leadership

Still linking ideas to Burns' work, the second track for future study may be to introduce the idea of dual leadership: leadership that fits an organizational setting and leadership that fits a more intimate or personal leadership experience. In this sense it may be reasonable to study leadership perspectives in terms of "units of focus" for both organizational and intimate leadership. Units of focus may include the system for Scientific Management, the group for Excellence Management, the individual-in-organizational-setting for Values Leadership, the team for Trust Culture Leadership, and the individual-within-community for Whole-Soul Leadership (see Column D in Table 9). These proposed foci may be placed in two umbrella units, namely Organizational Leadership and Intimate Leadership, with Values Leadership being the point of overlap (see Column E in Table 9). Table 9 shows this new approach to leadership research as it relates to past and present approaches. This future research approach links the Leadership Perspectives Model to past efforts of understanding leadership while building on the exploration of this study into the nature of the leadership perspectives and how they relate to each other.

Understanding leadership in terms of "units of focus" and in terms of the organizational or the personal may lend added illuminating language to help better describe and prescribe our leadership activities. Such an approach may help individuals begin the process of unpacking what they believe to be an unwieldy, complex concept like leadership. For instance, it might help one interview subject who consistently described leadership in terms of transactional or scientific management principles, but then, at the end of the interview, felt compelled to talk about one man who was "incredible," someone who has changed his life forever. He said, "I met this one president of an organization I belonged to and he was an exceptional leader....He was young, the greatest speaker, a motivator, and his vision was right. He was extremely gifted. You know, I think I'll never measure up to his standards, though I think I try to sometimes. There are certain leaders for certain times, I guess." Perhaps this was an experience of intimate leadership rather than organizational leadership. The interview subject understood how to lead an organization: Scientific Management was his perspective. But when he ran up against intimate leadership, he could not verbalize it. He knew it was leadership, but it surpassed his organizational experience.

Typical Values of Each Leadership Perspectives and the Four V's

To unravel some of the nuances of the perspectival approach to leadership theory, it may be appropriate to center attention on another research track: the personal and organizational values that differentiate each perspective. Burns (1978) and

Table 9 Future research – unit of focus in leadership relationships

Past research	Present research	Future research		
Burns' dichotomy (Column A)	Current literature distinction (Column B)	Leadership perspectives (Column C)	Proposed units of focus in leadership relationship (Column D)	Proposed umbrella units of focus (Column E)
Transactional leadership	Management Technology	Scientific Management	System	Organizational leadership
Bridge – elements of transactional and transforming leadership (or management and leadership)		Excellence management	Group	Organizational leadership
Transforming leadership	Leadership Technology	Values Leadership	Individual-in-Organizations	Organizational leadership/ Intimate Leadership
		Trust Culture Leadership	Team membership	Intimate leadership
		Whole-Soul Leadership	Individuals-in-community	Intimate leadership

Greenleaf (1977) consistently speak of values, motives, and aspirations, and recent leadership literature is replete with references to values, and even spiritual dimensions to leadership (see Fairholm 1997; Jacobsen 1994; Vaill 1989). One way to focus this attention on the values component of leadership is to understand whether certain values sets (see Rokeach 1979) are distinct within each perspective and whether those values sets relate in holarchical ways. Such a research track would combine elements of Burns' transactional and transforming leadership typology, the organizational leadership and intimate leadership notions posited earlier, and the issues of holons and holarchies as applied to social systems and patterns of behavior. This focus on values may also provide more depth to the issues of vision and mission (see DePree 1989; Kouzes and Posner 1990; Manz and Sims 1989), and also to the issue of relationship and followership (see Gardner 1990; Pittman et al. 1998; Rost 1991) that are evident in contemporary leadership literature.

Which values are and should be at play in leadership practice is the first question for this research track. However, it begs the question of how to fulfill those values. What mechanism, framework, or skill can operationalize those values and make them real in the lives of leader and led? One potential answer is the notion of vision – not vision statements, but vision itself. If we understand vision as the picture in our mind's eye of how values play out now and in the future in the lives of leader and led, we can see that visions become more than statements on a wall; they are the embodied story of what the values actually mean in practice. Such visions give leaders the wherewithal to inspire, to teach, to encourage, and to set standards of behavior.

But visions, too, must be realized if leadership is to be useful. Visions must also be put into practice, or operationalized, by those who hear and agree. In this sense, visions must be given direction and magnitude, purpose and bounds. Such direction and bounds might be thought of as the vectors that serve to make concrete the visions of leaders. These vectors are the tasks that must be done to make the vision come alive, be achieved, or be realized. Vectors serve visions in much the same way visions serve values: they make possibilities real to those involved in the relationship of leadership.

Because leadership is a relationship, because it deals with intimate notions of values and beliefs and behaviors among people, we need to understand the basic nature of that relationship. As outlined earlier, management is about control and prediction. If leadership is different, then the relationship must be one of freedom and liberation. In fact, leadership is best understood as a volunteer relationship in which the people involved retain their own voice and express this voice throughout the leadership activity: as they choose values, as they agree to adopt certain visions, and as they put forth effort to accomplish vectors. Indeed, maintaining and encouraging individual voice is requisite to leadership. When it is gone, something other than leadership is taking place. The degree of inner voice encouraged to be exercised and developed may be an indicator of the specific leadership perspective at play.

Together, then, the four V's of Values, Vision, Vector, and Voice outline a general framework to analyze the phenomenon of leadership as people see it, as they experience it, and as they practice it (Fairholm 2008). In essence, it is a descriptive and prescriptive tool – descriptive in that it offers avenues of analysis and prescriptive in that it helps us see how we and others may practice leadership in more transcendent and encompassing ways. Again, this framework offers a comprehensive but simple way to analyze whether leadership (rather than a leader) is at play or not. The Four V's help us see upon what foundation a person's leadership perspective is based and whether that particular conception fits with contemporary views of what leadership really is. No matter the perspective of leadership one may hold, using the four concepts described earlier may provide a useful framework to understand and apply that leadership in interpersonal endeavors. This combination of concepts reveals common elements of social interaction that help define what is meant by the term "leadership."

Summary: The Philosophy of Leadership

These research tracks may continue to refine basic understanding of the leadership phenomenon encompassed in the Leadership Perspectives Model. However, such research is not inherently valuable; it must be applied. The activities and impact of leadership are real and influence the lives of people everyday, everywhere. The perspectives of leadership apply to leadership in all organizations, whether economic, social, familial, or governmental. For that reason, research into each perspective of leadership has direct application to how people view and fulfill their leadership opportunities.

Leadership is a realistic philosophy adopted by some and implicitly understood by most. Defining leadership not as a quality, technique, or methodology but rather as a philosophy in no way implies leadership is something we cannot learn or apply. As a philosophy, leadership can be learned, studied, understood, and applied by people who are so inclined. The ethics of leadership is not found only in its philosophical underpinnings but also in its application by would-be leaders.

The first attempts to codify leadership and determine what "makes a good leader" centered on the belief that leaders are born, not made. This gave rise to various forms of trait theory: the idea that leadership depends upon personal traits, personality, and character. The great person theory and many of the psychology-based theories of leadership depend on this point of view. However, because it was so difficult to come up with a definitive list of traits or qualities that all leaders held in common, theorists shifted to studying behavior instead of inborn traits. Along with behavior theory in general were specific theories based on interaction and expectancy of roles, exchange activities between leader and follower, and the perceptions that followers have of leaders. These behavior-based theories did provide a way for people to copy what other leaders have done, but the behaviors did not prove to be generalizable. Therefore, studies began to focus on the environments in which leadership takes place. Situational theory, contingency theory, and the more humanistic models of leadership emerged. It was during this emphasis in leadership study that the desire to differentiate between managers and leaders emerged. The unique elements and foci of leadership and managementsuggest that the two are different and require divergent explanatory theories.

As we observe organizations, two critical competencies seem to emerge that past theory has labeled management. Fairholm (1991) explains the need for competent, dedicated managers to provide continuity of process, to insure program productivity, and to control and schedule the materials needed for production or service delivery. Our corporate and government organizations also need people who can (1) infuse them with common values which define the organization, determine its character, link it to the larger society, and (2) ensure its long-term survival. However, the skills and competencies required to do the first are substantially different than those needed to do the second. When theorists and practitioners do not make that distinction, they confuse the issue of organizational success and set individuals up for failure. This distinction helps clarify the contributions of such writers as Greenleaf and Burns. These two authors approach leadership as a phenomenon to be understood independent of a particular leader. In fact, the test of who is or is not a leader depends upon how one uses or implements the technologies of leadership.

The need for leadership cries out in our societies, groups, nations, and families. But there is also much progress in understanding what it is. The Leadership Perspectives Model places the leadership phenomenon in a context that can be easily understood so that the debate will be more useful, more enlightening, and more productive in the quest to understand the true nature of leadership. The model says that people do see leadership differently and their perspectives certainly matter in theory and practice. The perspectives reflect both management and leadership ideas and leadership studies past, present, and future help (and will help) elucidate various characteristics of the different perspectives. Understood separately, these perspectives are insightful and helpful. However, the model does not stop there. As understanding increases about how the different perspectives relate, so does ultimate understanding of what leadership really is. That is the key. Leadership, then, is best understood, described, and even applied as a system of ever-more encompassing and transcendent perspectives of leadership. It is pervasive in life and is revealed as each of us, collectively and independently, reflects on its theory and engages in its practice.

Appendix: Research Approach and Methodology

Much of the data validating the efficacy of the five perspectives in the Leadership Perspectives Model come from original research done by Fairholm (2002). A summary of the project follows.

Research Approach

The purpose of the study was to explore the phenomenon of leadership by examining and enhancing the descriptive power of Fairholm's (1998a, 1998b) model of five virtual leadership realities using a dual approach of essay content analysis and semi-structured interview data compiled from selected middle and senior managers and staff of local government jurisdictions. The exploration of the five leadership conceptions focuses on two different methods to provide corroborating evidence – a type of methodological triangulation, if you will (see Mitchell 1993; Denzin and Lincoln 2000; Hinds and Young 1987; Webb et al. 1966). The two general approaches or research methods used in this study are content analysis and semistructured interview research.

Content Analysis

Content analysis is a method that involves counting communication phenomena and categorizing them according to a taxonomy or typology scheme. As with most other research methods, content analysis begins with identifying research questions and choosing a sample or samples. Once chosen, the text must be coded into manageable content categories. By reducing the text to categories consisting of a word, set of words, or phrases, one can focus on and code for specific words or patterns that are indicative of the research question. The process of coding is basically one of selective reduction, which is the central idea in content analysis (see Krippendorff 1980; Weber 1990).

Semistructured Interviews

The second method of addressing the research questions is semistructured interviewing. Standard qualitative interviewing protocols usually refer to in-depth, semistructured forms of interviewing with the goal of exploring and elucidating specific research questions by allowing the interaction between interviewee(s) and interviewer to shape the data collected (see Mason 1996; Burgess 1984; Creswell 1998; Miles and Huberman 1994). This methodology allows for in-depth exploration of individual perspectives about the operational categories and constructs, thus providing rich data regarding the research questions and testing of the theoretical model's efficacy.

Review of Questions, Methods, and Model

The research focused on whether different conceptions of leadership exist and whether they are useful in describing leadership as practiced by local government managers. The following research questions guided this research:

1. To what extent do an individual's perceptions of leadership philosophy, defined in terms of (1) Leadership in Action/Implementation Descriptions, (2) Tools and Behaviors, and (3) personal Approaches to Followers, differentiate particular perspectives of leadership?
2. How well do the ways in which individuals describe leadership reflect the model of leadership virtual realities outlined by Fairholm (1998b)?
3. To what extent do the different perspectives of leadership reflect five views that, though different, relate to each other in a hierarchical manner?

Table 10 summarizes the methodologies used to answer the research questions.
The research's constructs include Fairholm's (1998b) five leadership virtual realities (perspectives) of leadership. These perspectives are defined as:

1. *Leadership as (Scientific) Management* – Leadership equals management in that it focuses on getting others to do work the leader wants done, essentially separating the planning (management) from the doing (labor).
2. *Leadership as Excellence Management*– Leadership emphasizes quality and productivity process improvement rather than just product, and people over either product or process, and requires the management of values, attitudes, and organizational aims within a framework of quality improvement.
3. *Values Leadership*– Leadership is the integration of group behavior with shared values through setting values and teaching them to followers through an articulated vision that leads to excellent products and service, mutual growth, and enhanced self-determination
4. *Trust Culture Leadership* – Leadership is a process of building trust cultures within which leader and follower (in an essentially voluntary relationship, even, perhaps, from a variety of individual cultural contexts) relate to each other to accomplish mutually valued goals using agreed-upon processes.

Table 10 Summary of methodologies

Methodology	Research questions explored	Subjects	Data collection and analysis	Appropriateness
Content analysis	Q1 and Q2	Random sample of 100 essays from a total population of about 230 essays	Collect data by reducing the text to categories consisting of a word, set of words, or phrases. Analyze by coding and classifying the data to focus on specific words or patterns that are indicative of the research questions	Verify and refine the theorized categories and elements of the leadership perspectives, thus allowing for more accurate data regarding the model being tested
Interviews	Q1, Q2, and Q3	Stratified sample ($n = 30$) of DC area public managers	Collect data through note taking and transcription of interview material. Analyze data through a form of content analysis that focuses on patterns of discussion points that speak to the research constructs and questions	In-depth exploration of individual perspectives about the operational categories and constructs, thus providing rich data regarding the research questions and testing of the theoretical model's efficacy

5. *Spiritual (Whole-Soul) Leadership* – Leadership is the integration of the components of work and self – of the leader and each follower – into a comprehensive system that fosters continuous growth, improvement, self-awareness, and self-leadership so that leaders see each worker as a whole person with a variety of skills, knowledge, and abilities that invariably go beyond the narrow confines of job needs.

These constructs were operationalized by examining three categories that help to define each construct. These operational categories are new to the original model and are as follows:

1. Leadership in Action/Implementation Description – implementation of this model of leadership is composed of key elements arranged in ways that allow each construct (leadership perspective) to have logical and practical meaning. These elements include the leadership task and goals.
2. Tools and Behaviors – the behaviors needed and/or tools for each leadership perspective point to the individual's capacity to "do leadership" in terms of the construct's essential characteristics.

3. Approach to Followers – the approach to others associated with each leadership perspective highlights the basic position one places him or herself in the leadership relationship as compared to another person in the leadership relationship.

These categories were further operationalized through the emergence of specific leadership elements. These leadership elements came from experience, observation, literature review, and the research itself. They are summarized in Table 11.

The Leadership Perspectives Model (LPM) combines the constructs, categories, and leadership elements (culled from experience and literature) into a cohesive whole. It operationalizes significant elements of the initial 1998 model and points a way not only to understand the phenomenon of leadership better but also to a way of teaching leadership and developing individuals in their leadership activities. In sum, this revised model, as a tool to explore leadership perspectives, is the study's main contribution. The LPM's categories and variables are reviewed in Table 11 and illustrated in Fig. 10.

The LPM model tested in this study is represented in Fig. 10. Together, the constructs, operational categories, and the variables identified enhance the original leadership virtual realities model. It includes the operational categories in an attempt to illustrate how the different implementation descriptions, tools and behaviors, and approaches to followers may influence the identification and differentiation of the perspectives and explicitly shows how the variables outlined in Table 11 help define the operational categories and the leadership perspectives.

Methodology: Conducting the Research

The study was conducted in two parts: the content analysis of randomly selected essays and semistructured interviews of local government public managers. The content analysis used randomly selected subjects of District of Columbia government managers engaged in, or recently completing, an executive development course operated in partnership between the District's Center for Workforce Development and The George Washington University Center for Excellence in Municipal Management (CEMM). This represents a purposive sampling of DC government managers and senior staff for an exploratory investigation of leadership conceptions. These employees represent a fairly even proportion of male and female managers and senior staff. Their years of service in the District government range from less than 1 year to over 30 years. Their ages range from the high twenties to low sixties and the ethnicity of participants is diverse, but predominately African American.

The semistructured interview portion of the research used subjects from Washington, DC area local governments. One-third had participated in the CEMM programming (those from DC). Two-third have not (those from Arlington County, VA, and Prince Georges County, MD). This population includes seasoned public managers working in a large metropolitan context. Their characteristics are largely the same as described earlier, though as a whole, somewhat less diverse in ethnicity

Table 11 Key variables in operational categories for each leadership perspective

Operational categories	Scientific Management (SM)	Excellence Management (EM)	Values Leadership (VL)	Trust Culture Leadership (TCL)	Spiritual (Whole-Soul) Leadership (WSL)
Leaders in Action/Implementation Description (LAD)	1. Ensure efficient use of resources to ensure group activity is controlled and predictable to 2. ensure verifiably optimal productivity and resource allocation	3. Foster continuous process improvement environment for increased service and productivity levels to 4. transform the environment and perceptions of followers to encourage innovation, high quality products, and excellent services	5. Help individual become proactive contributors to group action based on shared values and agreed upon goals to 6. encourage high organizational performance and self-led followers	7. Ensure cultures conducive to mutual trust and unified collective action consistent with the 8. prioritization of mutual cultural values and organizational conduct in terms of those values	9. Relate to individuals such that concern for the whole person is paramount in raising each other to higher levels of awareness and action so that the 10. best in people is liberated in a context of continuous improvement of self, culture, and service delivery
Tools and Behaviors (TB)	1. Measuring/appraising/rewarding individual performance 2. Organizing (to include such things as budgeting, staffing) 3. Planning (to include such things as coordination and reporting)	4. Focusing on process improvement 5. Listening actively 6. Being accessible (to include such things as managing by walking around, open door policies)	7. Setting and enforcing values 8. Visioning 9. Focusing communication around the vision	10. Creating and maintaining culture through visioning 11. Sharing governance 12. Measuring/appraising/rewarding group performance	13. Developing and enabling individual wholeness in a community (team) context 14. Fostering an intelligent organization 15. Setting moral standards
Approaches to Followers (AF)	1. Incentivization 2. Control 3. Direction	4. Motivation 5. Engaging people in problem definition and solution 6. Expressing common courtesy/respect	7. Values prioritization 8. Teaching/coaching 9. Empowering (fostering ownership)	10. Trust 11. Team building 12. Fostering a shared culture	13. Inspiration 14. Liberating followers to build community and promote stewardship 15. Modeling a service orientation

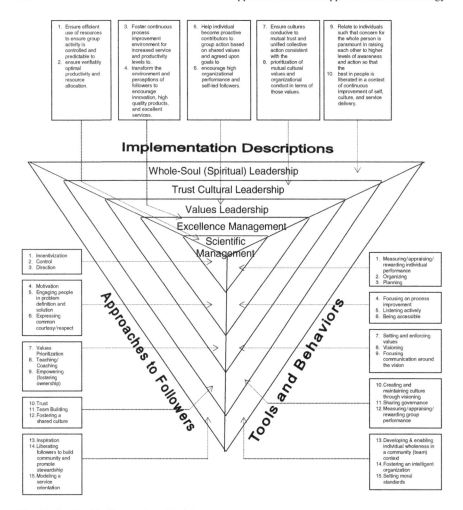

Fig. 10 Leadership Perspectives Model

(predominantly white). Studying public managers in these three jurisdictions may lend theoretical generalizability as results may reflect commonalities across the municipalities.

Methodology I: Content Analysis of Time-Controlled Essays

The content analysis design was used to explore whether written responses to the question "What is leadership?" reflect distinct, identifiable leadership perspectives. Disadvantages of this approach are that the essays may be incomplete reflections of the subjects' thoughts and that some subjects may be better writers than others, leading to potential misinterpretations of the written products. Advantages of this approach include the researcher's ability to accurately obtain the language and words of the subjects in an unobtrusive manner that can be stored over time for future reference (Creswell 1994).

Background

As a part of the application process for CEMM's *Program for Excellence in Municipal Management*, prospective participants of the training are required to write a time-controlled essay answering the question, "What is leadership?" The applicants are allowed 75 min to respond to the question. The responses are pre-pared in a computer lab setting which allows for a controlled environment. The environment, context, and time constraints are designed to elicit more intuitive responses. Such an approach is thought best to capture an applicant's "gut" reaction to the question of what leadership is. Each participant is informed that the essay may be used in research related to leadership and is able to state whether or not the essay may be used. Not allowing the essay to be used in the research effort has no bearing on the participant's likelihood to be accepted into the program. Approximately 100 essays were used in this research, representing a random sam-pling of the essays written by applicants. The District government's Center for Workforce Development provided the random sampling of essays.

Coding Mechanism

As suggested before, Carney's (1972) 8-category coding process informed the coding of this research. The coding mechanism was developed based on the definitions, operational categories, and variables of the study's constructs. These were deter-mined by a review of the relevant literature and framed by Fairholm's (1998b) model. Table 12 summarizes how this part of the research was structured in response to Carney's steps. The coding mechanism was pretested on a selected sample of essays collected from federal government managers and municipal man-agers gathered through consulting experiences.

After securing the essays, the researcher analyzed essay texts based on the veri-fied coding mechanism. The coding guided the analysis by helping the researcher highlight words or phrases that depict unique conceptions of leadership. Because leadership has always been difficult to define and describe, subjects have a difficult time writing a consistent response to the question. For this reason, an individual essay may reflect elements of multiple conceptions. The researcher coded the essay in its entirety for all occurrences of the specified variables. After that specific review, the researcher also makes an overall assessment of the essay and places it in the context of one of the five conceptions. Further analysis of the coding for each essay aggregates the coding sheets and determines the intensity of coded responses within each construct. This process was conducted with the aid of commercially

Table 12 Carney's 8-category process and the structure of the research

Carney's 8-category coding process	Result
1. Decide the level of analysis	Variables that cross operational categories within the constructs.
2. Decide how many concepts to code for	Total of 40 variables: 10 under Implementation Descriptions; 15 under Tools and Behavior; and 15 under Approaches to Followers
3. Decide whether to code for existence or frequency of a concept	Will code for both frequency and existence of the variables
4. Decide on how you will distinguish among concepts	Variables will be distinguished through exact wording and through phrases that carry the same meaning as informed by the literature that refined the variables
5. Develop rules for coding your texts	Assisted by NUD-IST software
6. Decide what to do with "irrelevant" information	Irrelevant information will be ignored except as it may help to understand the entire context of the essays and/or interviews. Irrelevance can only be determined after careful review of the all the data
7. Code the texts	Assisted by NUD-IST software
8. Analyze your results	Assisted by NUD-IST software

available software designed to assist qualitative analysis of text and interview information. The software is called Non-numerical Unstructured Data Indexing Searching and Theorizing (NUD-IST). Using this software allows for a level of objectivity and replication not available if the researcher conducted the coding of the texts himself.

Methodology II: Semistructured Interviews of Selected Public Managers

The purpose of the semistructured interview technique was to gather in-depth understanding of how selected public managers understand and engage in leadership to explore the theory that different perspectives of leadership exist and, as a whole, help to elucidate the leadership phenomenon. The advantages of interviewing include the potential for subjects to provide historical and contextual information. However, interviews do pose limitations as not all subjects are as articulate as others and the presence of the researcher may lead participants to offer "socially acceptable" responses. Another commonly held disadvantage of interviewing is that information is filtered through the views of the interviewees (Creswell 1994). For this study, however, this was a decided advantage because it is the very perspectives of the subjects that are being explored. The interviewer was keenly aware of the limitations and used proper interviewing skills to explore the interviewees' responses.

Background and Sample

Rather than focusing on only one jurisdiction as with the essay analysis, interview subjects were taken from three Washington Metropolitan areas, namely Arlington County, VA; Washington, DC; and Prince Georges County, MD. Using three jurisdictions in this study lends credibility to research findings in that results will take into account different organizational and municipal environments. It also assists in the transferability of the research because it enhances the potential contexts in which the findings may be valid. All the participants in the research are similar in their public sector focus and general responsibility level throughout the three jurisdictions. The strata used for sampling this group include government function and personnel grade level. Efforts were made to balance gender and ethnicity in the sample. Stratifying this group of managers allows for potential comparisons and clarifications of the data obtained (see O'Sullivan and Rassel 1989). Subjects are divided into classes according to the government function they work in. The government functions include: government direction, support and finance, economic development, regulation and public works, public safety and justice, public education system and human support services. From this initial division, equal numbers of subjects were randomly selected based on personnel grade level. The personnel grade-level classes used in this study include: first-line supervisor and lower-level manager (for example, DS 12 or below in DC government); midlevel manager (for example, DS 13-14 in DC government); senior manager/executive (for example, DS 15 or above in DC government). Table 13 summarizes the classes used for stratification.

Interview Protocol Instrument

To help ensure that each interview was conducted in the same manner, a standard interview protocol was used at every interview. The protocol assists the researcher

Table 13 Stratification classes for interview subjects

Class (strata)	Class elements	Purpose for using class
Government function	• Government direction, support, and finance • Economic development, regulation, and public works • Public safety and justice • Public education and human support services	Explores individual perspectives accounting for potentially different leadership conceptions depending upon different types of government services delivered
Personnel grade level	• First-line supervisor and lower-level manager (for example, DS 12 or below in DC government) • Midlevel manager (for example, DS 13-14 in DC government) • Senior manager/executive (for example, DS 15 or above in DC government)	Explores individual perspectives accounting for potentially different leadership conceptions depending upon the level of the organization in which the subjects are working

in verifying that the interviewee is aware of the purpose and structure of the study as a whole and the interview in specific. It also ensures compliance by the interviewee that the information gathered can be used in the research. The interview process begins with initial telephone conversations to schedule an appointment. At that time a short description of the purpose of the study and the interview was given. Where possible, a copy of the interview questions is e-mailed or faxed to the participants before the appointed time for the interview. At the meeting, the researcher gives to the participant and reads aloud a description of the study and the purpose of the interview. The questioning then proceeds. The interview is semistructured and the interviewer is prepared to alter the sequence of questions if necessary. Further clarifications of responses are requested if needed and the interviewer ensures that all questions are asked. The interview should take not more than 1 hour to complete. At the close of the interview, while the interviewer prepares to leave, he asks the participant to fill out a short form to capture key demographics of the participants. The interview protocol instrument, description, and participant attributes form are found in Appendix C. Interview information is compiled from the notes taken by the interviewer. This information is compiled into a field notes document for each interview. The researcher makes an initial overall assessment of each interview and places it in the context of one of the five leadership perspectives to facilitate the analysis. These documents are analyzed using the NUD-IST software to search and index on the same coding schemes as for the essay content analysis. Specific attention is given to interview data that may indicate to what extent the different perspectives reflect a hierarchical ordering of the five leadership perspectives. Table 14 contains the letter of purpose, interview questions, and demographics requested.

Verification, Trustworthiness, and Validity Issues

Though threats to validity are diminished and the trustworthiness of the research is enhanced by the research design, there remains a reasonable concern about the generalizability of the findings due to the characteristics of the subjects and the environment in which they operate. However, as the purpose of the study is to explore and develop theory regarding perspectives of leadership, these concerns are decreased. The notion of verification of qualitative research is comparable to the issues of validity in quantitative designs (see Creswell 1998; LeCompte and Schensul 1999; Lincoln and Guba 1985; Wolcott 1994). Verification is related to validity concerns in traditional quantitative research. The goal of verification is to underscore that the procedures used to gather qualitative data and that the conclusions derived from the data are useful and appropriate to the demands of the research purposes.

Verification, then, is related to the idea of an inquiry's trustworthiness. Three issues of trustworthiness are relevant to the research, especially in terms of the content analysis: dependability, credibility, and transferability (see Lincoln and Guba 1985). The issue of dependability ensures that the researcher takes into

Table 14 Interview Protocols

Interview Protocols

Purposes

Thank you for scheduling time to speak with me. In the letter or phone call requesting this appointment, I mentioned I would be taking notes during our discussion. The notes are for recording our conversation to help me remember as I write about the findings of this study. Please be assured that our conversations are confidential and your comments will only be used in **non-attributable, anonymous** ways.

As we begin let me explain a little about this study. I am working on my doctoral dissertation and am interested in exploring what public managers think leadership is. My research is being supported in part by the GWU Center for Excellence in Municipal Management. This research will be helpful in evaluating and refining the training and advisory services conducted by the Center. It will also, more broadly, help public administrators deal with the complex issue of leadership as they engage in leading complex public organizations. The following questions will be examined:

1. To what extent does an individual's perception of leadership philosophy, implementation descriptions, tools and behaviors, and personal approaches to followers differentiate particular perspectives of leadership?

2. How well do the ways in which individuals describe leadership reflect the model of leadership virtual realities outlined by Fairholm (1998b)?

3. To what extent do the different perspectives of leadership reflect five views that, though different, relate to each other in a hierarchical manner?

This part of the study involves interviewing a sample of public managers. The interviews are designed to gather in-depth understanding about the individuals' perspective of leadership. Another portion of the study involves analyzing essays written by public managers about what they think leadership is. Together, these data are to be used to build theory regarding the nature of the leadership phenomenon and to enhance leadership and management training of public managers. Today I would like to talk with you about your personal views on leadership. Please know that there are no necessarily right answers. Your experiences may have shown you that there are various, often conflicting, views of leadership. Today, I am interested in what **you personally** have to say about what it means to "do leadership." I would like to ask you some specific questions about leadership including such things as leadership goals, tasks, activities, and relationships with others, and then I would like you to answer a few questions about your professional background. These questions are designed to elicit a focused conversation about the leadership phenomenon and assess how representative the conversations may be.

Semistructured Interview Questions

1. What do you think is the goal(s) or task(s) of leadership?

2. What types of activities or sets of skills do you think describes leadership?

3. If you were to define leadership, what would your definition be?

4. In describing leadership, how do you think leaders should relate to followers? In other words, how should a leader approach the relationship between leader and follower?

5. A senior executive in the organization has assigned a branch chief, who oversees 5 professional and 2 support staff, the job of redesigning a service delivery process to be presented to the executive committee in two weeks. You are the branch chief. How would you most effectively accomplish the assignment?

(continued)

Table 14 (continued)

Interview Protocols

6. Your ideal boss would be the kind of person that saw leadership as what.... Please fill in the blank.

7. If you were to describe a leader, what words, phrases, or statements would you use?

8. Do you feel leaders can be developed? To what extent do you think leadership training improves the performance of leaders?

9. What impact do leaders have on organizations, groups, or individuals?

10. Are there any other comments you wish to express about the research in general or this interview in specific?

11. If time... Are there any "leadership stories" from work or any other aspect of your life that have made an impression on you? If so, would you tell me about them?

Participant Descriptions

1. How long have you been in your current position in government?

   ___ 0–2 yrs ___ 3–5 yrs ___ 5–10 yrs ___ 10–15 yrs ___ 15–20 yrs ___ 20–25 yrs ___ above 25 yrs

2. What is your current title?_____

3. Have you had any other positions in this government? If so, what?

4. Have you worked in other governments? If so, which ones and in what positions?

   Government   Position   Amount of Time

5. Have you worked in the private or non-profit sectors? If so, where and in what types of positions?

   Company   Positions

6. Can you tell me about your professional preparation, like degrees, certifications, training....?

   Degree/Training Emphasis/Subject

account factors of change in environment and subject that may influence the consistency of the findings. The detailed coding mechanism based in theory and the standard data collection protocols allow for replication and consistency in other settings or within changing environments. Credibility refers to the effort to gain enough evidence in reasonable ways to lend more and more confidence that the data are accurate and relevant and that conclusions derived from the evidence are reasonable and compelling (see Eisner and Peshkin 1990). To relieve such concerns, this research design employs the NUD-IST software to ensure that the coding scheme captures key variables and to ensure that a consistent interpretation of the coding scheme is applied to all of the texts. The interview protocol also ensures that throughout the process interview information and the initial interpretations of the information are discussed between sender and receiver so that both approve of the findings gathered during the interview process. Using public managers from three different local governments also minimizes threats to credibility because it involves different organizational situations and municipal contexts. The third issue includes potential threats to transferability. Overcoming such depends upon recognizing and explaining the context of the study so that any transfer of findings will be sufficiently grounded in what Lincoln and Guba (1985) describe as empirical evidence of contextual similarity.

Though a qualitative design, a number of traditional validity issues may also be addressed in this research, especially with the interview methodology, though many authors may use alternative terms as outlined earlier. Two potential threats to internal validity include selection bias and design contamination. Two potential threats to external validity are also of special note in this research design: effects of setting and effects of history (see Cook and Campbell 1979). The DC government and surrounding jurisdictions (the setting for this research) may be a unique municipal environment, which, then, may affect the survey responses. Since this research is qualitative in nature, does not test any cause-and-effect relationships, and employs purposive sampling techniques rather than probability samples, statistical validity is not an issue.

Summary of Methodology

The study used essay content analysis and interview research to explore and offer evidence for different conceptions of leadership as constructed from Fairholm's model of leadership virtual realities. The subjects included DC government managers and senior staff who have completed or are currently engaged in leadership development training and public managers from Arlington County, VA, and Prince Georges County, MD. Threats to validity have been minimized and the trustworthiness of the analysis has been enhanced by the research design. Data collected from these research efforts lend evidence related to the research questions stated earlier and refine the assumptions upon which they are based.

Key Research Findings

The key research findings are found in Chap. 2 and throughout the book. Following is a brief summary of some general findings.

- Five leadership perspectives are identified via content analysis and interview data. Four are found in "pure" forms; Excellence Management is a bridge perspective. See Tables 15– 20 for a summary of leadership element "hits" in the content analysis and a sample of the comments retrieved from participant essays that reinforce the leadership elements.
- The five perspectives of leadership tend toward a hierarchy. Data illustrate that adopting a new perspective transcends the previous one. For instance, the tools and behaviors of a "lower order" perspective may be the building blocks for the tools and behaviors of succeeding perspectives, but they are not adopted unchanged from one perspective to another. As one moves up the hierarchy of leadership perspectives, the tools, behaviors, and approaches one uses are themselves encompassed and transcended and can at certain levels be totally sublimated by other tools and behaviors so as to be obsolete or even antithetical to the work of a leader in higher order perspectives.
- The perspectives can be distinguished by understanding how someone describes the implementation (or doing) of leadership, the tools and behaviors used, and the approaches to followers taken in the leadership relationship. Specific leadership elements within the Approaches to Followers category most distinctly distinguish a person's leadership perspectives (such as giving orders, motivating, team building, inspiring). However, the tools and behaviors that individuals describe in "doing leadership" are more helpful generally in differentiating leadership perspectives than either of the other two.
- The higher in the organizational hierarchy managers are, and the more time in service they have, the more likely they are to subscribe to higher order perspectives. People can and do move from one perspective to another; that movement is toward higher order perspectives – perspectives that are more encompassing and transcendent than previous conceptions.
- All five perspectives are evident in Male and Female public managers at the same relative frequencies. However, females tended slightly more toward the Excellence Management Perspective, while males tended slightly more toward the Scientific Management Perspective. All five perspectives are evident in African-American and White public managers at the same relative frequencies.
- The data reveal that the functional area of government in which public managers operate may influence leadership perspectives. Managers in the public safety and justice function tend toward the first three perspectives in the hierarchy only: Scientific Management, Excellence Management, and Values Leadership. Managers in the government support, direction, and finance function revealed all but the Trust Culture Leadership perspective. Managers in the human service/education, economic regulations and public works functions reflected all five leadership perspectives, though tending more toward the lower order perspectives.

Table 15 Summary of hits within each perspective by leadership elements and categories

Leadership perspective	Operational categories	Leadership elements	No. of hits	Percentage for element	Percentage for category
Scientific Management	Leadership in Action Description	Ensure efficient use of resources to ensure group activity is control-led and predictable	39	11	
		Ensure verifiably optimal productivity and resource allocation	24	7	18
	Tools and Behavior	Measuring/appraising/rewarding individual performance	57	17	
		Organizing (to include such things as budgeting, staffing)	54	16	
		Planning (to include such things as coordination and reporting)	64	19	51
	Approaches to Followers	Incentivization	15	4	
		Control	15	4	
		Direction	74	22	30
Total			342	100	
Excellence Management	Leadership in Action Description	Foster continuous process improvement environment for increased service and productivity levels	18	10	
		Transform the environment and perceptions of followers to encour-age innovation, high quality products, and excellent services	38	21	31
	Tools and Behavior	Focusing on process improvement	25	14	
		Listening actively	6	3	
		Being accessible (to include such things as managing by walking around, open door policies)	9	5	22
	Approaches to Followers	Motivation	59	32	
		Engaging people in problem definition and solution	15	8	
		Expressing common courtesy/respect	13	7	48
Total			183	100	
Values Leadership	Leadership in Action Description	Help individual become proactive contributors to group action based on shared values and agreed upon goals	59	17	28
	Tools and Behavior	Encourage high organizational performance and self-led followers	35	10	
		Setting and enforcing values	19	6	
		Visioning	81	24	
		Focusing communication around the vision	44	13	42
	Approaches to Followers	Values prioritization	15	4	
		Teaching/coaching	61	18	
		Empowering (fostering ownership)	26	8	30

(continued)

Table 15 (continued)

Leadership perspective	Operational categories	Leadership elements	No. of hits	Percentage for element	Percentage for category
Total			340	100	
Trust Cultural Leadership	Leadership in Action Description	Ensure cultures conducive to mutual trust and unified collective action	16	7	13
		Prioritization of mutual cultural values and organizational conduct in terms of those values	15	6	
	Tools and Behavior	Creating and maintaining culture through visioning	28	12	37
		Sharing governance	23	10	
		Measuring/appraising/rewarding group performance	37	16	
	Approaches to Followers	Trust	24	10	50
		Team building	77	32	
		Fostering a shared culture	18	8	
Total			238	100	
Whole-Soul Leadership	Leadership in Action Description	Relate to individuals such that concern for the whole person is paramount in raising each other to higher levels of awareness and action	28	12	20
		Best in people is liberated in a context of continuous improvement of self, culture, and service delivery	19	8	
	Tools and Behavior	Developing and enabling individual wholeness in a community (team) context	20	8	46
		Fostering an intelligent organization	36	15	
		Setting moral standards	55	23	
	Approaches to Followers	Inspiration	51	21	34
		Liberating followers to build community and promote stewardship	14	6	
		Modeling a service orientation	17	7	
Total			240	100	

Table 16 Sample essay quotations – top three scientific management leadership elements (2002 research)

Leadership element	Sample statements from essays – verbatim
Direction	"The final aspect of leadership is direction. Direction is one of the most important facets of leadership. Without direction your employees, projects, programs and organization's mission, may come to a standstill." "…confidence to make decisions." "Leadership through instruction is when a leader can give clear defined instructions to those employees under his command. A leader must be able to define what is necessary to those employees so the project can be completed on time and within budget."
Planning	"The superiors gave out the orders and basically planned out the work strategy and the subordinates followed." "Staff should have a clear idea about time limits and the completion of projects. Clear goals help employees to avoid wasting energy, and it avoids confusion. The department manager should establish goals for the staff." "Construct a plan of action for achieving the desired results, considering the resources required and available. The plan should include benchmarks, milestones and factors for measuring the success of the plan."
Measuring/ appraising/ rewarding individual performance	"Leadership is, and can encompass rewarding efforts from those who have put in extra time on special projects, and extra time used to succeed with positive results for both personal and organizational needs." "A leader must never show favoritism or be biased when counseling and disciplining. They must be able to show each individual what they did wrong, explain why it was wrong and then administer positive reinforcement when a situations dictate. Their actions must be quick." "All staff or group members are individuals. They should be treated as such without playing favorites."

Table 17 Sample essay quotations – top three excellence management leadership elements (2002 research)

Leadership element	Sample statements from essays – verbatim
Motivation	"The leader has to change their leadership style to motivate staff." "Most importantly leaders must stay abreast of the latest techniques and philosophies that will help them motivate and lead their employees." "Management tools are essential for a leader to motivate people."
Transform the environment to encourage high quality	"Leadership in government also requires individuals to move beyond processes that hinder progress and move towards challenges that help organizations thrives and succeed." "The leader must facilitate continuous improvement in staff performance and continued input from staff and customers to keep the vision relevant as it moves along. "The leader takes the necessary actions to promote excellence in the organization or community in which he plays a leadership role."
Focusing on process improvement	"The findings [are] to be conveyed, analyzed, an a proper tool to be used to refine the findings and recommend the best applicable method." "Leadership is also a state of constant education. Not only of oneself but also of a process, the act of charging or trying to improve a system or process is one that needs to be a focus point of a leader. There is nothing worse than hearing 'it's the way we have always done it.'" "[always] best methods or processes to use in the accomplishment of specific tasks."

Table 18 Sample essay quotations – top three values leadership elements (2002 research)

Leadership element	Sample statements from essays – verbatim
Visioning	"A leader is an individual who envisions a change and helps a group move toward that goal."
	"They provide vision of 'how it should and could be' and influence other people in support of their mission and vision."
	"The person in a leadership position first and foremost has the capacity to 'see' a future – however that future is defined for that organization. People in a leadership positions therefore try to determine what the future direction of an organization should be. They typically express their vision in conceptual from, that is, as ideas, because their concern is not with planning and how to get to the future, but with painting a picture of what the future will be."
Teaching/ coaching	"A leader should be willing to become a teacher. There should be little hesitation in teaching staff…"
	"A good leader should be a coach for his or her staff and recognize and develop the potential of each person on the team.
	"This teacher will be able to fully leverage the energy and abilities of their entire agency."
Help individuals become proactive based on values and goals	"A good leader explains or present the task in such a way that the subordinates want to undertake the task and are excited about reaching the goal."
	"After everyone is in agreement with the proposed solution to address the situation, he gives you the opportunity to go away, and develop a plan of action."
	"Workers need to be seen as mature, desirous, of being productive, wanting to identify with the job and contribute to its success, and willing to accomplish the organizational goals."

Table 19 Sample essay quotations – top three Trust Culture Leadership elements from (2002 research)

Leadership element	Sample Statements from Essays – verbatim
Team building	"You need a team to lead therefore you must accomplish team building."
	"They must promote and build cooperation between themselves, the team they lead, and other competing work groups."
	"Team oriented: He has the ability to build and construct teams to perform with clarity and uniformity for a mission."
Measuring/ appraising/ rewarding group performance	"The team that brought you to today's mishap or failure will be the team that has to bring you to tomorrow's success."
	"…to reinforce the concept that everyone on the team is a contributor to the end product and that all work as all recognition is a group a effort."
	"Leadership is the ability to guide a team or team members, in a focused effort to achieve new levels of individual and team performance."
Creating and maintaining culture through visioning	"They already know the vision and the sub-goals needed to move forward. They work in partnership with their co-workers, because they understand the integral parts of the vision."
	"Within this process the leader will elicit input and feedback to mold the group members into an invested and participatory team to define respective roles, responsibilities, and objectives which each part must play in accomplishing the goals and the purpose previously defined."
	"People within a group or team work effectively and efficiently when there 3 is a link between their personal goals and the goals or state desired by the larger group. A leader is not so much able to create this link, as to foster the recognition of the existence of the link, and its importance to the individual."

Table 20 Sample essay quotations – top three Whole-Soul Leadership elements (2002 research)

Leadership element	Sample statements from essays
Setting moral standards	"Leadership is also possessing an ethical code and following that code even if it may not be the most popular or most politically astute way to proceed." "[Leadership] must maintain a high level of integrity and must conduct itself under the brightest moral standards." "A leader is a trendsetter. He sets the standards and motivates others to live up to those standards. He leads by example and encourages those around him to always reach to a higher level."
Inspiration	"Inspiration – A leader must be able to enthuse, inspire, and instill a sense of urgency and importance in those individuals that he or she is entrusted to lead." "It includes the capacity of an individual to inspire." "A leader is an individual that possesses certain qualities that inspire individuals to achieve and accomplish goals in life that seem insurmountable."
Fostering an intelligent organization	"Allowing your employees the freedom to make a mistake yet learn from them, is better for them and the organization in the long run." "I also believe that leadership is the ability to acquire and effectively use knowledge….I feel this way because an individual or organization cannot make informed and confident decisions without knowledge." "The most important aspect of leadership is the ability of individuals and groups to build the capacity of an organization or a community…"

References

Ackerman, L. (1985). Leadership vs. managership. *Leadership & Organization Development Journal, 6*(2), 17–19

Adair, J. (1986). *Effective Teambuilding*. Brookfield, VT: Gower Publishing

Argyris, C. (1957). *Personality and Organization*. New York, NY: Harper & Row

Autry, J. A. (1992). *Love and Profit: The Art of Caring Leadership*. New York: Avon Books

Badarraco, J. and Ellsworth, R. (1992). Leadership, integrity, and conflict. *Management Decision, 30*(6), 29–34

Barker, J. A. (1992). *Future Edge: Discovering the New Rules of Success*. New York: Morrow

Barnard, C. (1938a). *The Functions of the Executive*. Cambridge, MA: Harvard University Press

Barnard, C. (1938b). A theory of authority. In *Organization and Management, Selected Papers*. Cambridge, MA Harvard University Press

Barnard, C. (1962). *Organization and Management*. Cambridge, MA: Harvard University Press

Barnes, L. (1981). Managing the paradox of organizational trust. *Harvard Business Review, 2*, 23–30

Baruch, Y. (1998). Leadership – is that what we study. *The Journal of Leadership Studies, 5*(1), 100–124

Bass, B. M. (1985). *Leadership and Performance Beyond Expectations*. New York, NY: The Free Press

Bass, B. M. and Avolio, B. J. (1994). *Improving Organizational Effectiveness Through Transformational Leadership*. Thousand Oaks, CA: Sage

Beaver, G. (2002). Strategy and management in the smaller enterprise. *Strategic Change, 11*(4), 175

Bennis, W. (1982). The artform of leadership. *Training and Development Journal, 36*(4), 44–46

Bennis, W. and Nanus, B. (1985). *Leaders: The Strategies for Taking Charge*. New York, NY: HarperCollins Publishers

Berry, L. (1997). Leading for the long term. *Leader to Leader, 6*, 30–36

Biberman, J. (2003). How workplace spirituality becomes mainstreamed in a scholarly. In R Giacalone and C Jurkiewicz (eds.), *Handbook of Workplace Spirituality and Organizational Performance*. Armonk, NY: M. E. Sharpe.

Bierly, P, Kessler, E, and Christensen, E. (2000). Organizational learning, knowledge and wisdom. *Journal of Organizational Change Management, 13*(6), 595–618

Bingham, W. (1927). Leadership. In H Metcalf (ed.), *The Psychological Foundations of Management*. New York: Shaw.

Blake, R. and Mouton, J. (1964). *The Managerial Grid*. Houston: Gulf

Block, P. (1993). *Stewardship: Choosing Service Over Self-Interest*. San Francisco, CA: Berrett-Koehler

Bogardus, E. (1934). *Leaders and Leadership*. New York: Appleton-Century

Bolman, L. and Deal, T. (1984). *Modern Approaches to Understanding and Managing Organizations*. San Francisco, CA: Jossey-Bass

Bolman, L and Deal, T. (1997). *Reframing Organizations: Artistry, Choice, and Leadership*. San Francisco, CA: Jossey-Bass

Bolman, L. and Deal, T. (2001). *Leading with Soul*. San Francisco, CA: Jossey Bass

Bowden, A. (1926). A study of the personality of student leaders in the United States. *Journal of Abnormal Social Psychology, 21,* 149–160

Box, R. (1999). Running government like a business: implications for public administration theory and practice. *American Review of Public Administration, 29*(1), 19–43

Boyce, W. (1995). The ecology of the soul. *National Forum, The Phi Kappa Phi Journal, 4,* 22–27

Bozeman, B. (ed). (1993). *Public Management: The State of the Art*. San Francisco, CA: Jossey Bass.

Bradford, D. and Cohen, A. (1984). *Managing for Excellence*. New York: Wiley

Brassier, A. (1985). Strategic vision: a practical tool. *The Bureaucrat, 3,* 23–26

Brown, J. (1992). Developing a corporate community. In *New Traditions in Business: Spirit and Leadership in the 21st Century*. San Francisco, CA: Berrett-Koehler

Burack, E. (1999). Spirituality in the workplace. *Journal of Organizational Change Management, 12*(4), 280–292

Burgess, R. (1984). *Field Research: An Introduction to Field Research*. London: Allen and Unwin

Burns, J. (1978). *Leadership*. New York, NY: Harper & Row

Cacioppe, R. (2000). Creating spirit at work: re-visioning organization development and leadership, part II. *Leadership and Organization Development Journal, 21*(2), 110–119

Calano, J. and Salzman, J. (1988). *Career Tracking*. New York, NY: Simon and Schuster

Cappelli, P. (1995). Can this relationship be saved. *Wharton Alumni Magazine, 2,* 31–37

Card, M. (1997). Toward a middle-range theory of individual-level strategic leadership transitions. *Leadership Quarterly, 8*(1), 27–48

Carney, T. (1972). *Content Analysis: A Technique for Systematic Inference from Communications*. Winnepeg: University of Manitoba Press

Cavanaugh, G., Hanson, B., Hanson, K., and Hinojoso, J. (2001). Toward a spirituality for the contemporary organization: implications for work, family and society. *Institute for Spirituality and Organizational Leadership: Proceedings from Bridging the Gap*. Retrieved 16 Nov 2002, fromhttp://lsb.scu.edu/ISOL/contemporary_organization.pdf

Chaleff, I. (1997). Learn the art of followership. *Government Executive, 29*(2), 51

Cheng, B. (1982). The contingency model of leadership effectiveness: the empirical study of the meaning of LPC score and of the validity of model. *Acta Psychologica Taiwanica, 24*(2), 111–120

Cleveland, H. (1972). *The Future Executive: A Guide for Tomorrow's Managers*. New York, NY: HarperCollins

Clemens, J and Mayer, D. (1999). *The Classic Touch: Lessons on Leadership from Homer to Hemingway*. Lincolnwood, IL: NTC/Contemporary Books

Cober, R, Hacker, S, and Johnston, C. (1998). Organization. In Giacalone, R and Jurkiewicz, C (eds.), *Handbook of Workplace Spirituality and Organizational Performance*. Armonk, NY: M.E. Sharpe.

Collins, J. and Porras, J. (1997). *Built to Last: Successful Habits of Visionary Companies*. New York, NY: HarperBusiness

Colvin, R. E. (1996). *Transformational Executive Leadership: A Comparison of Culture-Focused and Individual-Focused Leadership Modalities*. Unpublished Doctoral Dissertation, Virginia Commonwealth University, Richmond, VA.

Conger, J. A. (1991). Inspiring others: the language of leadership. *Academy of Management Executive, 5,* 31–45

Conger, J. and Kanungo, R. (eds.), (1988). *Charismatic Leadership: The Illusive Factor in Organizational Effectiveness*. San Francisco, CA: Jossey-Bass.

Cook, T. and Campbell, D. (1979). *Quasi-Experimentation: Design and Analysis Issues for Field Settings*. Boston, MA: Houghton Mifflin

Cook-Greuter, S. (2002). A detailed description of the development of nine action logics. Retrieved 31 Jan 2004, from http://www.harthillusa.com/

Cound, D. (1987). A call for leadership. *Quality Progress, March,* 11–14

Covey, S. (1992). *Principle-Centered Leadership*. New York, NY: Simon and Schuster

Creswell, J. (1994). *Research Design: Qualitative and Quantitative Approaches*. Thousand Oaks, CA: Sage

Creswell, J. (1998). *Qualitative Inquiry and Research Design: Choosing Among Five Traditions*. Thousand Oaks, CA: Sage

Crosby, P. (1984). *Quality Without Tears: The Art of Hassle-Free Management*. New York, NY: McGraw-Hill

Culbert, S. and McDonough, J. (1985). *Radical Management: Power Politics and the Pursuit of Trust*. New York, NY: The Free Press

Cuoto, R. (1993). The transformation of transforming leadership. In T Wren (ed.), *The Leader's Companion: Insights on Leadership Through the Ages*. New York, NY: The Free Press.

Danforth, D. (1987). The quality imperative. *Quality Progress*, 2, 17–19

Davis, T and Luthans, F. (1984). Defining and researching leadership as a behavioral construct: an idiographic approach. *Journal of Applied Behavioral Science*, 20(3), 237–251

Day, D. (2000). Leadership development: a review in context. *Leadership Quarterly*, 11(4), 581–611

Delbecq, A. (1999). Christian spirituality and contemporary business leadership. *Journal of Organizational Change Management*, 12(4), 345–354

Deming, W. (1986). *Out of the Crisis*. Cambridge, MA: Massachusetts Institute of Technology Center for Advanced Engineering Study

Dent, E, Higgins, M, and Wharff, D. (2005). Spirituality and leadership: an empirical review of definitions, distinctions, and embedded assumptions. *The Leadership Quarterly*, 16(5), 625–653

Denzin, N. and Lincoln, Y. (2000). *Handbook of Qualitative Research*, 2nd ed. Thousand Oaks, CA: Sage

DePree, M. (1989). *Leadership is an Art*. New York: Doubleday

DePree, M. (1992). *Leadership Jazz*. New York: Dell

Dowd, J. (1936). *Control in Human Societies*. New York: Appleton-Century

Drath, W. and Palus, C. (1994). *Making Common Sense: Leadership as Meaning-Making in a Community of Practice*. Greensboro, North Carolina: Center for Creative Leadership

Dreilinger, C. (1998). Beyond cynicism: building a culture which supports both ethical business practice and high performance. In W. Rosenbach and R. Taylor (eds.), *Contemporary Issues in Leadership, 4th ed.* Boulder, CO: Westview.

Drucker, P. (1954). *The Practice of Management*. New York, NY: Harper

Drucker, P. (1966). *The Effective Executive*. New York, NY: HarperCollins Publishers

Drucker, P. (1990). *Managing the Non-Profit Organization: Practices and Principles*. New York, NY: HarperCollins

Dunphy, S. and Aupperle, K. (2000). Using theatrical films to bring management concepts to life: a new pedagogy. *Decision Science Institute 2000 Proceedings*, 1, 215–217

Eadie, D. (1983). Putting a powerful tool to practical use: the application of strategic planning in the public sector. *Public Administration Review*, 5, 447–452

Eisner, E. and Peshkin, A. (1990). *Qualitative Inquiry in Education: The Continuing Debate*. New York: Teachers College Press

Erteszek, J. (1983). The common venture enterprise: a western answer to the Japanese art of management. *New Management*, 1(2), 4–10

Etzioni, A. (1996). *The New Golden Rule: Community and Morality in a Democratic Society*. New York: Basic Books

Evans, M. (1970). The effects of supervisory behavior on the path-goal relationship. *Organizational Behavior and Human Performance*, 5, 277–298

Fairholm, G. (1991). *Values Leadership: Toward a New Philosophy of Leadership*. New York, NY: Praeger

Fairholm, G. (1993). *Organizational Power Politics: Tactics in Organizational Leadership*. Westport, CT: Praeger

Fairholm, G. (1994). *Leadership and the Culture of Trust*. Westport, CT: Praeger

Fairholm, G. (1997). *Capturing the Heart of Leadership: Spirituality and Community in the New American Workplace*. Westport, CT: Praeger

Fairholm, G. (1998a). Leadership as an exercise in virtual reality. *Leadership and Organization Development Journal, 19*(4), 187–193

Fairholm, G. (1998b). *Perspectives on Leadership: From the Science of Management to its Spiritual Heart*. Westport, CT: Quorum Books

Fairholm, G. (2001). *Mastering Inner Leadership*. Westport, CT: Quorum Books

Fairholm, M. (2002). *Conceiving Leadership: Exploring Five Perspectives of Leadership by Investigating the Conceptions and Experiences of Selected Metropolitan Washington Area Municipal Managers*. The George Washington University: Washington, DC

Fairholm, M. (2004). Different Perspectives on the Practice of Leadership. *Public Administration Review, 64*(5), 577–590

Fairholm, M. (2007). Trans-leadership: linking influential theory and contemporary research. In R. Morse and T. Buss (eds.), *Transforming Public Leadership for the 21st Century*. Armonk, New York: M.E. Sharpe Publishers.

Fairholm, M. (2008). *The Four Vs and Public Administration Practice: A Framework for Discerning Leadership in a Transformational Age*. Paper presented at the Annual Conference of the American Society for Public Administration, March 7–11, Dallas, TX

Fairholm, M. and Fairholm, G. (2000). Leadership amid the constraints of trust. *Leadership and Organizational Development Journal, 21*(2), 102–109

Fayol, H. (1916). General principles of management. In J. Shafritz and J. Ott(eds.), *Classics of Organization Theory*, 5th ed. Fort Worth, TX: Harcourt

Felton, K. (1995). *Warrior's Words: A Consideration of Language and Leadership*. Westport, CT: Praeger

Fiedler, F. (1967). *A Theory of Leadership Effectiveness*. New York, NY: McGraw-Hill

Flom, E. (1987). Look and listen: a personal primer on leadership. *Vital Speeches of the Day, 53*(19), 594–596

Follett, M. (1926). The giving of orders. In H Metcalf (ed.), *The Scientific Foundations of Business Administration*. New York: The Williams and Wilkins Co.

Follett, M. (1998). *The New State: Group Organization – The Solution of Popular Government*. University Park, Pennsylvania: The Pennsylvania University Press

Fowler, J. (1995). *Stages of Faith: The Psychology of Human Development and the Quest for Meaning*. San Francisco, CA: HarperCollins Publishers

Fraser, C. (1978). Small groups: I. Structure and leadership. In C. F. Henri Tajfel (Ed.), *Introducing social psychology: An analysis of individual reaction and response*. (pp. 176–200): Penguin Books, Inc, Middlesex, England

Freshman, B. (1999). An exploratory analysis of definitions and applications of spirituality in the workplace. *Journal of Organizational Change Management, 12*(4), 318–323

Friedman, H. (2004). Moral leadership: ancient lessons for modern times *Journal of College and Character*. Retrieved 5 Nov 2006, from http://www.collegevalues.org/articles.cfm

Frost, P. and Egri, C. (1990). Appreciating executive action. In S. Srivastva and D. Cooperrider (eds.), *Appreciative Management and Leadership: The Power of Positive Thought and Action in Organizations*. San Francisco, CA: Jossey-Bass.

Fry, B. (2003). *Mastering Public Administration: From Max Weber to Dwight Waldo*. Chatham, NJ: Chatham House Publishers

Gardner, J. (1987). The tasks of leadership. *New Management, 4*(4), 9–14

Gardner, J. (1990). *On Leadership*. New York, NY: The Free Press

Georgantzas, N. and Ritchie-Dunham, J. (2003). Designing high-leverage strategies and tactics. *Human Systems Management, 22*(1), 1–11

George, C. (1968). *The History of Management Thought*. Englewood Cliff, NJ: Prentice-Hall

Giacalone, R. and Jurkiewicz, C. (2003). Right from wrong: the influence of spirituality on perceptions of unethical business activities. *Journal of Business Ethics, 46*(1), 85–91

Gibb, J. (1978). *A New View of Reason and Organizations Development*. New York: The Guild of Tutor's Press

Gibbons, P. (1999). *Spirituality at Work: A Pre-theoretical Overview.* M.Sc. Dissertation, Birkbeck College, University of London: London

Gilbreth, F. (1912). *Primer of Scientific Management.* New York: D. Van Nostrand Company

Gini, A. (1997). Moral leadership: an overview. *Journal of Business Ethics, 16*(3), 323–330

Gitlow, H. and Gitlow, S. (1987). *The Deming Guide to Quality and Competitive Position.* New York, NY: Prentice-Hall

Goleman, D. (1995). *Emotional Intelligence.* New York: Bantam Books

Good, D. (1988). Individuals, interpersonal relations and trust. In *Trust Making and Breaking Cooperative Relations.* Oxford, MA: Basil Blackwell

Gouldner, A. (1954). *Patterns of Industrial Bureaucracy.* Glencoe, IL: The Free Press

Graen, G. and Uhl-Bien, M. (1995). Relationship-based approach to leadership: development of leader-member exchange (LMX) theory of leadership of, 25 years, applying a multilevel multi-domain approach. *Leadership Quarterly, 6*, 219–247

Graves, C. (1970). Toward humanism from animalism: an open systems theory of values. *Journal of Humanistic Psychology, 5*, 25–39

Greenleaf, R. (1977). *Servant Leadership: A Journey into the Nature of Legitimate Power and Greatness.* New York, NY: Paulist Press

Greenleaf, R. (1998). *The Power of Servant Leadership.* San Francisco, CA: Berrett-Koehler

Gulick, L. (1937). Notes of the theory of organization. In L Gulick and L Urwick (eds.), *Papers on the Science of Administration.* New York: Institute of Public Administration.

Gulick, L. and Urwick, L. (1937). *Papers on the Science of Administration,* 2nd ed New York: Institute of Public Administration

Handy, C. (1994). *The Age of Paradox.* Cambridge, MA: Harvard University Press

Haney, W. (1973). *Communication and Organizational Behavior.* Homewood, IL: Richard D. Erwin

Hawley, J. (1993). *Reawakening the Spirit in Work: The Power of Dharmic Management.* San Francisco, CA: Berrett-Koehler

Heerman, B. (1995). Spiritual core is essential to high performing teams. *The New Leaders.* (2), 4–5

Heifetz, R. A. (1994). *Leadership Without Easy Answers.* Cambridge, MA: Belknap

Heifitz, R. A. & Laurie, D. L. (1998). The work of leadership. In W. E. Rosenbach & R. Taylor (Eds.), *Contemporary Issues in Leadership* (4th ed., pp. 179–197). Boulder, CO: Westview Press

Heilman, M. Hornstein, H. Cage, J. and Herschlag, J. (1984). Reactions to prescribed leader behavior as a function of role perspective: the case of the Vroom-Yetton model. *Journal of Applied Psychology, 69*(1), 50–60

Hemphill, J. (1950). *Leader Behavior Description.* Columbus, OH: Ohio State University

Hemphill, J. (1954). *A Proposed Theory of Leadership in Small Groups.* Columbus, OH: Ohio State University

Herman, R. & Gioia, J. (1998). Making work meaningful: secrets of the future-focused corporation. *The Futurist, 32*(9), 24–38

Hersey, P. and Blanchard, K. (1979). Life cycle theory of leadership. *Training and Development Journal, 6*, 94–100

Herzberg, F. (1984). Why me? whom do I turn to? mystery systems shape loyalties. *Industry Week,* November, 12, 101–104

Herzberg, F. (1987). One more time: how do you motivate employees? *Harvard Business Review, 6*, 109–120

Herzberg, F. Mausner, B. and Snyderman, B. (1959). *The Motivation to Work.* New York: Wiley

Hinds, P. and Young, K. (1987). A triangulation of methods and paradigms to study nurse-given wellness care. *Nursing Research, 36*(3), 195

Hitt, W. (1988). *The Leader-Manager.* New York: Battelle Press

Hofstadter, R. (1955). *The Age of Reform.* New York: Vintage Books

Hofstede, G. (1993). Cultural constraints in management theories. *Academy of Management Executive, 7*(2), 81–94

Hollander, E. (1978). *Leadership Dynamics: A Practical Guide to Effective Relationships.* New York, NY: The Free Press

Hollander, E. (1997). How and why active followers matter in leadership. In E. Hollander and L. Offermann (eds.), *The Balance of Leadership and Followership.* University of Maryland, College Park, MD: Kellogg Leadership Studies Project

Homans, G. C. (1950). *The Human Group.* New York, Harcourt Brace & World

Honderich, T. and Burnyeat, M., Eds. (1979). *Philosophy as It Is.* London: Penguin Books

House, R. (1996). Path-goal theory of leadership: an examination of a prescriptive theory. *Leadership Quarterly, 7*(3), 323–352

Howard, S. (2002). A spiritual perspective on learning in the workplace. *Journal of Management Psychology, 17*(3), 230–242

Hughes, R, Ginnett, R, and Curphy, G. (1993). *Leadership: Enhancing the Lessons of Experience.* Boston, MA: McGraw-Hill, Irwin

Hunt, J., Osborn, R., and Marton, H. (1981). A multiple influence model of leadership. *US Army Research Institute for the Behavioral & Social Sciences Report.* TR, 520 (182)

Jacobsen, S. (1994) *Spirituality and Transformational Leadership in Secular Settings: A Delphi Study.* Unpublished Doctoral Dissertation, Seattle University, Seattle, WA

Jay, A. (1968). *Management and Machiavelli: An Inquiry Into the Politics of Corporate Life.* New York: Holt Rinehart and Winston

Jaques, E., & Clement, S. D. (1991). *Executive Leadership: A Practical Guide To Managing Complexity.* Arlington, VA: Cason Hall.

Jernigan, J. (1997). *Trust-Based Values Leadership: A Case Study in Productivity of a Public Sector Line Organization.* Unpublished Doctoral Dissertation, Virginia Commonwealth University, Richmond, VA

Juran, J. (1989). *Juran on Leadership for Quality: An Executive Handbook.* New York, NY: The Free Press

Kaltman, A. (1998). *Cigars, Whiskey and Winning: Leadership Lessons from Ulysses S. Grant.* Paramus, NJ: Prentice-Hall

Kaufman, H. (1969). Administration decentralization and political power. *Public Administration Review, 29*(1), 3–15

Kegan, R. (1982). *The Evolving Self.* Boston, MA: Harvard University Press

Kee, J. and Black, R. (1985). Is excellence possible in the public sector? *Public Productivity Review, 2,* 25–34

Kidder, R. (1995). Universal human values: finding an ethical common ground. *Public Management, 77*(6), 4–9

Kilbourne, C. E. (1935). The elements of leadership. *Journal of Cost Artillery, 78,* 437–439

Kirkpatrick, S. and Locke, E. (1991). Leadership: do traits matter? *Academy of Management Executive, 5,* 48–60

Koestler, A. (1970). Beyond atomism and holism: the concept of holon. In A. Koestler and J. Smythies (eds.), *Beyond Reductionism: New Perspective in the Life Sciences.* New York, NY: Macmillan.

Kohlberg, L. (1984). *The Psychology of Moral Development: The Nature and Validity of Moral Stages.* San Francisco, CA: Harper & Row

Kohn, A. (1993). *Punished by Rewards: The Trouble with Gold Stars, Incentive Plans, A's Praise, and Other Bribes.* Boston: Houghton Mifflin Co.

Konz, G and Ryan, F. (1999). Maintaining organizational spirituality: no easy task. *Journal of Organizational Change Management, 12*(3), 200–210

Korac-Kakabadse, N., Kouzmin, A., and Kakabadse, A. (2002). Spirituality and leadership praxis. *Journal of Managerial Psychology, 17*(3), 165–182

Kotter, J. (1990). What leaders really do. *Harvard Business Review,* (May–June), 45–56

Kotter, J. (1996). *Leading Change.* Boston, MA: Harvard Business School Press

Kouzes, J. and Posner, B. (1990). *The Leadership Challenge: How to Get Extraordinary Things Done in Organizations.* San Francisco, CA: Jossey-Bass

Kouzes, J. and Posner, B. (1993). *Credibility: How Leaders Gain and Lose It, Why People Demand It*. San Francisco, CA: Jossey-Bass

Krippendorff, K. (1980). *Content Analysis: An Introduction to its Methodology*. Beverly Hills, CA: Sage

Krishnakumar, S. and Neck, C. (2002). The what, why and how of spirituality in the workplace. *Journal of Managerial Psychology, 17*(3), 153–164

Kuritz, S. (1992). A holistic approach to process safety. *Occupational Health and Safety, 61*(10), 28–32

Lammermeyer, H. (1990). *Human Relations: The Key to Quality*. New York: ASQC Quality Press

Lasswell, H. and Kaplin, A. (1950). *Power and Society*. New Haven: Yale University Press

LeCompte, M. and Schensul, J. (1999). *Analyzing and Interpreting Ethnographic Data*. Walnut Creek, CA: AltaMira Press

Levinson, H. (1968). *The Exceptional Executive: A Psychological Conception*. Cambridge, MA: Harvard University Press

Levit, R. (1992). Meaning, purpose, and leadership. *International Forum for Logotherapy, 15*(2), 71–75

Lewin, K. (1951). *Field Theory in Social Science: Selected Theoretical Papers*. New York, CA: Harper

Lincoln, Y. and Guba, E. (1985). *Naturalistic Inquiry*. Beverly Hills, CA: Sage

Ludeman, K. (1989). *The Worth Ethic*. New York: E. P. Dutton

Luke, J. (1998). *Catalytic Leadership: Strategies for an Interconnected World*. San Francisco, CA: Jossey-Bass

Maccoby, M. (1976). *The Gamesman*. New York: Bantum Books

Maccoby, M. (1981). *The Leader*. New York, NY: Simon and Schuster

Magaziner, E. (1994). New thinking, not just new insight. *The New Leaders, 1*, 6

Malmberg, K. B. (1999). *A Vision for the Future: The Practice of Leading in the Federal Workplace*. Paper presented at the American Society for Public Administration, Orlando, FL

Manz, C. and Sims, J. (1989). *Superleadership, Leading Others to Lead Themselves*. New York, NY: Prentice-Hall

Marko, K. (2002). *Romance and Reality: The Pursuit of Personal Fulfillment in the New Millennium Workplace*, Royal Roads University, Victoria, BC, 147

Martin, M. (1996). *Leadership in a Cultural Trust Chasm: An Analysis of Trust Directed Behaviors and Vision Directed Behaviors That Lead to Positive Follower Attitudes and Responses*. Ph.D. Dissertation, Virginia Commonwealth University, Richmond, VA

Marquardt, M. and Reynolds, A. (1994). *The Global Learning Organization*. New York, NY: Irwin

Maslow, A. (1943). A theory of motivation. *Psychological Review*, 50, 370–396

Mason, J. (1996). *Qualitative Research*. London: Sage

Mayo, E. (1945). *The Social Problems of an Industrial Civilization*. Boston, MA: Division of Research, Graduate School of Business Administration, Harvard University

McFarland, L., Senn, L., and Childress, J. (1993). *Twenty-First Century Leadership: Dialogues with, 100 Top Leaders*. Long Beach, CA: The Leadership Press

McGregor, D. (1960). *The Human Side of Enterprise*. New York, NY: McGraw-Hill

McGregor, D., Bennis, W., Schein, E., and McGregor, C. (1966). *Leadership and Motivation: Essays*. Cambridge, MA: MIT

McMurray, R. (1973). Power and the ambitious executives. *Harvard Business Review*, 140–145

Merrell, V. (1979). *Huddling: The Informal Way to Management Success*. New York, NY: AMACOM

Miles, M. and Huberman, M. (1994). *Qualitative Data Analysis*. Thousand Oaks, CA: Sage

Miller, M. and Cook-Greuter, S. (1999). *Creativity, Spirituality, and Transcendence*. Westport, CT: Greenwood Publishing

Millett, J. D. (1954). *Management in the Public Service: The Quest for Effective Performance*. New York, NY: McGraw-Hill

Mintzberg, H. (1975). The manager's job: folklore and fact. *Harvard Business Review*, July–August, 19–32

Mitchell, T. (1993). Leadership, values, and accountability. In R. Martin and M. Chemers (eds.), *Leadership Theory and Research: Perspectives and Directions*. San Diego, CA: Academic.

Mitroff, I. and E. Denton (1999). *A Spiritual Audit of Corporate America: A Hard Look at Spirituality, Religion, and Values in the Workplace*. San Francisco, CA: Jossey-Bass

Mohrman, A., Resnick-West, S., and Lawler, E. (1989). *Designing Performance Appraisal Systems*. San Fransisco, CA: Jossey-Bass

Myers, S. (1970). *Every Employee a Manager*. New York, NY: McGraw-Hill

Nadler, D. and Tushman, M. (1990). Beyond the charismatic leader: leadership and organizational change. *California Management Review*, *32*(4), 77–97

Nair, K. (1994). *A Higher Standard of Leadership: Lessons from the Life of Gandhi*. San Francisco, CA: Berrett-Koehler

Nanus, B. (1992). *Visionary Leadership: Creating a Compelling Sense of Direction for Your Organization*. San Francisco, CA: Jossey-Bass

Neal, J., Bergmann-Lichtenstein, B., & Banner, D. (1999). Spiritual perspectives on individual, organization, and societal transformation. *Journal of Organizational Change Management*, *12*(3), 175–185

Nelson, B. (1997). Creating an energized workplace. *Leader to Leader*, *5*(3), 34–39

Newcomer, K. (1997). *Preparing Public Managers for the, 21st Century: Holding Ourselves Accountable for Their Performance*. Paper presented at the International Symposium on Performance-based Management in Public Administration and its Training Implications, September, 24–26, Caserta, Italy

Nicholls, J. (1985). A new approach to situational leadership. *Leadership and Organization Development Journal*, *6*(4), 2–7

Nirenberg, J. (1998). Myths we teach, realities we ignore: leadership education in business schools. *The Journal of Leadership Studies*, *5*(1), 82–99

Nolan, J. and Harty, H. (1984). Followership > = leadership. *Education*, *104*(3), 311–312

Odom, R., Boxx, R., and Dunn, G. (1990). Organizational cultures, commitment, satisfaction, and cohesion. *Public Productivity and Management Review*, *14*(2), 157–169

Offermann, L. (1984). Short-term supervisory experience and LPC score: effects of leader's sex and group sex composition. *Journal of Social Psychology*, *123*(1), 115–121

O'Sullivan, E. and Rassel, G. (1989). *Research Methods for Public Administrators*. New York, NY: Longman

O'Toole, J. (1996). *Leading Change: The Argument for Value-Based Leadership*. New York, NY: Ballentine Books

Ott, J. (1989). *The Organizational Culture Perspective*. Homewood, IL: The Dorsey Press

Palmer, P. (1998). *The Courage to Teach: Exploring the Inner Landscape of a Teacher's Life*. San Francisco, CA: Jossey-Bass

Pascerella, P. (1984). *The New Achievers*. New York, NY: The Free Press

Peters, T. and Austin, N. (1985). *A Passion for Excellence: The Leadership Difference*. New York, NY: Random House

Peters, T. and Waterman, R. (1982). *In Search of Excellence: Lessons from America's Best-Run Companies*. New York, NY: Warner Books

Pfeffer, J. (1977). The ambiguity of leadership. *Academy of Management Review*, *2*(1), 104–112

Pinchot, G. and E. Pinchot (1994). *The End of Bureaucracy and the Rise of the Intelligent Organization*. San Francisco, CA: Berrett-Koehler

Pittman, T., Rosenbach, W., and Potter, E. (1998). Followers and partners. In W. Rosenbach and R. Taylor (eds.), *Contemporary Issues in Leadership*, 4th ed. Boulder, CO: Westview

Porter, E., Sargent, A., and Stupak, R. (1987). Managing for excellence in the federal government. *New Management*, *4*(4), 15–18

Price, D. K. (1965). *The Scientific Estate*. Cambridge, MA: Belknap

Prince, H. (1995). Moral development in individuals. In J Wren (ed.), *The Leader's Companion*. New York, NY: The Free Press

Quinn, R. and McGrath, M. (1985). The transformation of organizational cultures: a competing values perspective. In P. Frost, L. Moore, M. Louis, C. Lundberg, and J. Martin (eds.), *Organizational Culture*. Beverly Hills, CA: Sage

Rago, W. (1996). Struggles in transformation: a study in TQM, leadership, and organizational culture in a government agency. *Public Administration Review*, 56(3), 227–234

Raspberry, W. (1995). Churches shouldn't neglect their strong inside game. *The Richmond Times-Dispatch, February*, 16, 15

Ready, D. and Conger, J. (2003). Why leadership development efforts fail. *MIT Sloan Management Review*, 44(3), 83–89

Rice, R. and Kastenbaum, D. (1983). The contingency model of leadership: some current issues. *Basic and Applied Social Psychology*, 4(4), 373–392

Roethlisberger, F. (1956). *Management and Morale*. Cambridge, MA: Harvard University Press

Roethlisberger, F., Dickson, W., and Wright, H. (1941). *Management and the Worker: An Account of a Research Program Conducted by the Western Electric Company, Hawthorne Works, Chicago*. Cambridge, MA: Harvard University Press

Rokeach, M. (1979). *Organizing Human Values*. New York, NY: The Free Press

Rosen, R. (1992). Developing a healthy organization. In *New Traditions in Business: Spirit and Leadership in the, 21st Century*. San Francisco, CA: Berrett-Koehler

Rosenbach, W. and Taylor, R. (eds.). (1989). *Contemporary Issues in Leadership*, 2nd ed. Boulder, CO: Westview

Rosener, J. (1990). Ways women lead. *Harvard Business Review*, (6), 52–59

Ross, J. (1993). *Total Quality Management: Text, Cases, and Readings*. Delray Beach, FL: St. Lucia

Rossiter, C. and Pearch, B. (1975). *Communicating Personally*. New York, NY: Bobbs-Merrill Co

Rost, J. (1991). *Leadership for the Twenty-First Century*. Westport, CT: Greenwood Publishing

Rutan, J. and Rice, C. (1981). The charismatic leader: asset or liability. *Psychotherapy: Theory, Research and Practice*, 18(4), 487–492

Samuelson, R. (1984). In search of simplicity. *Newsweek, April 30*, 70

Sanchez, A. (1988). *The Contribution of Personality Type (Preference) and Selected Situational Factors to Visionary Leadership*. Unpublished Doctoral Dissertation, University of Colorado at Denver, Denver Co.

Sashkin, M. (1982). *A Manager's Guide to Participative Management*. New York, NY: AMA Membership Publications Division

Sashkin, M. (1989). Visionary leadership: the perspective from education. In W. Rosenbach & R. Taylor (eds.), *Contemporary Issues in Leadership*, 2nd ed. Boulder, CO: Westview

Sashkin, M. and Rosenbach, W. (1998). A new vision of leadership. In W. Rosenbach and R. Taylor (eds.), *Contemporary Issues in Leadership*, 4th ed. Boulder, CO: Westview

Sashkin, M. and Sashkin, M. (1994). *The New Teamwork: Developing and Using Cross-function Teams*. New York: AMA Membership Publications

Sathe, V. (1983). Organizational culture: some conceptual distinctions and their managerial implications. Working Paper, Harvard Business School, Division of Research, Boston, MA

Schein, V. (1989). Would women lead differently? In W. Rosenbach and R. Taylor (eds.), *Contemporary Issues in Leadership*, 2nd ed. Boulder, CO: Westview

Schein, E. (1992). *Organizational Culture and Leadership*, 2nd ed. San Francisco, CA: Jossey-Bass

Scott, W., (1973). The theory of significant people, *Public Administration Review* (August), 24–32

Scott, W. and Hart, D. (1979). *Organizational America*. Boston, MA: Houghton-Mifflin

Seckler-Hudson, C. (1951). *Processes of Organization and Management*. Washington, DC: The American University Press

Seckler-Hudson, C. (1955). *Organization and Management: Theory and Practice*. Washington, DC: The American University Press

Selznick, P. (1957). *Leadership in Administration*. New York: Row, Peterson

Senge, P. (1990). *The Fifth Discipline: The Art and Practice of the Learning Organization*. New York: Doubleday

Senge, P. (1998). Leading learning organizations. In W. Rosenbach and R. Taylor (eds.), *Contemporary Issues in Leadership*, 4th ed. Boulder, CO: Westview

Shouksmith, G. (1983). The factor structure of "Most Preferred Co-worker," and "Assumed Similarity of Opposites" scores. *Psychological Reports*, *53*(1), 255–258

Steers, R. (1985). *Antecedents and Outcomes of Organizational Commitment*. Unpublished Doctoral Dissertation, University of Iowa, Iowa City, IA

Stimpson, D. and Reuel, L. (1984). Management style: modeling or balancing? *Journal of Psychology*, *116*(2), 169–173

Stogdill, R. (1974). *Handbook of Leadership: A Survey of Theory and Research*. New York, NY: The Free Press

Stogdill, R. and Coons, A (eds.), (1957). *Leader Behavior: Its Description and Measurement*. Columbus, OH: Ohio State University

Stoney, C. (2001). Strategic management or strategic Taylorism? a case study into change within a UK local authority. *International Journal of Public Sector Management*, *14*(1), 27–42

Sullivan, G. and Harper, M. (1996). *Hope is Not a Method: What Business Leaders Can Learn from America's Army*. New York, NY: Broadway Books

Tannenbaum, R. & Schmidt, W. H. (1973). How to choose a leadership style. *Harvard Business Review, May/June*, 162

Taylor, F. (1915). *The Principles of Scientific Management*. New York, NY: Harper & Row

Terry, R. (1994). Authentic leadership: courage in action. *The New Leaders*, (1), 13–14

Thayer, F. (1980). Values, truth and administration: God or mammon. *Public Administration Review*, *45*(1), 91–98

Thompson, C. (2000). *The Congruent Life: Following the Inward Path to Fulfilling Work and Inspired Leadership*. San Francisco, CA: Jossey-Bass

Thornberry, N. (1997). A view about "vision". *European Management Journal*, *15*(1), 28–34

Tichy, N. M. (1997). The mark of a winner. *Leader to Leader*, *6*(3), 24–29

Tolley, H. (2003). Doing business in Babylon. *BYU Magazine*, (3), 36–40

Triandis, H. (1993). The contingency model in cross-cultural perspective. In R. Martin and M. Chemers (eds.), *Leadership Theory and Research: Perspectives and Directions*. San Diego, CA: Academic

Tuckman, B. (1965). Developmental sequence in small groups. *Psychological Bulletin*, *63*(6), 384–389

Uttal, B. (1983). The corporate culture vultures. *Fortune*, *108*(8), 66

Vaill, P. (1989). *Spirituality in the Age of the Leveraged Buyout*. Paper presented at the Spirituality in Life and Work, July 21, Washington, DC

Vaill, P. (1996). *Learning as a Way of Being: Strategies for Survival in a World of Permanent White Water*. San Francisco, CA: Jossey-Bass

Vaill, P. (1998). *Spirited Leading and Learning: Process Wisdom for a New Age*. San Francisco, CA: Jossey-Bass

Valle, M. (1999). Crisis, culture and charisma: the new leader's work in public organizations. *Public Personnel Management*, *28*(2), 245–257

Vecchio, R. and Gobdel, B. (1984). The vertical dyad linkage model of leadership: problems and prospects. *Organizational Behavior & Human Performance*, *34*(1), 5–20

Vroom, V. and Jago, A. (1988). *The New Leadership: Managing Participation in Organizations*. Englewood Cliffs, NJ: Prentice-Hall

Vroom, V. and Yetton, P. (1973). *Leadership and Decision-Making*. Pittsburgh, PA: University of Pittsburgh Press

Wagner-Marsh, F. and Conley, J. (1999). The fourth wave: the spirituality-based firm. *Journal of Organizational Change Management*, *12*(4), 292–301

Webb, E., Campbell, D., and Schwartz, R. (1966). *Unobtrusive Measures*. Chicago: Rand McNally

Weber, M. (1921). *Theory of Social and Economic Organization* (Hendeson, A. M. Parsons, T., Trans.). London: Oxford University Press

Weber, R. (1990). *Basic Content Analysis*, 2nd ed. Newbury Park, CA: Sage

Weinberg, L. (1996). Seeing through organization: exploring the constitutive quality of social relations. *Administration and Society*, *28*(2), 117–124

Weisbord, M. (1987). *Productive Workplaces: Organizing and Managing for Dignity, Meaning, and Community*. San Francisco, CA: Jossey-Bass

Wharff, D. M. (2003). Spirituality: Implications for Organizations and Leadership Development, Conference Paper. University of Maryland University College, Rockville, MD

Wharff, D. M. (2004). *Expressions of Spiritually Inspired Leadership in the Public Sector: Calling for a New Paradigmin Developing Leaders*. A Dissertation Submitted to the Graduate School of the University of Maryland University College, Rockville, MD

Wheatley, M. (1997). Goodbye, command and control. *Leader to Leader*, *5*(3), 21–28

Wheatley, M. (1999). *Leadership and the New Science: Learning about Organization from an Orderly Universe*, 2nd ed. San Francisco, CA: Berrett-Koehler

Wheatley, M. and Kellner-Rogers, M. (1998). Bringing life to organizations. *Journal for Strategic Performance Measurement*, (3), 41–49

Whetton, D. and Cameron, K. (1998). *Developing Management Skills*, 4th ed. Reading, MA: Addison-Wesley

Whyte, W. (1956). *The Organization Man*. New York, NY: Simon and Schuster

Wilber, K. (2000). *A Brief History of Everything*, 2nd ed. Boston, MA: Shambhala Publications

Wildavsky, A. (1984). *The Nursing Father: Moses as a Political Leader*. Birmingham: University of Alabama Press

Wilsey, M. (1995). Leadership and human motivation in the workplace. *Quality Progress*, *28*(11), 85–88

Wolcott, H. (1994). *Transforming Qualitative Data: Description, Analysis, and Interpretation*. Thousand Oaks, CA: Sage

Wolf, F. (1989). *Taking the Quantum Leap: The New Physics for Non-Scientists, Revised*. New York, NY: Harper and Row

Yamigichi, T. and Yamigichi, M. (1994). Trust and commitment in the United States and Japan. *Motivation and Emotion*, *18*, 129–166

Yukl, G. (1988). *Leadership in Organizations*, 4th ed. Englewood Cliffs, NJ: Prentice-Hall

Zaleznik, A. (1977). Managers and leaders: are they different? *Harvard Business Review*, *55*, 67–78

Zand, D. (1972). Trust and managerial problem solving. *Administrative Science Quarterly*, *17*(2), 229–39

Zwart, G. A. (2000). *The Relationship Between Spirituality and Transformational Leadership in Public, Private, and Nonprofit Sector Organizations*. Doctoral Dissertation, University of La Verne, La Verne, CA

Index

CPSIA information can be obtained at www.ICGtesting.com
Printed in the USA
LVOW01*0901040115

421433LV00007B/395/P

9 780387 849010